DONALD DEWAR

DONALD

Scotland's *first* First Minister

DEWAR

Edited by WENDY ALEXANDER MSP

MAINSTREAM
PUBLISHING

EDINBURGH AND LONDON

First published in Great Britain in 2005 by
MAINSTREAM PUBLISHING COMPANY
(EDINBURGH) LTD
7 Albany Street
Edinburgh EH1 3UG

ISBN 1 84596 038 6

A catalogue record for this book is available
from the British Library

Typeset in Garamond

Printed in Great Britain by
William Clowes Ltd, Beccles, Suffolk

This is about more than our politics and our laws. This is about who we are, how we carry ourselves. There is a new voice in the land, the voice of a democratic Parliament. A voice to shape Scotland as surely as the echoes from our past:

the shout of the welder in the din of the great Clyde shipyards;

the speak of the Mearns, with its soul in the land;

the discourse of the Enlightenment, when Edinburgh and Glasgow were a light held to the intellectual life of Europe;

the wild cry of the Great Pipes;

and back to the distant cries of the battles of Bruce and Wallace.

Walter Scott wrote that only a man with soul so dead could have no sense, no feel of his native land. For me, for any Scot, today is a proud moment: a new stage on a journey begun long ago and which has no end.

Extract from speech by Donald Dewar at the Opening Ceremony of the Scottish Parliament on 1 July 1999

Contents

Donald and Devolution

Donald and Scotland

Donald's Legacy . . .

Appendices

Acknowledgements

I would like to thank all those who contributed to this book. Without their enthusiastic participation, it would never have happened. Their views are diverse, engaging and their own. Many contributors knew Donald longer and more intimately than I did but all saw the value in trying to bring together a wide-ranging collection recalling his life and times. I am also indebted to Adam Elder for his expert assistance in compiling the photographs for this collection.

I would also like to thank Maggie Pearlstine, who helped crystallise the idea of the book; Bill Campbell of Mainstream, who agreed to publish; and Agnes Robertson, who contributed her time, energy and skill to putting the collection together. In my office, Lorraine McFarlane gracefully accepted the arrival of yet another 'extra' project with equanimity and good humour, ably assisted by Monica Arduini, Sean O'Conor, and later Liz Hodge, Stuart McCallum and Conor Magowan. Jamie Crawford, Shonaig Macpherson, Jim Cassidy, the staff of the Scottish Parliament's Information Services and the Dewar Library also contributed their time and expertise, as did Maureen Morton in reviewing the manuscript.

Grateful thanks and appreciation also go to the following for their invaluable assistance with researching and supplying the photographs: *The Herald*; Iain Martin, Alan Macdonald and Pamela Grigg at *Scotland on*

Sunday; Jean Smith at the Scottish Parliament; Joe Quinn at the Press Association and Judith Tewson at Scottish Viewpoint; and to Graeme Murdoch for the cover design.

Finally, I would like to thank Marion Dewar for her interest, Andrew Hamnett and the University of Strathclyde for their continuing support and my husband, Brian Ashcroft, who graciously endured the disruption a book brings to the life of the editor and the editor's family.

All authorial proceeds from this volume are being gifted to the Dewar Arts Awards, established in his memory. The awards are open to anyone under 30 who has talent in any art form but not much money. They have already assisted gifted young people in the fulfilment of their creative dreams in Boston, Strasbourg, Chicago, Miami, New York and Canada.

I hope all readers will find here aspects of Donald's life that were hitherto unfamiliar to them. Many who saw only the public face of 'Dour Donald' will discover for themselves his private, humorous, irreverent side. Reflecting upon Donald's life illuminates how significant a period in Scotland's history we are living through. Future generations will look back with interest and, I believe, more empathy than is sometimes our wont today. I hope this collection inspires readers not simply to look back but also to look forward with renewed ambitions.

Five years after his untimely death his legacy affirms that it is possible to oppose, as Donald did, with courtesy; to disagree, as Donald did, without personal animus; and to fight for one's beliefs, as Donald did, with conviction untainted by malice. As contributors, we will have succeeded if his memory, recalled here by friends, colleagues, commentators and opponents, serves to illuminate some of what is best in politics and most precious in public service.

Wendy Alexander
September 2005

'There shall be a Scottish Parliament'

The people of Scotland will remember Donald Dewar for many reasons but the above six words were a commitment that became a testament to this private, cultured man who, in his 63 years, touched the hearts and minds of a nation. Donald Campbell Dewar was born in Glasgow on Saturday, 21 August 1937, the son of a doctor. Elsewhere Adolf Hitler was about to set the world on fire; America's President Franklin D. Roosevelt was fighting with the Senate; the Spanish Civil War escalated with the Falangists bombing Madrid; Eamon de Valera was elected President of Eire; Leon Trotsky called for the overthrow of Soviet leader Josef Stalin; and Glasgow was emerging from the dark years of the Great Depression.

Over the coming 60 years Donald Dewar was to become a champion in the fight against inequality, poverty and deprivation.

From Glasgow Academy he progressed to Glasgow University, where he became President of Glasgow University Union. After qualifying as a lawyer, he served as MP for the highly marginal seat of Aberdeen South from

1966 to 1970. With the loss of the seat in 1970 he returned to the law, after some years working as a reporter to the children's panel, an experience that reinforced his abiding interest in the welfare of Scotland's children. He also had a short foray on to the airwaves as a political presenter for Radio Clyde. In 1978 he returned to Westminster, winning a by-election in Garscadden, a result many saw as turning the tide of Scottish Nationalism. He became chairman of the Select Committee on Scottish Affairs and succeeded Bruce Millan as shadow Secretary of State for Scotland in 1983, a post he held until 1992 when he became shadow Secretary of State for Social Security under John Smith. Tony Blair made him shadow Chief Whip, before he returned to the Scottish Office as Secretary of State following Labour's election victory of 1997.

Whether rushing along the corridors of power in Westminster, or striding through the fledgling Parliament on the Mound, or strolling across George Square in his beloved Glasgow, people looked up to Donald Dewar. The fact he was a soaring 6 ft 5 in. helped but this unassuming, unpretentious man had a great vision for Scotland, great personal integrity and a great intellect. He was a softly spoken socialist and a passionate Scot, a man of great compassion who worked for change. He strove to offer hope to those disadvantaged through birth, social background or the vagaries of economic change. For his native land, he saw devolution not so much as the righting of a past wrong but the beginning of a new road ahead. When the people of Scotland agreed with Donald Dewar in the devolution referendum of September 1997, a foundation was laid for Scotland's future. In 1998, he was elected Scottish Labour's leader in the forthcoming Scottish Parliament and in May 1999, he became Scotland's First Minister.

Moulded by the turbulent times of the twentieth century it fell to him to lead Scotland into the twenty-first.

There is a Scottish Parliament.

Introduction

Wendy Alexander

'The wrong side of the social arithmetic' was a phrase Donald Dewar used relentlessly when talking about poverty. He hated the smooth words of modern marketing almost as much as he disdained the rhetorical flourishes of those who prefer hyperbole to practical action. Yet for all his political pragmatism 'Big Donald' loathed poverty. It offended him to his core. The simple sense that 'it does not have to be like this' drove him throughout his political life and ultimately to an early death.

Donald was a big man in every sense of the word. He was 'big' in his vision for Scotland, in his love of country and in his conviction that the purpose of politics was to right the social arithmetic of Scotland. Despite his cerebral private pursuits – literature, history and art appreciation – Donald's commitment to politics, and social justice in particular, was always practical. As essay upon essay attests, Donald was a stranger to the trappings of greatness. He cared little about the paraphernalia of wealth or power. His car looked as if it had been rescued from the scrapyard. Inside, the detritus of every by-election and general election campaign for the last decade lay fading on the back seat. The frugal discomfort of his home, despite the books and paintings, was a constant source of anxiety to his friends.

Donald Dewar was a conviction politician rather than a follower of prevailing political fashions: his political life a testimony to the fact that the price of leadership is responsibility. This book explores the paradox of a man often derided in his day but now recalled with respect. It tells us something about the nature of leadership and also about the character of the Scots, because it is only posthumously that Donald's essential style – serious, understated, free of hyperbole, willing to stand apart and committed to the common weal – has found favour.

Donald the man contrived to be pessimistic, honest, loveable and irascible all at once – it was a beguilingly Scottish combination. As contributors testify, many have missed his wisdom, humanity and personal humility almost as much as his acerbic wit! He was a patriotic Scot with an admiration for Gladstonian liberalism and the political philosophy of a Croslandite social democrat. A man frequently dogged by personal self-doubt and sometimes depression, he was dedicated to delivering better days ahead. He gave his political life to the Labour Party because he believed it had been the most civilising force in the lives of British people in the twentieth century.

I first met Donald at Glasgow University Labour Club more than 20 years ago. Like many a student before me, I asked this famous former club chairman a pretentious question about the nature of socialism. Donald responded with characteristic vigour, remarking that he had just come from a morning at Yarrows and Barr & Stroud, and he could tell me that the shop stewards at both were more interested in jobs, health and housing than socialist theory. It was a characteristic riposte from a man who knew what mattered to Scots and above all to his constituents. For Donald, politics was about changing real lives of real people.

Five years later in 1987, our paths crossed again when I was a Labour sub-agent attempting to win back Hillhead from Roy Jenkins. Despite Donald's personal distaste for our candidate, he regularly turned up at the rooms from his safe neighbouring seat to volunteer his services for canvassing. He was positively wilful in his determination to muck in and not stand on ceremony, despite the fact that he was already shadow Secretary of State for Scotland. But it was only in the following year that I began to know him really well, when I became Labour research officer in September 1988. A month later, Donald made his seminal speech at Stirling University telling the country that 'Scots are going to have to live dangerously for a while' if they wanted a Scottish Parliament.[1] I was given my instructions and left in no doubt that it would please the then shadow Secretary of State for Scotland if the consultation underway in the Labour

Party about possible participation in the embryonic Scottish Constitutional Convention would come down firmly in favour.

But if Donald was a Scot through and through, he also believed in Britain. His politics were never about taking Scotland out of Britain. First and foremost, they were about taking poverty out of Scotland. If he were reviewing this volume – and book reviewing was one of his real pleasures – he might muse that his significant political contribution was made not during the heady days of preparing the Devolution White Paper following Labour's 1997 victory but much earlier. If he were only remembered as the Father of Devolution or for what he put in train post-devolution it would be to overlook Donald's other gift to Scotland: keeping the flame of social justice alive in the wilderness years of the 1980s and early '90s. In those hard times, he toiled hard for Scottish Labour; the frequent melancholy of those years suited Donald. Perhaps because he had known hard times himself he could thole the hard times of the nation. As steel, coal and shipbuilding suffered and unemployment rose and rose, Donald simply kept going, opposing, in his own way and with dignity, whilst believing that better times would come. Many colleagues have recalled that in the daily grind of opposition politics Donald typically pushed himself harder, with a stamina perhaps only exceeded by Gordon Brown in the Scottish Labour Party.

More than a decade later, when it came to drafting the Scotland Bill, Donald knew there was only one chance to get it right and for him it was entirely personal. It was his way of saying 'never again' to the waste of the 1980s and early '90s.

Contrary to expectation and past practice, the Devolution White Paper Scotland's Parliament was pored over – indeed crafted line by line – by its lead minister. He argued over every dot and comma with sceptical colleagues and Whitehall officials alike, and, as others describe later, his absolute mastery of arcane detail was decisive in the critical Cabinet committees. He would return to the Scottish Office's London base in Dover House with a furrowed brow that melted into a wry smile as he described his battles with colleagues over the detail. Time and time again his grasp of the minutiae had disarmed and outmanoeuvred the sceptics. This well-informed, understated and yet winning style was not so different from the one he deployed during his later stewardship of First Minister's questions in the infant Scottish Parliament.

When in early June 1997 he recoiled in exasperation at the tone emerging from the delicate cross-Whitehall official negotiations, I was instructed to take a laptop computer home to Glasgow so we could work on a redraft over a weekend. It was unprecedented; there were rumblings of resignations, but by then Civil Service colleagues had been won over by his style, commitment and his vision for the Act. More late-night drafting sessions were to follow before Donald was content with the package.

The White Paper and subsequent Scotland Act have already proved more durable than many predicted. The Act provided the Scottish Parliament with real clarity about its powers and responsibilities, creating both the basis for a new confidence about Scotland and new levels of critical self-awareness about the nation's aspirations. Success was not a foregone conclusion, as many more fully federal nations have stumbled in their initial attempts to enshrine a durable assignment of legislative powers and responsibilities. As the Economic and Social Research Council in the first major research study of devolution recently noted:

> The formal division of powers gives Scotland possibly the widest range of competences of any devolved or federated government in Europe, with the striking exception of fiscal powers . . . the Scottish Parliament can repeal and alter Westminster laws in devolved matters; in other countries there are usually state-wide framework laws within which devolved Parliaments must operate.[2]

Nor has the far-reaching character of the settlement been an impediment to its effectiveness. Devolution has been successfully implemented without the legal wrangling about the division of powers between Scotland and the rest of the United Kingdom that so many authoritatively predicted, largely as a result of Donald's visionary decision *not* to specify the devolved powers but instead to extend the Scottish Parliament's competence to all matters which were not explicitly reserved to Westminster.

The durability of the Scotland Act has given Donald a permanent place in the Scottish political firmament. So much so that it is easy to overlook the fact that he was in office as First Minister for less than eighteen months and for the latter six months battling ill health. This volume reappraises that legacy in office, both as Secretary of State for Scotland and as First Minister. Despite the tightness of the fiscal restraints in those early years his own political priorities of social justice and economic efficiency are clearly discernible.

I recall one evening in July 1997, having attended his first Highlands and Islands Convention at Lochgilphead, Donald was tired – it had been a frustrating day. Our inability to find a reliable fax machine had almost scuppered a highly charged tripartite drafting negotiation between Argyll, Edinburgh and the Cabinet Office. The last of these three, charged with producing a workable devolution scheme, was understandably inclined to advocate whatever Whitehall colleagues would wear. Donald was having none of it, hence the need to be alert to every seemingly inconsequential detail. If all that backroom activity was not enough, the Highlands and Islands Convention participants had their own demanding agenda. Having waited 18 years to have a Labour Secretary of State before them once again, Highland Scotland's representatives were in no mood to wait any longer. Their impatience was palpable, although Donald had barely clocked up two months in office. The only thing that appeased the assembled crowd was Donald's promise of quick action on radical land reform. It was a promise kept with the creation of Scotland's first national parks, the abolition of feudal tenure, radical community land-ownership plans and a wide-ranging right to roam all underway by the time of his death.

Later, somewhat tired and irritable, we stopped for a pre-arranged private supper at the Loch Fyne Oyster Bar with Peter McKinlay, the outgoing chief executive of Scottish Homes. Peter was a rather atypical public servant. He had been pestering me for a private meeting with the Secretary of State and I think Donald began the evening disappointed that I had relented! By the end of the evening, I felt less guilty – Donald had at least been intrigued by the reams of data on housing debt, on staff morale and on tenant empowerment and repairs with which he had been bombarded. Peter's proposition was that if Scottish Homes under the Conservatives could move thousands of homes to housing associations, then it was possible to develop a more radical model of community ownership to tackle Glasgow's historic housing problems. He was clear: this was not a 'big bang' solution of the sort that had failed the city so often in the past. Essentially, it was founded on empowering tenants to make decisions about their own homes and communities. It would build upon the existing housing association movement, which had been pioneered by sympathetic radicals and community activists in the

1970s, and Scottish Homes' own experience in disposing of its housing stock.

It became a theme of Donald's time in office but there is nothing surprising about Donald's interest in Glasgow housing – it had dominated his Saturday surgeries of the previous twenty years. Just under three years later in April 2000, only weeks before his heart operation, Donald launched Labour's plans for community ownership in Glasgow.[3] He said then, 'This gives us the chance to build better housing for the city, under the control of tenants. It will give a boost of confidence to the city's people and build stronger and safer communities . . . it offers the opportunity to eradicate the images of steel shutters and boarded-up houses. These images have no place in Scotland in the twenty-first century.'[4]

Indeed, the last meeting I ever had with Donald, on the Friday evening before his death, was about Glasgow housing. He was as enthusiastic as ever about the concept of community ownership, if somewhat worn down by the opposition it was encountering – not least within Labour's own ranks.

The events of that single July day in 1997 – when he demonstrated support for radical land reform and for the community ownership of social housing, while at the same time fighting a Whitehall rearguard action on some aspect of devolution – come close to capturing the essence of Donald's premiership. Donald never would have put it this way, he was far too self-effacing, but on that day he was starting to right some of the worst wrongs in the Scottish social arithmetic. He was bringing together the fight for a Scottish Parliament and the start of an assault on those twin scars of rural and urban Scotland – the unconscionable concentration of land ownership in a few hands and substandard urban housing. These wrongs had haunted the Scottish Labour Party since its inception. He was quietly getting on with the job of reversing those iniquities.

Donald, once regarded as a Labour right-winger in the battles of the 1980s, therefore eluded the easy labels of Old or New Labour. In fact, he confounded them. He exhibited precious few of the downsides of New Labour, such as a fascination with modern marketing or spin, and there is little doubt about the purpose of his politics being to challenge inequality wherever it stunted life chances. But he also believed that Labour had for two decades lost the trust of voters not because people were unconvinced that Labour cared about social justice but because Labour failed to carry conviction about its economic competence and its commitment to pursuing economic efficiency. These vital strands in Donald's personal political philosophy are themes that I return to in the concluding section.

Donald was not only Scotland's first First Minister he was also a Labour First Minister. He tried to put his convictions into action – and contributors assess his achievements in office in tackling housing debt; launching a social justice strategy; guaranteeing meaningful apprenticeships; providing a central heating system for all pensioner households without one; and introducing free local bus travel for pensioners. Donald sometimes bridled at the demands of high office but these things gave him real pride.

Donald was the very antithesis of showy. I recall on the Millennium Hogmanay he chose to attend a local Glasgow street party. Donald, Scotland's First Minister, was in an old holey pullover, nursing a plastic cup of mulled wine, chatting to residents and watching the fireworks in the back garden around the corner from Sam Galbraith's home. At one point, I nipped inside to try to find him a jacket to borrow against the cold night air. He was, as ever, without one. My eye caught the television coverage of the champagne and black-tie glitter of the Greenwich dome. Donald was contemptuous – he was happy where he was at an impromptu street party in his constituency. Well, not quite happy – he was also fretting about getting to Edinburgh sometime in the wee sma' hours to thank in person those civil servants condemned to be on 'Millennium Bug' duty in a bunker that night.

At the Parliament's opening in 1999, Donald said Scotland's Parliament should aspire to be 'a voice that shapes Scotland and a voice for the future'. But the issue that shaped Scotland for some time became the saga of the Holyrood building project. It came to settle over his legacy and indeed haunt the whole devolution project, at least until the conclusion of the Fraser Inquiry and the opening of the building.[5] Of course, one can only speculate about his possible reaction to unfolding events but I am drawn back to that speech at the Parliament's official opening in 1999, when he said, 'This is about more than our politics and our laws. This is about who we are, how we carry ourselves.' And in his next breath he continued even more prophetically, 'We are fallible. We will make mistakes.'

Even before the Parliament got down to business, Donald knew that the new nation would make mistakes. A man berated in his day as dithering Donald and derided for a lack of political vision came ironically after his death to be lambasted by many for wanting an iconic home for the Parliament. But Donald understood the power of history and symbolism. More than 200 years ago, Edinburgh would never have become the Athens of the North, so soon after the defeat at Culloden, without the visible symbolism of the New Town's visionary architecture. Donald never wanted the grandiosity of the Palace of Westminster for the devolved Scotland but he appreciated the understated grandeur of the New Town. He believed that a new era demanded a new start.

How he would have reacted had he lived to see the painful unfolding of the building process, as I have already said, can only be a matter of speculation. Many believe he would have banged heads together, addressed escalating costs and sought to hasten completion. He would certainly have exhibited his characteristic candour and humility. For good or ill, in 1997 he undoubtedly felt that if he left the decision about a new Parliament building until its members were elected, then the Parliament's first year would inevitably be dominated by an unseemly squabble between the parties about sites, architects and designs. But I believe Donald would also have accepted responsibility for any part that he felt he had played in the subsequent cost escalation. As a political 'old pro', he would not have been surprised by opponents charging him with fiddling the figures, fixing the architect and choosing the contract – all, incidentally, charges rejected by the Fraser Inquiry. He would have been more concerned about how to learn the lessons of the inquiry, notably how to create the capabilities the new Scotland needs. That would require complementing the undoubted expertise of officials (so critical in turning the hopes of the Scottish Constitutional Convention into the legislative reality) with the new and different skills now required to procure infrastructure, reform institutions and better manage public services.

Donald would have been shocked by the expense of the Parliament building but he would also have celebrated it as one of Britain's most exciting buildings: a work of architecture built at a high cost, in both cash and public credibility terms, yet also iconic, moving and modern. All this he sought but it was to be secondary to what was achieved within the building.

Donald was an essentially private man. He would have hated anyone poring over his private life and this book respects that sentiment. He was dismissive of the biography, or even autobiography, for which friends sometimes canvassed. However, Donald's very Scottish liking for personal privacy should not be assumed to mean he had no life beyond politics, as can be glimpsed in so many of the following chapters. And in life, the place of his children was clear to those around him. Sir Russell Hillhouse, former Permanent Secretary at the Scottish Office, recounts how on his first full day in office – Saturday, 3 May 1997 – Donald broke off from designing devolution to take his children, Marion and Iain, to lunch. And the birth of his first grandchild in January 1999 brought him the greatest pleasure.

Malcolm Rifkind and Neil MacCormick in their generous tributes acknowledge that Donald commanded respect and affection across the political spectrum more because of who he was than because of the office he held. Political foes described him as a 'cultured, civilised and . . . thoroughly decent man'. His shyness would have led him to cringe at the merest hint of political 'sainthood'. The well-meaning title 'Father of the Nation' resulted only in bluster, disdain and a dismissive wave of the hand; statues and memorials would have fared little better.

No doubt in due course a biography will appear. The purpose of this book is rather different: a series of essays in tribute to the man, reflecting upon both his life and his political legacy. Together they examine Donald's achievements, his style of politics, his vision for Scotland, and where the nation stands five years after his death. Organised into five sections, it traces his life, his links to Labour, to devolution, to Scotland and his legacy. I am very grateful to all who have contributed to that effort. Whilst Donald eschewed a biographer for himself (perhaps Donald the good gossip had enjoyed too many revealing biographies over the years), contributors provide many fresh insights. Five years on is too early for a definitive judgement but the right point to reflect on the contemporary relevance of his legacy. It is a legacy big enough to bear contributors' candour about his legendary rudeness, his intermittent indecision and his occasional depression.

I hope a book dedicated not only to looking back but also forwards with understanding about where Scotland has come from would have found favour with Donald. And if the early chapters reveal much about Donald the man, the closing ones say something about Scotland today. I believe Donald would have been cheered, relatively speaking, of course, if his legacy became a prism through which devolution, his, and Labour's, achievements were sympathetically and fairly re-assessed as a source of inspiration for this and future generations.

And, of course, any book that touches on the political life of the nation does so against a backdrop of some disappointment with devolution. Donald knew all too well, particularly in his private contemplative moments, how far the new Scotland had to travel. Yet the momentum surrounding devolution between 1997 and 2000 compelled him, in the words of Robert Louis Stevenson, to keep his fears to himself but share his inspiration with others. The playing out of some of those fears since his untimely death and the continuing inspiration he offers today are the subject of the concluding chapter.

Like so many contributors to this book, I thought I knew Donald well. But as memory is translated into legacy I've discovered something that I had never before fully appreciated. Donald was a politician typically renowned for his caution – and yet he also knew how to live dangerously when it really mattered.

His legacy should record that Donald was remarkably 'right' on the really big decisions of his political life: for example, beginning in 1988, by taking Labour into the Scottish Constitutional Convention, despite the party's widespread misgivings. Two years later, he persuaded Labour, against its own electoral interests, to support proportional representation for the future Parliament. In 1996, he was a prime mover in arguing that a referendum, and ultimately a two-question referendum, would be the only effective way to signal popular assent to – and so entrench – a future Parliament. It was a decision almost universally reviled by pro-devolutionists at the time. The following year, as Scotland's new Secretary of State, in his only significant departure from the Scottish Constitutional Convention's plans, he rejected the specifying of the Parliament's powers in favour of a more radical approach: devolving to Holyrood all matters not specifically reserved to Westminster. Imagine the subsequent frustrations that a more restrictive approach would have wrought. And more controversially, also in 1997, came his commitment to constructing an iconic parliament building, convinced that a new era demanded a fresh start. In 1998, his backing for Labour's radical plans to select equal numbers of male and female candidates led to a Parliament that was immediately catapulted into the bronze medal position internationally for women's representation. In 1999, he refused to leave at Westminster the social liberalism that had characterised his record since the earliest days and backed simultaneously repeal of section 2A (sometimes known as Clause 28) in both Scotland and Westminster in the same session of each Parliament.[6] In 2000, he signalled his antipathy to both old-style landlordism and old-fashioned municipal control with his championing of radical land reform and community ownership of Glasgow's social housing.

Looking back the pattern is clear. Donald did not deliberately court controversy and disliked confrontation. But he was also a politician unafraid to act in what he believed to be the national interest. No matter that such stances were deeply unpopular with his party, the public or the press of the day, all provoking howls of outrage and many calls for his political head. Yet which of these decisions have not been vindicated with the passage of time? For Donald, the big picture came before partisan considerations or the prevailing consensus. A man who by instinct was gentle on the people, he had the wisdom to be hard on the issues when it mattered, however much it sometimes hurt.

Such is the nature of true leadership. For all his apparent caution, Donald knew how, and when, to lead public and party opinion. These were not Old Labour or New Labour decisions – simply the right decisions. Decisions, of a conviction politician attempting always to act in the nation's interest, whilst also seeking to reinforce the common weal, and Scotland's collective commitment to fair chances for all.

Today he would be sanguine, laconic, sympathetic but still impatient for social justice. The memorial he would have cared most about was for Labour to hold the trust of the Scottish people in its efforts to right the social arithmetic and to see the Scottish Parliament grow into the heartbeat of the whole nation.

Donald, the man . . .

Even at university Donald always struck me as a rather old-fashioned Edwardian figure with a world-weary manner and a sardonic humour which he carefully cultivated and which never really left him. I opened the door to him on New Year's Day and greeted him conventionally with 'Happy New Year, Donald' to be answered by 'I see no reason, Meta, to assume that it will be.'

Baroness Meta Ramsay – friend

My untypical residence in an Adam mansion in the Borders must have appealed to his curiosity. He arrived at Berwick station on a winter evening, inevitably without an overcoat, devoured everything that Catherine had cooked, commented on our lamentable taste in wallpaper and then lay down on the floor to browse through books from the library of Patrick Home, who had been MP for Berwickshire in 1780. Later, he sent me an extract from a contemporary survey describing my embarrassing forebear's political allegiances.

John Home Robertson MSP – colleague

I always found him, especially in private – humorous and serious at the same time, and never, ever, patronising.

Bill Spiers, STUC – colleague

Donald didn't tell jokes. He told stories. He came out with some wonderful aphorisms, once describing the corps de ballet of a distinguished Russian company we had just seen as 'reminiscent of Knightswood Primary School'.

Ken Munro – friend

A Strange Childhood

Charlie Allan

My parents met Donald's parents when my father was working as a reporter and then feature writer on the *Glasgow Herald* and my mother was on the *Express*. I remember Dr Dewar as a Tory who thought he got a blue do when the health service was formed. My parents were both socialists. What they had in common was love of Scotland (as opposed to Scottish Nationalism) and the arts and literature of all sorts. Both sets of parents were active in the Glasgow Arts Society and the Saltire Society. The issue of each couple was a single boy.

For about four years between the ages of perhaps eight and twelve, Donald came to our farm in Aberdeenshire for holidays, which I remember as being long and fun. Dr Dewar, who seemed old, showed us how to make better bows and arrows, and even made a split cane fishing rod out of bamboo. He designed treasure hunts for us. And Mary Dewar, who was beautiful, brought sweeties.

But mostly we two were left to our own play with the half-dozen or so cottar bairns who by chance were all boys. We swam in the North Sea, caught bandies with nets in the River Ythan and made traps for trout out of the empty wine bottles, which our parents generated in abundance during those visits. We chased the pigeons in the barn till they dropped and we could wring their necks. Then we plucked them and cleaned them, my mother cooked them and we all ate them. We played kick-thecannie, tak-ye and heist-the-green-flag. We fought with insults and stones.

There were hours and hours of football, for which Donald had some inclination but no aptitude. I remember in particular Donald trying to keep goal against Joe Low, a few years our senior and much the best footballer among us. The future First Minister of Scotland, close to tears and nursing his stinging hands, upbraided the future First Plumber of Methlick for 'firing rockets at me'.

It wasn't an easy environment for the boy from Glasgow who had been at a boarding school (Beverley School near Bonchester Bridge) from about five years old because both his parents were too ill to look after him. His mother had a brain tumour and I was told that his father had had tuberculosis. He couldn't speak the Doric and 'talking' was a distinct disadvantage for a boy in Buchan in those days.

And yet, when the year came when it was announced that the Dewar family holiday would be enjoyed somewhere else, Donald cried so much that the plans were changed and he came once again to the farm.

Donald was different from the rest of us. He could read, for a start, and I don't just mean a few words. At eight years old, he could read whole books without pictures. He seemed to know all of Scotland's history as well as much of its literature. When he was back in Glasgow, we loons played at 'Bobbies and Burglars'. But when Donald came for his holidays we had William Wallace, Edward Long Shanks, the Duke of Montrose, John Knox, Alan Breck and, best of all, Colin Campbell, the Red Fox.

Instead of the typical bairns' housie, Donald designed a grand fort. It had a drawbridge, represented by a bentwood frame, which we could raise or lower with a rope. But this was such a pest to operate that Donald decided we should just creep in round the back and save the drawbridge for the arrival of 'distinguished visitors'. I think about that often and the irony that he was the only one of us then who knew what 'distinguished' meant and the only one who came remotely close to becoming himself 'distinguished'.

He was so well read that I asked Donald Dewar, when he was studying law at Glasgow University, why he had not done history. With all his knowledge I thought it would have been a cushy number for him as well as being in line with his interests. He told me that he had intended to read history but that he had been put right off by the first lecture. In that, the professor had said that to understand European history you had to know about an important family. He then wrote the word HABSBURG in block capitals on the board and told them to note the spelling. Donald couldn't see how this course was going to teach him much. I'm sure he was right. He didn't go back.

The young Dewar was not what is now called 'touchy feelie'. Duty kisses for old aunties were out. He was not above letting his intellectual superiority show and he could be bated into a rage. The charm and the patience with fools, which I found so unusual and so appealing in his political persona, came later. At the age of ten, when I was eight, I remember Donald telling me in very dismissive terms that I shouldn't say 'funnily enough'. 'Only authors and silly people like that say "funnily enough".' Such was the force of his personality that to this day I have not and would not say 'funnily enough'. And that despite the fact that even then I saw that he was not on firm ground. My father, his host, was John R. Allan, the author of that Scottish classic *Farmer's Boy*. I could see that it wasn't the most tactful of Donald's lessons.

We competed in everything, even the sweeties that Mary Dewar brought each summer. Because I ate so quickly she divided them in half. And so developed a keen competition to see who could make them last longest. I might have beaten the budding First Minister at football but when it came to still having lots of sweeties left long after I had finished mine, he was the master.

Donald and I enjoyed an aspect of childhood that is not open to young boys today. We were twice taken, by a very nice bachelor schoolmaster called Mr Mac, on a youth hostelling holiday. We travelled all over the west coast of Scotland and down as far as England in his little green car, which may have been a Morris Eight. We swam in the warm waters of the Gulf Stream one rainy night at dusk and we parked our car and walked the last few hundred yards in England because there you weren't supposed to youth hostel by car. Those were wonderful holidays and I saw no evidence of whatever it is that obsesses modern parents.

The other part of my boyhood relationship with Donald Dewar is more vivid for me because then I was the stranger. I stayed with him in Glasgow on at least three occasions.

By this time, he had left boarding school and was attending Glasgow Academy. There he had been introduced to the mysteries of rugby football. Donald seemed to find it easier to play with an oval ball than a round one. He showed his country cousin how to tackle properly with a most convincing demonstration. He grabbed me round the waist and told me to run away. That I did rather effectively. But when he grabbed me by the ankles I couldn't move one inch. I see him clearly still, on the floor in the corridor of his parents' top flat in Lacrosse Terrace, my ankles trapped and he looking earnestly up at me to be sure that I had got the point of 'tackling low'.

Donald took me to see Glasgow Academicals tackling low at Anniesland and to see George Young, Tiger Shaw and Willie Waddell tackling hard at Ibrox. But he was curiously embarrassed by his affection for Glasgow Rangers. He told me several times that he was a Partick Thistle supporter really, as Firhill was just up the road.

Donald also took me to a real golf course for my first ever round. It was a sore trial for the host. His athletic young guest halved the first hole and won all the rest.

But what I remember best was the bizarre fight that Donald organised for me.

He had this acquaintance who came from Partick on the other side of the River Kelvin. He was not only tough but also the leader of a small gang. Donald encouraged me that I too was quite tough and might manage to handle him. The venue was the back green of the tenement. I was introduced to Tom and we proceeded to fight. I can vouch for the fact that he was strong but thank goodness he wasn't nasty. In fact, as fighters go, he was very nice. Under the watchful eye of the future First Minister he would wrestle me to the ground, establish mastery and then let me get up saying, 'fair's fair', whereupon he would knock me down again.

In the 50 years in which I knew Donald subsequently, the great fight was never mentioned so I am only guessing. But I think that while Donald was quite proud of the plucky show his friend from the country had put up, he was even more proud of the way that Tom had shown me how tough Glasgow was.

I often produce tears. It only takes a sentimental passage in a book, the sight of Steve Redgrave winning his fifth gold medal or my old friend walking with the Queen at the opening of his life's work, and down they roll. But I can only remember twice in my life crying. The second time was when I heard the official announcement on Radio Scotland that Donald was dead. I was driving and I should really have stopped as wave upon wave of shuddering sobs shook me. We weren't close friends as adults and I don't really think I was crying for those boyhood days. I think

I was crying for Scotland. I could easily imagine our devolved status descending into chaos and I couldn't see a queue of Donald Dewars waiting to take his place.

I have always been proud of my early association with Donald, although we didn't choose one another. It was our parents who were close friends. As adults, we were only in touch intermittently. Although Donald was two years older than me, there was a short period in the early 1960s when I was a very junior lecturer at Glasgow University and Donald was a very senior law student, since in those days law was invariably a second degree. We did meet at least once and memorably for me. He had a den in his parents' house at which he introduced me to his friends John Smith and Jimmy Gordon.

I told Donald not to waste time replying to my congratulatory letter when devolution was won but to get on with making a good job of running Scotland. Nevertheless, he took precious time for a long reply, 'because I want to'.

I cherish my boyhood memories of Donald. But much more than that, I was so very proud of having a First Minister who had read so much that he could write his own speeches and had a Cadell over his fireplace. And how long will it be before we have another First Minister particular enough to say Scotland with a t in the middle?

At School: 1947–57

John Kerr

The Glasgow Academy was formally dedicated to those who had died in the First World War. I was therefore educated literally inside a war memorial. Each morning, the first thing I saw as I approached the school was a pale granite slab which stood at the corner of Great Western Road and Colebrooke Street and bore the names of former pupils of the school who had died in the war. There was a similar 'roll of honour' on the second floor of the main school building, a cavernous neo-classical edifice. Sometimes, on the way from algebra to Latin, we walked right past it. The balcony was so narrow that we had to go in single file and each time I had a chance to read one of the names, above all of which there was the legend 'Say not that the Brave Die'. I think my first serious historical thought was an objection to that stern injunction. But they did die. Why deny it? Thus Niall Ferguson, in the introduction to his book *The Pity of War*, explains how history hung heavily in the Academy air, particularly the history of a tragedy that unfolded half a century before his birth, and how it led enquiring minds both to respect the past and to question the lessons authority drew from it.

The haze of history was thicker when Donald Dewar started his ten years in the war memorial in Colebrooke Street, only two years after Hiroshima and Nagasaki and the discovery of Auschwitz and Bergen-Belsen. The new names on the 'roll of honour' glinted freshly. Trams stood still on the silent Great Western Road at 11 a.m. For 11 November, the cadet force honour guard marched the wreath of poppies down to the granite slab, the whole school watching. Playground lore, not always wrong, ascribed to certain younger masters heroic Second World War roles and attributed to First World War horrors the evident eccentricities of certain of their older colleagues. No one objected when, once a week, we all came to school in military uniform and learned how to shoot or to name the parts of a Bren gun: it all seemed entirely natural, with two years of compulsory national service in prospect when one left the Academy. I don't remember any of this making us worried, but it did perhaps make us more conscious, than are present-day schoolboys, of events, past and present, in the political world beyond Colebrooke Street. Donald was an arch-example of someone aware of wider dramas and of the continuity of past and present. But he was not alone; and it is probably no accident that the Academy produced not just great academic historians like Ferguson (or Norman Stone or Neil MacGregor) but also a striking number of public servants. To say that the place preached responsibility and taught a sense of being heirs to a great tradition would sound pompous. But memorials do have such effects.

All this produced, in many of us, a rather douce 'West End' respect for convention. Not in Donald. In him, the dual effect described by Ferguson was clear. It made him a historian but also a critic. The Upper VIth, in which he was an academic star, provided the cadet force with its sergeants and sergeants-major; and Corporal Dewar. Drill was impeccable, except for Cpl Dewar's distressing habit of marching with first left arm and left leg, then right arm and right leg, coming forward together, a skill that must have taken hours of practice. He dominated the debating society but was happiest memorably proposing the motions that 'Life is Dull' and 'The Old School Tie should be Burned'. He was never a school prefect: to try to exercise petty authority would have been alien to its wittiest critic. And yet he wasn't really a rebel: real rebels don't take on the chore of writing the record for the school magazine. Lacking sporting talent, other than an enthusiasm for rough golf at Knightswood Corporation course (9d for nine holes and another nine for nothing if the man in the hut was feeling charitable), he poked fun at the heroes of the XV and XI; yet he regularly went to watch them play and it was he who kept the cricket scorebook. Not a natural actor like MacGregor or Bob Maclennan, he nevertheless regularly volunteered for a part in the summer Shakespeare play and the Christmas pantomime. Few *Dreams* can have been enlivened by a gloomier Quince, and few *Aladdin*s featured as disdainful a genie, viewing his wizardry with such detachment and distaste.

Donald and I started at the Academy on the same day but I was four years below him in the school; he was my older brother's friend and to me a distant giant. Trying now to define what, apart from the lanky, almost gawky, look, made him stand out so much from the blue-blazered ranks of the respectable, I don't think it was his cleverness: others too were clever and all tigers seem smart to the cubs. I don't think it was even his unusual ability to be at the same time both loquacious and lugubrious. I suspect it was the enthusiasm, so inadequately concealed by the assumed pessimism. Nothing bored him, except mathematics, of course. He was a master of exaggeration: with a straight face he would vigorously pursue an argument well beyond the point of absurdity, maintaining the self-evident truth of an assertion that no solemn son of the Kelvin could conceivably concede. My mother, no mean conversationalist herself, and not short of a view on the issues of the hour, was on her mettle when my brother brought Donald home for tea after school but his technique would fox her every time. He would let her identify the subject for discussion and draw her into explaining what all right-thinking folk thought. Then, very politely and starting quite hesitantly, he would build a crescendo of arguments all leading ineluctably to precisely the opposite conclusion. She fought in vain. She knew it was a tease. When he left, a dismissive 'Och, he's nothing but a long cold drink of water' would be followed by her urging my brother to bring Donald home again soon.

He was probably a bit of a loner until quite late in his career at the Academy. Those who started as five year olds tended to stick together and he was a latecomer. Academic prowess cuts no playground ice and prizes win no plaudits there. The ill health which kept him, at fourteen, away for much of one year, left him formidably well read, but required him to repeat that year's classes, separated from former friends and older than most new classmates. Probably some masters let their irritation show (as may well have been his hope) when his critical barbs hit home. But I think he enjoyed swimming against the tide and by the time he reached the Vth Form, writing essays already at university honours level, he had clearly found his niche, and I think he felt at home in the school.

In fact, I know he did. Forty years later, and by then Scotland's number one politician, Donald sat in a Washington summer garden, talking about

Glasgow Academy. 'Terrible place, wasn't it?' he started, and then demonstrated, at considerable length, that he thought no such thing. The gentle classicist rector he had teased so imaginatively turned out to have been an admired guide to Roman history. The shy modern linguist who had wasted love for the language of Racine on stolid schoolboy ears was revealed as the inspiration for a lifelong interest in modern France. He recalled tears in our English master's eyes at an A.E. Housman verse; he could still mimic the electric delivery of Lord Reith's prizegiving speech; even the absurdities of cadet force summer camp were remembered with affection.

The Pity of War had not then appeared, and I never thought to ask Donald whether, like Ferguson, he had felt a sense of being heir to the names on the walls. Because solemnity was hardly his style, my guess is that he would have first dismissed the thought as pretentious but then, if pressed, would have acknowledged its force. He was an unconvincing Diogenes. The cynicism, well honed in years of being 'agin the government' at the Academy, was the surface: underneath, even then, and encouraged then, was the sense of history and responsibility, as well as the enthusiasm and energy, in which lay the seeds of his commitment to public service. What a tragedy that the harvest was so cut short.

Coming of Age

Jimmy Gordon

It was through John Smith that I first met Donald Dewar. Donald and John followed the same academic courses at Glasgow University in the late 1950s and early '60s – MA (Hons) in history, followed by an LLB, which in those days was done concurrently with serving an apprenticeship in a law firm, for which, as I recall, they were paid the princely sum of £50 a year in the first year, rising to £75 in the second and £100 in the third!

It was John I knew first and best, from the summer before he started at Glasgow University in 1955, and we became firm friends. But, whereas John and Donald were united by a common interest in the Labour Party, manifest at that stage by membership of the Labour Club, of which both eventually became President, by contrast at university I was a Distributist. More importantly, I also felt conscious of a class difference between myself and Donald and some of his other friends. I felt more at ease with John's immediate circle of friends than with Donald's – who even played bridge! It seems silly now, and was undoubtedly more due to a chip on my working-class shoulder rather than any discernible behaviour pattern on their part, but I felt acutely conscious that Donald was definitely middle class. I am not thinking so much of material matters – although he had his own flat in the basement of his parents' home in Royal Terrace and the use of a car – but rather his almost inherited sense of the importance of Scottish culture and familiarity with it and his knowledge of Scottish history. Later, perhaps when I had caught up a little on my own reading, I began to appreciate more and more how profoundly Donald was attached to Scotland's cultural past. He had old-fashioned values, even at university, and in some respects I think he might have been happier living in the age of the Scottish Enlightenment! He was most definitely a Lowland Scot who felt uncomfortable with public displays of emotion and used his disparaging sense of humour to disguise his embarrassment. His love of things Scottish was cerebral and aesthetic rather than romantic. Indeed, he could be fairly dismissive of the more romantic Scottish myths which some mistake for our heritage. He was very good on Burns but again dismissed the 'poor untaught ploughman wearing the hodden grey' myth well before it became the fashion to do so. His sense of the distinctiveness of Scottish culture was reinforced by his respect for, and knowledge of, Scotland's Presbyterian traditions, on which I sometimes feel he would have liked to write a book.

If his personal qualities and values derived from his home background, it was Glasgow University and, more particularly, the debates there, which gave him the skills to use them to impact on a wide audience.

At Glasgow University in the late 1950s, debating and social activities, formal or informal, were run by Glasgow University Union, whereas in many other universities these were the province of the students' representative council (SRC). The union was, on paper, anachronistic: a club, though in fact open to all (provided they were male – although that was to change in the 1960s). At Glasgow, the SRC, by contrast, represented students' interests to the university authorities and was affiliated to other more political bodies like the Scottish Union of Students. Although relations between the SRC and the union were generally good, the fault lines of dispute were already beginning to show. John and I were more identified with the union cause than was Donald.

After serving on the SRC, Donald switched to the union, where he became assistant secretary in the year in which John Smith was convener of debates. Donald later went on to be president of the union. Incidentally, Donald always kept up with Mrs Whiteford, who had been the fulltime secretary at the SRC, and would continue to visit her right up to her 100th birthday.

Anyone meeting Donald for the first time would, of course, be struck by his tall gangling frame and angular appearance – usually slumped untidily in the most comfortable chair available. When he spoke, you were suddenly conscious of someone with the best command of the English language I have encountered – particularly his selection of witty and felicitous adjectives to describe and mock any particular scene or individual normally used to more reverential treatment. He had also a very rapid machine-gun delivery that frequently meant that you didn't have time to laugh at his first description before he had trumped it with an even finer phrase in the next clause. Malcolm Rifkind, for the Conservatives, had an equally rapid delivery and I have often felt that Hansard reporters, covering clashes between them in the House of Commons, must have felt they were taking part in the Hansard Olympics.

Donald undoubtedly honed his debating skills, which were to stand him in such good stead at both Westminster and Holyrood, in the Glasgow University Union, where he was a member of yet another Glasgow team to win the Observer Mace National Debating Tournament, open to all universities in Britain and Ireland.[1]

Despite Donald's enviable command of the English language, he had a curious inability to spell properly. John once told me that in a history essay Donald had spelt Garibaldi four different ways, all of them wrong! When the Labour Club was running Clement Attlee as a candidate in the rectorial election, Donald again managed to spell his name incorrectly.

When he was a law apprentice in the firm of Wright, Johnston and McKenzie, I remember him sidling off from an elongated coffee break with an 'I'd better get back to R J and M.' His frequent absences from the law office were usually explained by the necessity of attending a grandmother's funeral, till one of the partners pointed out that three such events was becoming a little excessive. He was also found on one occasion crumpled up in the company safe reading a morning newspaper.

He rejoiced in the affectionate nickname of 'the Gannet', a reference to his prodigious appetite, which miraculously and unfairly never seemed to leave its mark on his spare frame. I have seen half a dozen of us having a curry or a Chinese meal and Donald unashamedly scooping up all the remains – and then looking for pudding. Puddings for Donald didn't necessarily come singly. He would opt for, say, trifle and then suggest 'and you could possibly add in a little fruit salad as well' and then as an afterthought 'and a spot of ice cream would do no harm'. Cheese was not an alternative, even when specified as such on the menu, but an additional course to be savoured. I recall one meal that John and Donald and I were having in an almost deserted hotel dining room. Puddings had been ordered but when the waiter went to the kitchen, Donald decided to pinch some cheese from the trolley and just made it back to the table where he sat transfixed like a startled rabbit with the immobility of the guilty as the door from the kitchen swung open to reveal the waiter who I am sure realised exactly what had happened.

I would imagine that, as a Labour supporter, Donald was a fairly solitary figure at Glasgow Academy but at university the Labour Club was going through a good period and Donald was one of its stars. Although he was obviously extremely interested in politics and deeply committed to the Labour Party, I do not know if at university he had harboured thoughts of a career in politics. All that would change with the East Fife by-election in 1961, when John Smith was standing as the Labour candidate in what was traditionally a safe Conservative seat (although now, of course, held by another Glasgow contemporary, Menzies Campbell, for the Liberal Democrats). Carloads of students and recent graduates from Glasgow went through each weekend to support John – some of us weren't even members of the Labour Party at that point. Whether that by-election sowed the seed in Donald's mind, as in others, that standing for Parliament might be a logical continuation of debating at Glasgow University, I don't know. Certainly the role of Willie Marshall, then secretary of the Scottish Labour Party, should not be underestimated. Willie had an almost godfather role in trying to ensure that some of the bright young students from Glasgow were at least fielded at constituency selection conferences in the hope that one or two might find their way through and be adopted as parliamentary candidates. Obviously, they had to cut their teeth on seats which at that point were thought to be unwinnable, and, if they did well, it would serve as an advertisement for selection committees in the safe Labour seats.

In 1964, John felt duty bound to stay and fight East Fife again, while Donald had been adopted for Aberdeen South, then held by Lady Tweedsmuir for the Conservatives, and more than halved her majority from just over 8,000 to just under 4,000. It is no disrespect to Donald to say that everyone anticipated that John would make it into Parliament first but, to many people's surprise, possibly including his own, Donald won Aberdeen South at the 1966 election by 1,799 votes, whereas John was rejected by one selection conference after another in safe Labour seats and had to wait till 1970 before he inherited North Lanark from Peggy

Herbison. John, as a supporter of Gaitskell in the early 1960s, was regarded as being too right wing.

Donald was now in Westminster and, although he kept on the flat in Cleveden Road where the parties at Hogmanay were legendary, he and Alison, whom he had married in 1964, set up a flat in Exhibition Road in London.

Needless to say, Donald's talents showed through quickly at Westminster, although the four years of the 1966–70 Labour government were perhaps too short for him to have any realistic hopes of ministerial office. I was, by this time, political editor of Scottish Television and featured Donald frequently in my weekly programme, *The Commons Touch*, simply because he was so good. My abiding recollection of that period, however, is of a Scottish Labour Party conference in 1970. The loss of Hamilton in November 1967 to the Scottish Nationalist Party, followed by SNP successes in the local elections in 1968, had sent shockwaves through the Labour Party, which made any rational discussion of devolution seem almost traitorous. By this time, the SNP, not the Conservatives, were the enemy and Jim Sillars was the hero of the day for holding on to South Ayrshire in the by-election of March 1970 and for his famous pamphlet 'Don't Butcher Scotland's Future', attacking the SNP case. At that conference, I can recall only two Labour MPs speaking up in favour of at least consideration of devolution as a better form of government for Scotland. One was the late John P. Mackintosh and the other was Donald Dewar. His commitment to devolution was a long-standing one.

If the fates had been unkind to John Smith in denying him a winnable seat for so long, 1970 was to deal Donald a cruel blow with the loss of Aberdeen South back to the Conservatives. He was not to re-enter Parliament until 1978, just in time for 18 years in opposition.

But the early '70s were bad for Donald in other respects. His marriage to Alison was beginning to break up, with divorce taking place in 1973. If that was not enough, I recall visiting him in hospital with the start of the back problem that was to plague him for virtually the next 25 years. He was frequently in pain walking and it often showed on his face, although some mistook it for his simply being in a bad mood.

From a career point of view, he worked again as a lawyer with his old friend Ross Harper and was also a reporter to the children's panel in Lanarkshire. I also asked him to do the political programmes on Radio

Clyde in the '70s, having been able to virtually guarantee his impartiality to the other political parties, not only because of his innate fair-mindedness but because of how he felt about the way the Labour Party in the 1970s when the Bennite trend was already gaining ground.

It was to be 31 years after he first entered Parliament in 1966 before he achieved the ministerial office he so clearly deserved and later became the first First Minister of the Scottish Parliament. He knew a lot about Scottish history and it is fitting that he was allowed to play such a significant part in the making of the latest chapter of it.

As a Friend

Fiona Ross

It was March 1966. I was 18 years old. It was a great time to be a teenager. A new youth culture was erupting – the Beatles, hippies, Carnaby Street, Mary Quant. My home in Ayr was a long way from all that. My father, Willie Ross, was Secretary of State for Scotland. He worried about political things that seemed even further away, such as the Highlands and Islands Development Board. I worried about how short I could make my skirts. All sorts of politicians visited our house but I didn't pay much attention.

The one who arrived that March day seemed different. A general election was in full swing. Dad had been campaigning in Aberdeen South and the candidate had driven him home to Ayr. This hopeful's suit was a shambles, his hair straggled in every direction and black thick-framed spectacles made him look like an extra from a low-budget 1950s film. Decidedly square, there was obviously nothing to be learned about rock and roll from him. Expecting a tedious election discussion, I decided to make an excuse and leave.

But then his limbs folded up in an extraordinary, inexplicable way. Collapsing inelegantly into a chair, he immediately launched into a torrent of stories about the miseries of electioneering in the rain; in damp meeting rooms with peeling wallpaper; in cars that broke down; with leaflets that turned to mush; and with bizarre, bumbling activists that sounded as though they came from the *Lord of the Rings*. Stories that were mildly amusing to begin with became shriekingly funny. He had the comedian's gift of turning the miserable into the hilarious. I had never met anyone quite so funny. I sat there spellbound. He must have talked for an hour, pausing only to munch his way through a vast quantity of my mother's shortbread. And then the verbal machine gun swept out again.

It was eight years later I really got to know him. Donald had lost the Aberdeen South seat in 1970 and was working first as a reporter to the children's panels in Lanarkshire and then as a solicitor with his old friend Ross Harper. While he continued to pursue his political ambitions, another friend, Jimmy Gordon, who was managing director of the new independent station, Radio Clyde, gave him the job of presenting the weekly political programme *Clyde Comment*. As a junior reporter, I was Donald's researcher, which meant I fixed the interviews. He did one with the new Tory leader in 1975 – Margaret Thatcher. It was not an experience she cared to repeat. Donald was put on her 'blacklist'. He professed outrage but he was actually quite proud.

It was during this time that we began our practice of meeting once a week or so and it continued until his death some 25 years later. Initially, it was a method of winding down after the programme. We discussed the performance of the various contributors and the issues to be tackled in the future. Donald was clearly the dominant figure in this friendship, with a wealth of knowledge and experience. He treated me as an equal; indeed, he treated everyone as an equal. Donald, throughout his life, was just as happy having a conversation with the cleaning lady as he was talking to a head of state. Despite that, I always got the impression he really thought I was an 'airhead' but it was Donald who suggested I take over the programme when he left Radio Clyde in 1978 to stand in the Garscadden by-election. Having a woman fronting a political programme in the '70s was almost unheard of.

Clearly he didn't think I was entirely stupid and he trusted me. Also, over the years I came to realise that Donald didn't do emotion. He could analyse a problem intellectually but when it came to determining motive he was at a loss. I think that was where I came in. Explaining why people behaved the way they did.

Donald was an impossible friend. To begin with, he was never on time, but the excuses were wonderful. On one occasion, he arrived very late at a dinner party. The hostess was furious and the guests starving. Most of them had never met him before and didn't know how to react when he explained, with a straight face, that he'd been at his tailor's. He would then glare at me, daring me not to laugh. While he had no interest whatsoever in his clothes, he was very good at criticising everyone else's. Mine seemed to hold a particular fascination. I recall a 20-minute interrogation about how much I spent every month, followed by the observation that the latest addition to my wardrobe made me look like an air hostess.

Donald had a novel method of demonstrating his friendship. He insulted you. He slagged off friends to their faces and behind their backs. I was 'very difficult'. Roy Hattersley looked and sounded like his dog, 'Buster'. Wendy Alexander was 'impossible'. Meta Ramsay was 'awkward'. Murray Elder was 'thrawn'. But at other times each was described as 'a good thing'. The test of friendship was that Donald could malign his friends but anyone who attempted to join in did so at his or her peril.

No one was spared his mischievous observations. The Queen was described as 'a plucky wee lady', while a political colleague who started to dye his hair was dismissed in the words of Oscar Wilde, 'he went quite gold with grief'. I did think that the arrival of the American President at a cabinet meeting might generate some excitement but as far as Donald was concerned Bill Clinton wasn't a charismatic politician, he was 'a happening'.

Friends talk on the phone. Donald barked. 'What are you doing? Do you want a curry? I'll pick you up in ten minutes.'

He called me one night from the ministerial car. Unusually, the conversation had no purpose. He finally admitted, like an excited child going to a party, that he was en route to Chequers. The following day I was given a detailed and hugely entertaining account of his fellow guests, although these were of secondary interest. The main attraction of Chequers was the library. Donald's love of books didn't simply extend to reading them. He would often buy a book because he liked the feel of it. One Sunday he read *Treasure Island*. Of course he'd read it before but, as he explained to me, this was a particularly fine leather-bound edition that he'd picked up in a second-hand bookshop.

Books and pictures were about the only things he ever spent money on and although the former were carefully stored on specially built shelves, or in glass-fronted bookcases, the pictures, for many years, lay on the floor. His house in Cleveden Road was horrendous. No creature comforts, it was reminiscent of a 1960s student flat. The carpets were threadbare and the paint peeling off the walls. There was no central heating. When the ancient electric fire in the sitting room broke, he bought another and put it in front of the original one. His television could have been a collector's item. It was enormous, with long spindly legs. It pre-dated the invention of remote controls. And everywhere there were piles of papers. Donald was in no doubt about how awful it was. Few people were allowed over the doorstep. He did eventually buy another house, just round the corner, and when he was in hospital for his heart operation, his two children Marion and Iain did what I suspect they'd wanted to do for years. They gutted Cleveden Road and organised the new flat, painting, decorating and buying furniture, including a state-of-the-art television, so when he came out he had no choice but to move to his new home.

Donald had dozens of friends. They saw an entertaining, amusing guest who would glory in 'holding court', telling scurrilous tales of colleagues past and present and turning mundane events into hilarious vignettes. But there was another side to Donald that few people saw. When Donald and I were, more usually, alone and without the audience, a very different person emerged. There were serious moments of self-doubt and black despair.

The first time I saw this was in the 1980s when he was facing reselection. The in-fighting in his Garscadden constituency was so poisonous that he considered resigning and causing a by-election. We had dinner the night before the final vote, which incidentally he won fairly easily, but he refused to be convinced. I gave up arguing and suggested that he shouldn't go quietly. He must resign and go out on a scandal by running off with a chorus girl. 'They're in very short supply,' was his response.

But perhaps the worst time was when he was Secretary of State for Scotland in the run up to the Scottish Parliament elections in 1998. Having raced through his first year in government with first the Scotland Bill and then the devolution referendum, he seemed to run out of momentum. He was under huge pressure at Westminster as various English colleagues suddenly woke up to the extent of the constitutional changes they'd agreed to. He was not good at keeping the media abreast of what was happening and so they turned on him and accused him of dragging his feet on policy issues. In the Labour Party, there was an endless series of rows over the selection of candidates for the Scottish Parliament, with many colleagues demanding he intervene on their behalf.

In short, Donald felt he was being bullied by everyone, but instead of confronting these people, he cowered in a corner. Confrontation on a personal level was something Donald avoided. He openly admitted to me that in terms of leadership qualities, he was lacking 'the killer instinct' and wished he had more of the personality of his old friend John Smith, who when it came to troublemakers was, in Donald's words, 'a bastard'. The personal attacks hurt Donald and caused him to slide into what I can only describe as a serious depression. He would sit up till 4 a.m. watching television, which is how he gained his encyclopaedic knowledge of Italian football. He was paralysed by indecision, totally convinced that everyone was against him – government colleagues at Westminster, activists in Scotland, the media and even his closest friends and advisers. Some were undoubtedly out to undermine him but the majority, like me, were trying to help. We were attempting to outline solutions rather than problems but he didn't want to hear any of it. To the outside world, he was irritable and irascible. In my house, he was talking of resigning.

Persuading Donald to open up was not easy. He would arrive at my house, lie on the floor and, having taken ownership of the television remote control, would feign interest in just about anything to stop me questioning him. And I mean anything. One night I was subjected to a documentary about an amateur theatre group in San Francisco who were preparing for a performance of *The Mikado*. Being deafened by a discordant version of 'The Lord High Executioner' did not strike me as the most effective way to combat depression. At this point, hardly a year into the Labour government, the Secretary of State who'd spent 18 years in the political wilderness, and finally had the job he'd always aspired to, was threatening to walk away. Donald was exhausted, and said on several occasions, 'I can't go on like this. This constant grind. On an endless treadmill.' He complained that in England, ministers could relax, as it would take the Tories some time to regroup, whereas in Scotland politics was on a war footing, with another year of campaigning up to the new parliament elections in 1999. The discussion of resignation was serious. He considered not standing for the Scottish Parliament and remaining at Westminster, where he would doubtless have been given another Cabinet position, possibly Leader of the House or Chief Whip. However, the option he favoured was to resign from the Cabinet and simply retire from politics at the next election. 'If I gave up this job,' he said, 'I would miss it but not much.'

But what would he do? He claimed he would take up writing and travelling, something he'd done little of. There was also vague mention of 'drifting' and 'getting a life'. This was a continuing theme over several months. The most difficult aspect of it was I couldn't tell anyone. That would have been regarded as an act of extreme disloyalty and loyalty was everything to Donald. It was when he announced that he'd finally decided that he would devote his retirement to sorting out his house that I realised he was coming out of the black despair. Such a notion was not remotely credible. As I look back on this bleak period, I now realise this was probably the start of his heart problems. He complained for weeks of being tired and having a chest infection but refused to visit a doctor.

When he was first admitted to hospital for tests in 2000, it was as much a shock to me as anyone else. He called me when he got out, explaining that he hadn't wanted to worry me but assured me he would tell me when his heart operation was scheduled, which he did. As he was recuperating from heart surgery, I saw him on a daily basis. Sam Galbraith told me it was imperative Donald take up walking to improve his circulation. Initially, it was a gentle stroll round the West End, with my personal architectural guide. These outings were fascinating. Donald was literally a walking expert in the history of the area. However, as the walks became five-mile hikes, I was excused. As Donald pointed out, I was in severe danger of getting fit.

During those brief few months before his death, we continued to visit restaurants all over Glasgow. We talked about everything and I found him reminiscing more and more. He never spoke directly about his own death but I do recall him saying that six weeks after anyone died, they were pretty much forgotten. It never really occurred to Donald that people regarded him as 'the Father of the Nation'. At his funeral, I could imagine him muttering disapproval at all the fuss. He wasn't vain or ambitious. This rather old-fashioned figure had old-fashioned values and loyalty was high on that list. The trappings and pressures of office were irrelevant. Friends were friends and he always had time for friends. He was unswervingly loyal to his country, his party and his friends.

There are many aspects of Donald that I still miss – even his spectacular rudeness – but no one could make me laugh quite like Donald.

As a Boss

David Whitton

To Donald Dewar the description of him as 'boss' would be anathema. He did not see himself in those terms and those of us privileged to work with him quickly discovered it was not a title that he liked. Call him boss and you'd be guaranteed one of those stares across the top of his glasses. A similar fate would befall you should you dare to describe him as 'Father of the Nation', another title bequeathed to him that he found perplexing.

Donald preferred to be called just that, Donald. Not for him fancy titles or any bowing or scraping. He would treat everyone the same: Cabinet colleague, civil servant, political adviser, constituent or someone he met in the street, and perhaps that is why he was so popular. In many ways, the song sung at the opening of the Scottish Parliament, 'A man's a man for a' that', could have been his theme tune.

I first met Donald Dewar shortly after moving to Glasgow to take up a job with *The Scotsman* newspaper when he was Labour's candidate in the famous Glasgow Garscadden by-election. In those days, his horn-rimmed glasses and trademark staccato speaking delivery punctuated with many umms and ahs did not instantly mark him out as the great figure he would become. Over the next few years I got to know him better, especially when I spent two years working for Scottish Television as their parliamentary correspondent at Westminster.

It was not until 1998, a year after he became Secretary of State for

Scotland, that I went to work for him. I had met him and Wendy Alexander, then one of his advisers, at the Scottish Council Forum being held at Gleneagles. Donald arrived late, still scribbling away at his speech. In truth, his delivery that night was not good and his remarks got a lukewarm reception. The press seized on one particular line about ring fencing Scottish companies to prevent their corporate headquarters being moved elsewhere.

Afterwards, I told Wendy what I thought of his performance and gave her my opinion on how things could be improved. Imagine my surprise when three days later I was invited to visit Donald in his favourite office, Meridian Court in Cadogan Street, Glasgow. We chatted over the speech, went through various issues, with him asking lots of penetrating questions about media coverage, and then he completely stunned me by saying, 'The Prime Minister says I can have a third adviser, do you want the job?' He promised me it would be exciting and that I would be getting the chance to be involved in a piece of history: the creation of Scotland's first parliament for almost 300 years. With an invitation like that who could refuse?

Although I had plenty of ideas on how to present Labour policies in Scotland, I quickly discovered that Donald could be a media manager's nightmare. For a start, he didn't really care what he looked like. That posed a problem or two in an age where television is a dominant medium. Then he wasn't that interested in what any paper other than *The Herald* was saying. He regarded it as Glasgow's paper; he was a Glaswegian representing one of the city's constituencies, so that's what counted.

He was not the type of politician who was always on the phone to pals in the media seeking to get them to write articles in his favour. He did have some close friends working in newspapers and television but they were of long standing and were not going to betray his confidences.

When we did have something really good to tell the press, more often than not he would not want to do it and had to be persuaded it was worthwhile. However, when he did make up his mind to do something he could be very stubborn. During the elections for the Scottish Parliament, all requests to interview him were carefully vetted. A request came from the Scottish *Daily Mail*, not a Labour-supporting paper, for Colette Douglas Home to do a profile. The campaign managers said no, as they feared a stitch up. Donald said yes, because he knew Colette and said she would not do such a thing. Donald won the day and when the interview appeared it was just fine.

On the night of the count for the Scottish Parliament elections, I went to collect him to take him to the Scottish Exhibition and Conference Centre in Glasgow for the declaration of his result. I found his flat in darkness, as the area was suffering a power cut. We floundered about with the aid of a torch as he got changed. Then as we went down the garden path to his car Donald slipped and fell but was fortunately not hurt. A similar type of fall just over two years later would have a more devastating outcome.

After he became First Minister of Scotland, the demands from the media intensified, as did the demands of the job. The work involved long hours but Donald would always want to make sure his members of staff were not overdoing it. Although he jealously guarded his own privacy, he also took a great interest in their lives, asking sometimes very personal questions about their backgrounds, their likes and dislikes. Then he took great delight in making teasing comments about a particular hobby or pastime. All of his staff were extremely loyal to him and would have done anything for him.

He had a particularly sparky relationship with Sandra Buckle, his administration assistant, who, amongst other things, typed his speeches, often having to decipher the famous Dewar handwriting. On many occasions, Donald found himself on the receiving end of a cutting put-down that would have him laughing out loud. I can't think of many other top-ranking politicians who would have encouraged that kind of verbal exchange; indeed, I can think of quite a few who wouldn't have tolerated it at all. But Donald took the view if you dish it out, you've got to take it.

In an age of modern communication, he was a Luddite. Although equipped with a pager he often forgot it. He had a mobile phone but wasn't entirely sure how to use it, especially when it came to recharging the battery. Every MSP was given a laptop but Donald's stayed in the box. This could sometimes cause problems, especially at weekends when I was under pressure to get a quote from him about some article or another that had appeared in the papers. Very often, calls were diverted to his message service and pager messages were not returned. Then, when I would meet up with him on the Monday, he would deny ever having had a call.

People worked hard for Donald not because he demanded it of them but because they wanted to. Everyone could see how much he put into his job and wanted to help him by doing their bit. He was not someone who would shout and demand things but he could let his displeasure be known more often than not with a heavily sarcastic put-down, as opposition politicians often found to their cost. He was not someone who enjoyed confrontation either and that was perhaps a weakness, especially with some political colleagues who took advantage.

Donald's greatest achievement was the Scotland Act, bringing devolution to Scotland. Yet having established the Parliament he didn't seem to know what to do next. I asked him if we had a plan for the first 100 days, a plan similar to that used by New Labour when it took power in 1997. The answer was no.

Instead, there was a week of consultation with the Liberal Democrats and from that emerged the first partnership agreement. It is doubtful if any other Labour politician at the time could have negotiated such a deal with Jim Wallace. Donald wasn't interested in headlines for his achievements; he just wanted to get the Parliament up and running.

The first legislative programme prompted a negative media response – 'Is that it?' Yet among those first Bills was the Adults with Incapacity Act, which made things much easier for those with relatives suffering from diseases such as Alzheimer's. As we walked back to the office down the Royal Mile, a couple stopped Donald in the street and thanked him for introducing legislation they had been waiting years for. That kind of response meant much more to him than any *Herald* editorial. His true leadership was shown during the row over the repeal of section 28 (section 2A of the Local Government Act 1986 was inserted by section 28 of the LGA 1988). Despite daily attacks from the *Daily Record*, Scottish *Sun* and Scottish *Daily Mail*, aided and abetted by a multimillion-pound campaign funded by entrepreneur Brian Souter, Donald never wavered.

There were divisions in his Cabinet, including leaks to the press, and Labour lost the Ayr by-election but Donald, while being careful always to seek the opinion of his colleagues, kept things together through consultation and negotiation. He believed it was the right thing to do. It had been Labour policy for years and despite the mud-slinging he stuck to his guns and got the repeal through Parliament. He regarded that as a proud moment for the new Scotland created by devolution.

After he became ill with his heart-valve problems, he was very reluctant to divulge any details, regarding it as a private matter. When I tried to explain that it was in fact a public matter, as he was First Minister, I got one of those stares. Once he returned to work, it wasn't too long before he was setting the same arduous pace as before. It was a mistake but he did it because as First Minister he felt a sense of duty to the people of Scotland: those who elected him and those who hadn't. Not a boss or Father of the Nation, but a leader, leading from the front, not hiding back in HQ using illness as an excuse for lack of activity.

Donald, my boss, only asked that you do your best. Yet, he inspired such loyalty amongst those closest to him that he didn't need to be constantly issuing instructions, as they would always go the extra mile to help him get results.

I cried on the day he died as I tried to write the announcement I had to make to the waiting media. Not something I've done often as an adult. I wasn't the only one. Many thousands of others whose lives had been touched by Donald Dewar cried with me. I still miss him and think about him a lot and wonder at times what he would have said about some of the situations that have arisen in the Scottish Parliament and beyond since his death.

My favourite recollections surround Friday afternoons in the Glasgow offices, where Donald would be sat, feet on the desk, not reviewing important government papers but mulling over the latest book catalogue wondering whether or not he should buy another title to add to his vast library. Laughing and joking with me and the private office team.

He could also hold his own in any conversation about sport, art or culture, a true lad o'pairts. He liked good Scots words like bauchle and maister man, as well as rich adjectives like thrawn and glaikit – all of which could be applied to Donald. For me, he was simply the best boss I ever had.

To See Ourselves . . .

Alf Young

Political tributes delivered from within the tribe usually run the risk of over-gilding the memory. I want this contribution to be, above all, as honest an appraisal as I can assemble of Donald Dewar's legacy to Scottish life. The man himself, while he would have tut-tutted at the very idea of a volume such as this, would expect nothing less. In his private moments, especially during the gloomier phases of his later life, no one doubted his true achievements more than Donald himself.

The main roots of my friendship with Donald were laid down during my three years as a Labour Party employee in the late 1970s. My role, as Labour's Scottish research officer, bridged my main careers in education and journalism. It was a turbulent time in Scottish politics. Despite Harold Wilson's referendum victory in 1975, endorsing the United Kingdom's renegotiated terms for membership of the Common Market, Labour remained deeply divided over Europe. Unemployment and inflation were rising inexorably. At Westminster, the Labour government clung to power thanks, latterly, to the Lib–Lab pact. In Scotland, Labour was struggling against a resurgent SNP and the breakaway Scottish Labour Party. The party was heading for a self-inflicted referendum rebuff over Scottish devolution, a successful vote of no confidence in Jim Callaghan's government and victory for a Thatcher-led Tory Party in the 1979 general election.

Donald, instinctively, unshakeably pro-Europe and pro-devolution, was a prominent member of Labour's Scottish Executive, the body for which I worked. In the 1966 general election, he had ousted a Tory grandee, Lady Tweedsmuir, from Aberdeen South, a seat held continuously by the Tories since 1918. But his first spell as an MP came to an abrupt end four years later, when the Tories won the seat back. Despite that, Donald continued to fight his corner within Labour's Scottish policy forums for what he believed to be right. He was one of the losing minority in that infamous vote in June 1974 when an extraordinary meeting of the Scottish Executive rejected – by six votes to five – all the London government's proposed schemes of devolution. It must have galled him even more that the meeting was maliciously convened on a Saturday when Scotland was playing (and drawing) with Yugoslavia in the World Cup finals in Germany. Donald loved his football. But by September, he and the other pro-devolutionists had got their own back, at the Dalintober Street Special Conference, when the party overwhelmingly endorsed 'the setting up of a directly elected Assembly with legislative powers within the context of the economic and political unity of the UK'.

It is easy to forget just how bitterly fraught the home rule debates of the 1970s were. Cynicism about the true motives for the policy change ran very deep, not just within Labour ranks. In 1975, the pro-devolution MP John P. Mackintosh recalled lunch with a senior Whitehall mandarin who, when asked what he was doing, replied, 'I am on the devolution caper.' It was no caper for firm believers in principled democratic renewal like Mackintosh and Dewar. They first entered Westminster at the same election, 1966. While Mackintosh had made much of the early public running, arguing the positive, reformist case for a Scottish Assembly in speeches, books and his *Scotsman* columns, Donald worked tirelessly within the party's Scottish machinery to keep the idea alive.

He returned to Westminster in April 1978, at the Glasgow Garscadden by-election, just months before Mackintosh, still the MP for Berwick and East Lothian, died prematurely. Symbolically, implicitly, Donald was inheriting prime responsibility for delivering a functioning model of home rule. And so began what, 21 years later, he himself called his 'long haul' towards his biggest single contribution to Scottish life – that there should, one day, be an elected Scottish Parliament reconvened in Edinburgh.

Never forget, however, that, between hope crystallising into belief and first becoming a firm political promise in the 1970s, and that promise maturing into constitutional reality in 1999, there were long years to be endured without the power to deliver anything. Donald died twenty-two years and six months after winning Garscadden. But for eighteen of those years he was in opposition. 'I know all about opposition,' he told the SNP's Alex Salmond, when introducing the Labour–Liberal Democrat programme for government to the new Scottish Parliament in September 1999. 'I relish the challenges of government.' But, apart from driving through the Scotland Act, winning decisive popular assent in the subsequent referendum and negotiating the terms of the first partnership Executive with the Liberal Democrats, Donald had very little time left to savour the challenges government would bring.

When the Bill to create that Parliament was finally published, its opening clause was a statement of blunt, decisive intent: there shall be a Scottish Parliament. 'I like that,' said Donald, with a broad grin. Those of us who had kept him company on parts of that long journey knew just how deep that sense of personal fulfilment ran. From the start Donald's commitment to the cause of devolution was heartfelt and enduring. He knew and understood his country's history and culture better than most nationalists. He recognised the significance of the great forces at work in a post-war Scotland that was fast losing another central pillar of its identity – its place in the world as a major manufacturing economy. Without significant constitutional change, he had long argued, the growing political challenges of our time could not be properly addressed. However, we also knew how much the great constitutional trek had taken out of him personally.

There had been plenty of bleak times along the way. His defeat in Aberdeen South in 1970 coincided with the end of his marriage. His children went off to live with his ex-wife and her new husband, future Labour Lord Chancellor Derry Irvine, in London. Derry and Donald had been good friends from university days. He still saw Marion and Iain regularly. Friends got used to helping Donald find ways to entertain them on their Scottish visits. But for him, real family life was over. And the pain of it never left him. Relations were still strained more than two decades later, at the time of John Smith's funeral. And as Secretary of State for Scotland he had to confront the Lord Chancellor, as chair of the key Cabinet committee on constitutional change, and fight for the kind of Scottish Parliament he wanted.

The devolution struggles of the 1970s hadn't just split the party. They also divided friend from friend. Our friendship flourished, in part, because we both thought from the beginning that a significant measure of Scottish home rule mattered, in principle. It was our shared belief that a strong dose of democratic renewal was vital if Scotland was to respond effectively to the many social and industrial challenges it was then confronting. Too many in the Labour Party at that time either opposed the whole idea of devolution or saw it as a tactical ploy to see off the nationalist advance. Those of us who really believed in the cause had to build our own mutual support networks.

I am writing this within weeks of Jim Callaghan's death in March 2005. His time as Prime Minister (1976–9) coincided almost exactly with my time as the Scottish Party's research officer. The tributes that have followed his passing, while critical of his political achievements, have been hugely flattering about his personal qualities. The legend of Sunny Jim lives on. Even Roy Jenkins, writing before his own death in January 2003, seeking to damn Callaghan achievements – as holder of all four major offices of state – with faint praise, was anxious to stress the dignity, kindness and humanity of the man before slipping in a well-polished stiletto or two.

Callaghan and I came face to face only twice in the three and a bit years I worked for the Labour Party. And on both occasions he treated me with the kind of bullying contempt that still faintly rankles to this day. On his first visit to Scotland as Prime Minister, he took exception to a paper I had written for the party's Scottish Executive, highlighting the political dangers in soaring unemployment. In my naivety, I had even cautioned against mass unemployment coming to be seen as an instrument of Labour government policy, something that would become apparent later in that telling Saatchi billboard campaign: Labour isn't Working. Everyone else in the room shared these concerns. But Callaghan made sure he aimed both barrels straight at me, a backroom researcher who had given up a much better-paid job to work for Labour. Predictably, Donald was quick to offer me personal support.

Then, in 1978, when the party was trying to dig its way out of the mess it had got itself into over home rule, I wrote another paper for Labour's Scottish Executive urging the use of two questions – one seeking endorsement of Labour's devolution settlement, the other seeking rejection of independence – in the referendum to come. Members agreed we should argue the two-question case with a sceptical Prime Minister and his senior ministerial team at a Downing Street summit. Before we got there my party boss, Helen Liddell, decided to leak the paper to the Fleet Street papers. It was front-page news the morning we walked into the Cabinet room. Callaghan was incandescent. Before the meeting got down to business, he demanded Labour's Scottish chairman, George Robertson, tell him who had leaked such a sensitive idea at such a provocative time. Robertson deflected the question to Liddell. She deflected it on to me, as the author of the offending message. For a second time, Callaghan tore into my motives rather than the substance of the case I was presenting.

I wasn't having it this time. So, across the Cabinet table a backroom party drone gave a Prime Minister as good as he got. I spelt out just how misguided his approach to the home rule issue had become. Like all bullies, he didn't know how to handle a rational shop-floor challenge to his lofty authority. In a sulk, he backed off. As we left the room, Michael Foot whispered to me, 'It's about time someone stood up to him.' And Donald Dewar, recently returned to Westminster and Foot's unlikely new lodger, again whisked me away for soothing words and a strong cup of tea.

A small informal group of us had helped Donald fight his 1978 by-election battle, bypassing the lacklustre official party campaign, planning our own rota of issues and impromptu leaflet campaigns, and bolstering Donald's faltering confidence, even on a snowy polling day afternoon, until the 4,552 Labour majority was secured. It was an astonishing victory, in a seat where all six council wards were held by the SNP. It was also fought in the teeth of a bitter offensive by the anti-abortion group, Society for the Protection of Unborn Children. I like to think we made it, in large measure, because Donald's patent decency and honesty shone through.

And yet, within a couple of years, with Mrs Thatcher in power and an increasingly factious Labour Party headed for the wilderness and doing its damnedest to tear itself apart, Donald was facing an insidious deselection challenge from sections of his own constituency party. I saw it from the inside. Although I had left my party job for a new career in journalism, I stayed on for a time as his constituency chairman. On a number of occasions, party bully-boys threatened me with physical retribution if I continued to fight Donald's corner. It was a very bleak time. When I moved home and had to give up the chair of Garscadden Constituency Labour Party, I gave up my party card too.

I had been a Labour Party member from my mid-teens. My brief time as a party insider, being kicked around by a Prime Minister and strong-armed by Militant elements in our local party, had cured me of all thoughts of a political career. I withdrew from active politics in part because I needed to earn a better living than the Labour Party could afford me and, in equal measure, because I had become disillusioned with what I had seen of politics from the inside. I also wanted my new career in newspapers to be free of any taint of party political preference. I happen to believe that the best journalism comes from those who maintain a degree of detachment from the things they write about. But I could not let that impulse to move beyond the Labour tribe terminate a personal friendship that meant so much to me.

Donald never once criticised my decision. He remained a regular visitor to our home and our table. He became an even more treasured friend. When our first son, Ewan, was born in 1982, Donald visited Carol in hospital. He came carrying a present. No, not flowers or a cuddly toy. Donald handed over, in his own words, 'a working copy, in doubtful condition' of J. Arnold Fleming's standard 1923 work *Scottish Pottery*. Whenever he came to our home, he had developed an exaggerated ritual of sternly critiquing the latest pot in our fledgling collection. Inside Fleming's book, on a sheet of House of Commons notepaper, he had written: 'To Carol and Alf – I take the firm view that it is the parents who deserve congratulation on occasions of this kind. I am not, however, sure that a collection of Scottish pottery and a young son are compatible interests.'

His own appetite for collecting books and Scottish art wasn't simply the material whim of a prosperous middle-aged Scot. I remember being with him once, at Alasdair Steven's treasure trove of antiquarian books in rural Perthshire, as he agonised over the cost of a set of the collected works of Hugh Millar, the nineteenth-century self-taught Scottish geologist and evangelical Christian. While Donald took pleasure from acquiring rare things, he saw his books primarily as a means to a greater end. He was assembling the tools to better understand, in a telling phrase from the speech he gave when the Queen opened the new Scottish Parliament, 'who we are, how we carry ourselves'.

When Donald's will was published, the casual cynics made much of his millionaire status. The properties, pictures and investment portfolio, including shares in some privatised industries like Railtrack, were cumulatively advanced as proof positive that Donald Dewar's political commitment to social justice could only have been skin deep. Had they really known him, they might have recognised a very different motivation.

Much of the wealth and many of the pictures he had inherited from his father, as the only child of a prosperous Glasgow consultant. In all the years I knew him, Donald showed scant regard for everyday possessions. His cars were always small and battered, his wardrobe often threadbare. When he came to dinner, he rarely thought to bring a bottle of wine. When he did, it might be a bottle of undrinkable white, made to be drunk young, which had lingered far too many years in a Cleveden Road cupboard.

Then why didn't he give it all away, the cynics will counter. I don't think he ever saw his worldly goods as his. He bought his aunt's house in Stirling on the pretext that he might retire there one day. For years, it lay empty, rarely visited. For over a year, Carol and I stored some surplus furniture in one of its echoing front rooms. I think he really bought it because he couldn't bear to see another substantive slice of Dewar family history disappear. If he thought about his personal wealth at all it was as the trustee of Dewar assets, to be preserved and passed on to his children, in the same way they had been passed on to him.

Ordinary Scots who had never even met him could sense Donald's instinctive commitment to social justice. His constituency contained many of Scotland's most deprived families. In the long years of opposition, Donald poured himself into the communities of Drumchapel, Yoker and Knightswood. He knew everyone. Stayed close to every local organisation. Handled mountains of family and personal problems. Perhaps, in part, he was diverting the energies he might have devoted to family life into his bigger constituency family. At his funeral, I encountered constituents praising his humanity who, 20 years before, had been threatening to see both of us outside.

When his friend John Smith became Labour leader and shocked Donald by moving him from his shadow Scottish brief, Donald held out for the social security portfolio instead. He held that role when Gordon Borrie was commissioned to think afresh about how Labour could achieve social justice in a changing world. I recall, from that period, the encyclopaedic knowledge he developed of every benefit, every wrinkle in Britain's welfare system. But I was never convinced that Donald saw himself continuing in that role, if Labour eventually regained power. Indeed, when he moved on and became an improbably successful Labour Chief Whip, I recall taking a *Herald* colleague to meet him for the first time, over an impromptu breakfast in his room in the Commons. He was in sparkling form as he guzzled eggs and dispensed tantalising gossip. This was Donald the ultimate party insider, never averse to a bit of fixing, who had stayed the course through thick and thin and could see his long haul finally reaching its hoped-for destination.

All his major political contemporaries, devolutionist and staunch unionist alike, had opted to climb to their political peaks on a United Kingdom or international stage. John Smith, David Steel, Gordon Brown, George Robertson, Malcolm Rifkind, Robin Cook, Menzies Campbell, Derry Irvine, John Reid, Alistair Darling. Of these, only Steel came back to be the Scottish Parliament's first Presiding Officer. Donald knew his long political haul had only one final destination – Edinburgh and the chance to seize that 'moment anchored in our history' when the new Parliament would finally open its doors.

Had he lived, he would have been mortified by the rammy over the cost of the Holyrood building but quietly proud that the building itself, such an extraordinary empowering space, is proving itself a home fit for any revitalised democracy. Had he lived, he would have been deeply troubled by the way in which home rule in action has proved a disappointment to so many Scots. But with the benefit of the long view – his powerful grasp of the great sweep of Scottish history – he would also have had the patience and confidence to wait for his great project to evolve and mature. Had he lived, I doubt Donald would have lingered long as the new Parliament's First Minister. He was hankering for relief from the years of relentless political commitment. I think he knew that, while he had turned a powerful belief into constitutional reality, he did not have the personal resources left to lead the new Parliament on its mission to make life better for more Scots. It was as if he had burned himself out delivering a devolved Scottish legislature and could not summon up the energy to shape the scope and reach of its deliberations. That said, the long haul to the bottom of Edinburgh's Canongate is journey enough for any politician. On that achievement alone, Donald can rest content.

Donald and Labour

A group of us were standing on the platform at Euston on a Thursday night waiting to board the sleeper back north when the subject came up of Isobel Lindsay leaving the SNP and applying to join the Labour Party. Donald bemoaned the arrival of a 'troublemaker'. I told him that I was also a 'troublemaker' – to which Donald responded, 'Yes, John, but you're our troublemaker.' Donald was at heart Old Labour – no New Labour true believer would ever have called me 'our' anything.

John McAllion, former MP/MSP Dundee East – colleague

Donald was a very quick thinker and a very fast talker. But he conveyed to people who needed him that he had all the time in the world for them. He was a good person as well as a generous politician.

Rev. Douglas Alexander – friend

My daughter will always remember him as the man who pinched her fish and chips, having first consumed his own, which prompted her to ask if he was always so hungry. For my part, I have long appreciated Donald's take on the subject of housework. Following a lengthy discussion about the properties of dust, we came to the conclusion that as it never accumulates to a depth greater than 5mm without falling over, there is little point in dusting. A great man and a great character too.

Jackie Baillie MSP – colleague

Campaigning with him was a pleasure – but could also be time consuming. During the Kincardine and Deeside by-election, it took us nearly a day to canvass a single street. Such was Donald's standing that he was dragged through every door on which he knocked and not allowed out again until he'd had a cup of tea and a biscuit.

Duncan McNeil MSP – colleague

Aberdeen's Candidate

George Whyte

I was introduced to Donald in the early summer of 1963, at the parliamentary selection conference for the Aberdeen South constituency. He had been nominated by the Garthlee Ward branch chair, Tom Fyfe, and was opposed by local candidate Jim Lamond, who had strong support. Donald, who had been the Glasgow University debating champion, won by 24 votes to 21, his words per minute creating an all-time record.

I was appointed as the constituency agent with a year or so to introduce Donald to the Aberdeen South electorate. The well-entrenched Conservative Lady Tweedsmuir was sitting with nearly a 9,000 majority and had polled 53.8 per cent of the vote in 1959. Labour had 36.6 per cent and the Liberals 9.6 per cent on an 81 per cent poll. We were up against a strong Conservative Party organisation that had one of Scotland's best full-time agents.

With Jim Lamond's supporters refraining from active work at branch level, it wasn't easy mobilising the grass roots of the constituency Labour Party. Jack Wood came over from the Aberdeen North constituency, a safe Labour seat, to become assistant agent.

Donald was residing in Glasgow and working as a law apprentice, which meant canvassing had to be done at the weekends when he was free. We had the offer of free offices and rooms in Marischal Street and however inadequate they were, we accepted the offer. When Harold Wilson won the 1964 general election, our vote in Aberdeen South, with Donald as the candidate, went up by 7.3 per cent and the Tory majority was cut in half.

By the time Wilson called a snap election in 1966, the pace of council-house development in the constituency was an important positive factor. In the run-up to the election, I was attending Labour Party agent training courses, where it was being made clear to us that an election was imminent, as Wilson could not sustain a parliamentary majority for much longer. Not requiring much convincing about this, I set in hand most of the printing and secured committee rooms at the junction of Holburn Street and Union Street at Holburn Junction. The location of the committee rooms facing Holburn Junction was a great hit, with a huge canvas banner 'Vote Dewar, Vote Labour' stretched across the building and visible to all traffic and pedestrians. Nothing of course is perfect and Donald had the humiliation of being charged (in the days before traffic wardens) with 'illegal parking'.

By this time, there was a much better atmosphere, with encouraging canvassing returns from reliable university canvassers and from Labour Party councillors like Councillor Jock Greig, an Aberdeen harbour board diver who secured the 'loan' of their pilot boat. One morning with a snowstorm in progress, Donald, armed with a loudhailer, with press and election workers aboard, proceeded to exhort the fishermen to vote Labour by proxy. These were the days of busy fishing boats landing their catch at the fish market.

Next morning a picture appeared in the Aberdeen *Press and Journal* with the headline 'Donald Chases the Floating Voters'. That same morning the harbour board manager threatened to throw the book at me. We had understood that Jock Greig had obtained the manager's authority. Anyway, with the help of Alan Thomson, the TGWU District Secretary, we were able to arrange a great number of trawler men with proxy votes.

There was great enthusiasm behind Donald throughout the campaign, with dozens of pupils from Aberdeen Grammar School calling at the committee rooms after school and volunteering to deliver literature. Donald had another surprise when he saw posters of himself posing with Harold Wilson. My wife Helen (who produced the art work) and the printer had done a great job. The poster must have meant a great deal to Donald, as 36 years later we were watching a television programme on Donald as First Minister and he appeared with one of these very posters on the wall behind him!

In 1964 and 1966, we had problems in ensuring Donald met enough of his prospective electorate, so I hit on the idea of a Sunday afternoon concert in the Music Hall. Here I introduced Donald to a packed hall from the platform of Aberdeen's Silver Brass Band. We also had the City Labour's *Clarion* giving Donald all the space he needed. By 1966, Lady Tweedsmuir seemed to be a good deal less popular and after the poll closed we were met by her agent, who conceded that Donald had won. The turn out was 81.3 per cent with Labour gaining 46 per cent of the vote. We had converted a Tory majority of nearly 10,000 in 1964 to a Labour majority of nearly 2,000.

I was appointed constituency secretary about this time and Donald asked if I would allow our flat and telephone in Victoria Road, Torry, to be the contact number for queries from constituents while he was at Westminster. This we did to the best of our ability.

They were interesting days, especially when Donald became parliamentary private secretary to Anthony Crosland, who was a Cabinet minister and visited Aberdeen on several occasions.

In early 1970, I was successful in moving to a better job with much more responsibility, thus leaving me with very little spare time. Jack Wood took over as Election Agent for the 1970 election, where regrettably we lost out to Iain Sproat and the Tories.

Garscadden's MP

Bill Butler

I first encountered Donald Dewar when he was Labour's candidate in the Glasgow Garscadden by-election of April 1978. I had returned home from university to spend the spring break campaigning for the party. If my memory serves, I think we exchanged a brief 'hello' at the main committee rooms located at Knightswood Cross before I was dispatched by the Scottish organiser, Jimmy Allison, to work under the direction of vastly more experienced members in the southern part of the constituency.

I do remember two things about the campaign: its intensity, especially around the issue of abortion, and Donald's resolution in the face of the opportunism of some of his political opponents. I recollect one especially large public meeting at a church hall in Knightswood where this highly charged subject was raised. Most of Donald's opponents tried to please everybody and ended up pleasing no one; only Donald and the Communist Party candidate, Sammy Barr, stated their positions straightforwardly. At the time, I felt the majority in the packed hall, no matter what their personal view, sensed and appreciated that honest approach. Such a conspicuously frank attitude was not without risk. The Glasgow Garscadden by-election occurred at a time of some upheaval in the political life of Scotland: SNP support was at its highest level, the Callaghan government had no overall majority, the Scottish Nationalists held all six of the local district council seats and Labour's national preeminence was under significant threat. In my mind, it came to typify Donald's method of dealing with the serious concerns that his constituents were to raise with him over the next 22 years as their elected member.

Donald's way of doing business never changed. His electors recognised in him a man of integrity and principle. He inspired trust, admiration and respect. And yet this was seldom expressed directly; most of Donald's constituents came to know instinctively that their Member of Parliament was an essentially reserved man and that overt praise would prove an embarrassment.

Two episodes from the general election campaign of 1987 provide examples of the means by which the people of Garscadden conveyed their admiration for, and trust in, the then shadow Secretary of State for Scotland. Both involved Donald's car.

At a sheltered housing complex on the day of the election, three cars arrived promptly to convey half a dozen of the female residents to the local polling station. One of the cars happened to be Donald's and this rendered the other two vehicles redundant, as the ladies insisted that they didn't mind waiting while Mr Dewar ferried them in twos to the polling station so, as one woman put it, 'we can all be taken to vote for Donald by Donald himself'.

Such admiration cannot possibly have been engendered by Donald's driving skills alone as evidenced by an incident a fortnight earlier. In order to avoid a stray shopping trolley that had trundled onto the road, Donald swerved straight into the path of an oncoming vehicle, which had just pulled out from its parking space. The resultant bump was inevitable. The driver of the other vehicle, a *very* large man, leapt from his seat ready, it seemed, at the very least, to state in unequivocal terms his opinion of the car-handling skills of the driver who had caused the collision. However, when he recognised Donald, getting out of the car to apologise and ask if he was all right, he refused even to exchange insurance details with him, as he knew 'Mr Dewar would sort things out'. Mr Dewar's fellow campaigners, seated in the back of his car, breathed an audible sigh of relief.

Those who were Donald's constituents – community activists, members of various organisations, the thousands who went to his surgeries over the years and on whose behalf he acted as advocate, members of all political parties and none, the religious and the irreligious – all tend to recall the same range of qualities and personality traits.

Ina Brodie, a community activist in Drumchapel, recollects his openness, his compassion and his diligence: 'Donald was one of the most approachable and friendly MPs you could ever meet. He always had time to have a blether. When you had a personal problem, Donald would always do his utmost to help . . . he worked tirelessly for all his constituents.'

This is echoed by Maureen Barr of Drumchapel Community Credit Union: 'He was a warm, compassionate man and always on hand to help out . . . whether he was stopped in the street or at a public meeting . . . he always carried a notebook . . . I never heard of anyone who didn't get a reply from him.'

John and Lily Hind, members of Scotstounhill Residents' Association, remember his love of debate and good company. After one meeting, Donald repaired to their house along with others who had been in attendance: 'Several small aperitifs were taken . . . Donald conducted proceedings and, by the end of a lively evening's discussion, he remained the only sober one. He then felt obliged to raid the biscuit tin.'

Jean Lickrish of Knightswood remarks on his 'commitment . . . and hard work' and then goes on to note Donald's unique dress sense: 'Formal dress was not his style. His long rangy figure was well known to have a casual, "thrown together" look. Colour coordinated – he never heard of it!'

Neil Macfarlane of Kelvindale Bowling Club reiterates the view of Donald as being 'totally dedicated to his constituency' and observes that: 'He rarely missed the opening day of Kelvindale Bowling Club . . . He was a well-kent face and well respected.'

Tom O'Connor, a former dockers' shop steward from Temple, conjures up a vivid memory of Donald's attendance at the final of an annual football tournament held on the Barr & Stroud Recreation Ground at Netherton Road: 'Donald turned up and began to chat with the crowd as was his way. At half-time, there he was sitting (or rather sprawling) on the grass, deep in conversation. Donald was a master at making himself comfortable whether on the grass or in an armchair. He stayed after the game for a cup of tea and a biscuit (a jaffa cake). Big Donald, our Donald, was just part of the people.'

Donald, of course, had his faults. We should avoid at all costs hagiography. He could be irascible. He could be very rude indeed –

usually, it must be said, to those who could stand it. He could on occasion be the very picture of inspissated gloom: on the night in 1987 when he achieved his highest percentage vote as a Labour candidate and before the count had begun he was heard to remark that he could 'sense a fall in support'. Nonetheless, the above are the comments of real people who actually knew Donald as their constituency member and they are by no means unrepresentative.

Throughout his tenure, Donald valued the relationship with his constituency Labour Party and its members: he rarely missed a general management committee meeting, often popped into branches when his heavy schedule allowed and was actively involved in every fundraiser and election campaign. Donald was no 'armchair general'. Undoubtedly, this close involvement proved invaluable when he faced his only reselection contest in the 1980s, a challenge which was decisively repelled.

Donald Dewar was by nature and instinct an intensely private man who followed a path dedicated to public service. He came from a very comfortable, middle-class background in the fashionable West End of Glasgow, and yet served with distinction, first at Westminster then at Holyrood, as the elected Labour member for a largely working-class constituency. He could never be described as being a follower of fashion, whether sartorial or political, but he developed an inimitable, unshowy style based upon firmly held political convictions. He was someone who did not court popularity but who inspired a widespread admiration and loyalty amongst his constituents. In an age of 'spin' and shallowness, Donald was straightforward whilst subtle: a man of considerable intellect who disliked intensely the superficial and, when the occasion dictated, said so, bluntly. He was in many ways a public relations disaster who in his dealings on behalf of those he represented proved a success. As an elected representative, he was cautious and considered. He was not prone to adopt dramatic policy positions in order to curry favour with those who like to see themselves described as astute political commentators, and yet he became the pre-eminent architect of the devolution settlement, quite the most radical constitutional rearrangement since the Reform Act of 1832. In short, Donald Dewar MP, MSP, First Minister of Scotland's first democratic parliament (the only MSP to have served in a British Cabinet) was a national politician of the first rank and a complex individual. Yet his constituents, whilst recognising, and taking pride in, their Member of Parliament's national standing, valued equally his worth as a remarkable constituency representative, a man of unimpeachable integrity, their trusted advocate.

Many an obituary of a political life contains the judgement 'a good, hardworking constituency member'. In the overwhelming majority of cases, this is neither an inaccurate nor an uncomplimentary verdict. It is simply an acknowledgement of a fact of political life: the vast majority of parliamentarians, although they may aspire to ministerial office, never play a part other than that of political spear carrier on the national stage and are confined, either by ability or circumstance, to the role of assiduous backbencher. Obviously, such an appraisal does not apply to the career of Donald Dewar. Nevertheless, an assessment of the politician, which ignored, or dismissed as peripheral, his constituency role, would lack a sense of critical balance. An understanding of Dewar the constituency member is as important as knowledge of Dewar the consummate parliamentarian. Both aspects of his political life are inextricably linked: his constituents and their hopes and concerns, how they viewed him and his efforts on their behalf, explain to a considerable degree his beliefs and his campaigning priorities when out of government and his political imperatives when he attained a position of power.

Donald believed in a more just, more equal society where people were allowed to exploit their talents, where potential was developed and not stifled. He expressed this belief in a very Dewaresque way: he wanted to correct 'the imbalance in the social arithmetic' so that his constituents would have the same opportunities as those in neighbouring Bearsden. His commitment to his constituents and their interests was unambiguous; it earned their respect during his lifetime, a respect that still endures amongst those whom Donald served.

An Unconventional Politician

Matt Smith

In *The Battle for Scotland*, Andrew Marr, writing of the devolution debate at the 1968 Scottish Labour Party conference, claims that Donald Dewar was 'regarded as a young Turk'. Even Marr comments that such a description was 'strange but true'. Few would use that description today, yet at that time, and particularly on the issue of devolution, the man who was to deliver the devolutionary settlement for Scotland was not a conventional campaigner.

Donald frequently operated outwith the usual constraints of a senior politician holding high office. But his unconventionality often related as much to the process as to the policy. In many instances, he held to mainstream political positions and could be frustratingly rigid in his attitudes; but not in all cases and, unlike others, he did not expect surrender as a means of achieving a false unity.

My own experience of working with Donald was both within the Labour Party and also as part of the wider trade union movement. These should not be fused together implying an always-common strategy. In the former, during our time together on the Executive of the former Strathclyde Labour Party, we operated as part of a political machine. In the latter, we operated from often differing standpoints, sometimes with a similar agenda, in many instances with disagreement and in a few cases with confrontation.

But in all political contexts, the characteristic that marked Donald out was his willingness to engage with an issue, allied to his accessibility. If there was an issue to be discussed, then Donald was available and he would sometimes make the first approach, thus ensuring that early engagement minimised the possibility of serious difficulties at a later stage. And, rather unusually, his willingness to engage increased rather than reduced as he took on high office.

Donald helped to create and shared in the values of the Labour Party and the wider Labour movement. He was very much a Labour Party man but one who could see beyond the immediacy of issues and understand other points of view.

Many knew him better and worked more closely with him than I did. Yet like so many in the Labour movement, our association extended for over a quarter of a century and I retain an affection and admiration for him today.

Amongst those with whom he came in contact it is uncanny how many not only share similar recollections but use the same language to describe their memories of him. People talk not just of acquaintance but of friendship; not just of discussing but of engaging; not just of understanding but of trust.

Donald could be frustratingly insulting and at times downright rude. He was argumentative sometimes for the sake of the argument, albeit a not uncommon trait in politics. His comments on colleagues were sometimes entertaining, occasionally scathing. Sometimes he appeared to be indiscreet and even five years after his death I do not feel inclined to repeat his comments on some senior colleagues. But that in itself is a reflection of the confidence I had in my dealings with him. This was not someone who, on attaining senior office, became a remote figure. Instead, our friendship, within the bounds of which we could share indiscretions, continued little changed.

I recall on one occasion when he was Secretary of State for Scotland arranging a discussion with Bill Spiers of the STUC. At the appointed time and place, Donald arrived but he was in fairly low humour and seemed to be carrying with him the problems of the world. We never did get down to our intended business but had a good time exchanging anecdotes, gossiping about people we all three knew and agreeing to meet again soon. The business was postponed to another day. With others, this would have been viewed as a deliberate ploy to avoid the issues. But with

Donald it was an accepted way of working and we knew that we would be able to pursue the intended business soon thereafter.

Inevitably there were major disagreements, as in the decision to take action against two direct labour organisations – East Ayrshire and North Lanarkshire. By chance, I had met Donald at Glasgow Airport and he had told me of his intention to act on the basis of reports he had received. I had protested that he was going too far and that his actions would undermine relationships with local government to say nothing of the impact on the workforce. Later, a full delegation of national officials and local trade unionists met with him in St Andrew's House, when we had the opportunity to fully outline our case. It became a crucial issue threatening to cloud our future dealings with government and Donald's response was to personally take charge of the issue.

Too many have taken from this and other incidents that Donald was anti-local government. That is a misreading of events, as the remit given to the McIntosh Commission in 1997 makes clear.

As a member of the commission, I can confirm that there was no established political interference and Donald stressed our independence. The timing of the establishment of the commission was important. Donald, like so many of us, had shared memories of the devolution debate pre-1978 when local government exhibited major reservations about devolution. So, two decades later, the McIntosh Commission was established to ensure that this key elected tier should not be left behind in a post-devolution Scotland. The aim was to strengthen local government. Amongst the recommendations was the proposal to introduce proportional voting, and were it not for the early work of the commission, the route to proportional representation in local government could have been even more difficult for many in the Labour Party to travel.

On the subject of devolution, Donald had few more enthusiastic friends than the Scottish trade unions. Trade unions played a key role both in keeping the issue alive in the difficult days and in creating the consensus and in securing victory in the 1997 referendum. There was nothing inevitable about the creation of a Scottish Parliament, as any reading of the history of devolution makes clear.

By supporting the Claim of Right and taking the Labour Party into the Scottish Constitutional Convention, he went beyond narrow party interests and embraced a wider consensus. A lesser politician could have at best resisted such a move; at worst, have scuppered Scotland's best chance to achieve devolution by a rigid adherence to the party line, particularly on issues such as proportional voting, without which change and certainly meaningful agreement would have been impossible.

Trade unions on the whole backed this consensual position and many today recognise that but for the stance Donald took, the initiative, as in 1978, would have been lost for another generation.

But in the process the Labour Party faced many difficulties in reaching a consensus position around issues where the situation was not always favourable to Labour's partisan interest. Throughout, few were as consistent as Donald in arguing the case for change. He and the trade unions, primarily, though not exclusively, operating through the STUC, could act as one. He was trusted and was on the same side.

In *Open Scotland?*, Philip Schlesinger describes Donald's vision of devolution as offering 'a stable settlement for Scots within the UK'. This also reflected the position of most of Scotland's trade unions. Yet Scottish trade unions are part of United Kingdom organisations, albeit those with Scottish identities, and the unease at a United Kingdom level about where devolution might lead was real. Those anxieties were assuaged by the terms of the 1998 settlement.

Donald was trusted and respected and this helped greatly when he took up office first as Secretary of State and then as First Minister. His standing within the STUC was high. We were to disagree on some issues, particularly in the early days after the 1997 general election over levels of public expenditure and the continuing use of PFI as a means of funding capital investment. But he was with us and we with him on the creation of a Scottish Parliament.

At the STUC in 2000 as president, I was able to welcome Donald as the *first* First Minister to address congress and he was particularly well received for a speech which dealt with key issues around devolution but also with matters of employment in Scotland. On a personal basis, of even greater significance was his acceptance of my invitation to address the President's Dinner. This annual event is attended by a wide cross section of Scotland's public life and is a key opportunity to present trade unionism to a wider audience. I particularly wanted Donald to attend and had asked him some months earlier. At first reluctant to be speaking at both the congress and at the dinner, he phoned to say that he would do so as a personal favour. I only knew after his acceptance, and not from Donald, that he was due to go into hospital the week after congress.

He made a witty and entertaining speech in which he hurled insults at a fair few of the guests. Those who had only experienced the serious politician were greatly entertained by his humour and his sometimes not totally politically correct asides. Others were to comment to me on his warmth and charm when they met him later that evening. It was a special occasion for me but sadly was to be his last address to the STUC. He would be dead within six months.

Accessibility was the trademark of our relationship. Neither before nor since have I had such regular contact with a senior minister. He would phone to discuss or advise of issues that might have an impact on public service workers.

Both as Secretary of State for Scotland and later as First Minister he would on occasion call to say that he was coming over from his Glasgow office to my office, near to each other in Glasgow city centre, to talk about a particular matter or just to have a general exchange. Even when we were attending meetings with other ministers it was not unknown for Donald to appear at the close of the discussion to find out what had been discussed and what was to be the outcome.

Donald was not by history or tradition a natural trade unionist. Yet there was no distancing from the wider movement. His contact was regular and, in my experience, far more prevalent than others who had a deeper historical trade union connection.

In the case of UNISON, he gave many hours to meet groups (often small groups) to explain policy, to discuss progress or to outline developments. The niceties of fine distinctions between affiliated and non-affiliated members were not for him; he always wanted to meet with the wider union, preferring to engage with the issues and not the structures.

He carried his offices with great dignity but did not expect dignity to attach to his offices. Not for him the call for cars and drivers to take him to and from meetings. He didn't seek special invites nor seek to restrict access. It was not exceptional for him to turn up unaccompanied, having arrived by public transport, and to stay beyond the agreed time. He gave of his time and for that many of us remain grateful.

Donald was unconventional in many ways. His lack of stuffiness could be surprising, particularly for those who did not know him. In the early days of the Scottish Parliament, I accompanied a delegation of senior Canadian trade unionists to Edinburgh and had advised Donald's office in advance that if time permitted, I would like to meet for a few minutes. Not knowing if this would be possible, we were taken aback when, immediately after First Minister's questions, he waved from the chamber to the gallery, indicating that he would see us in the corridor thereafter.

On my first visit to Bute House with Donald as resident, I turned up with the late John Lambie and a few other lost souls. None of us knew the number of the official residence. Having had no success with the local traffic warden, we commenced chapping doors only to see the Secretary of State himself appear at his front door beckoning us to his presence and then escorting us into his home.

On the eve of the state opening of the Scottish Parliament, my wife and I were attending a service in St Giles in Edinburgh. We were seated towards the back of the church near the main entrance and discussing with other guests events of the following day. In particular, we were being asked for our views on the First Minister, whom they had not met. To our surprise, Donald suddenly appeared for a chat, having entered the church and recognised some well-kent faces. Within minutes he had to go to join the royal guests who were just about to enter. He certainly made an impression on those to whom we were speaking. I don't believe the incident would register at all with Donald as being in any way unusual.

His informality did not lead to disrespect. It enhanced his standing and was one of his many strengths. Indeed, this often ensured that in our dealings with him we gave to him the same respect and did not trouble him unnecessarily with issues best left to others.

I felt his loss personally. Gone was someone with whom I could talk through key issues in confidence and in detail. I was not part of the inner circle nor was I in anything like daily contact. Nor should I have been. But I knew him to be available when there was a need.

On a very personal basis, I still recall the most important man in Scotland who had the time to join me, my wife and teenage children for Sunday lunch at my home. His company was a delight, his presence most welcome. I also had the privilege of working with him, particularly at such a crucial time for Scotland.

As a Colleague

Gordon Brown

I first met Donald Dewar when my brother and I walked with him on the UCS (Upper Clyde Shipbuilders) March for Jobs 33 years ago in 1972. I had never met Donald before and had known of him only by reputation. But John, who knew him for his work as a reporter to the children's panel in Lanarkshire, introduced us – and for three decades he was my friend.

In 1972, at our first meeting, the reporter to the Lanarkshire children's panel was marching for shipyard jobs. And strangely enough my last conversation with Donald was about exactly the same concern: Donald's worries about the future of naval orders and the effect on shipbuilding jobs on the Clyde.

And there is a symmetry as well as a constancy about the whole of Donald's life.

His first job as an MP was as parliamentary private secretary to Anthony Crosland, whose books on equality and social justice enthused a whole generation of young people. When he lost his Aberdeen South seat as Labour lost in 1970, he could have retreated into the more comfortable life of a solicitor but he chose instead to make Scotland's children's panel system work in one of our poorest communities: to help young people in trouble.

Then back in Parliament from 1978 – moved by the plight of people who needed him, the hundreds of meetings, the thousands of letters – he devoted more time than any MP I knew to fighting for social justice for his constituents. He did this first as MP for Garscadden and latterly as MSP for Anniesland: the only titles he really valued.

And through years of opposition, as he moved from shadow Secretary of State for Scotland, then Social Security Secretary, to Chief Whip, he used his unquestioned mastery of the debating chamber of the House of Commons to speak up consistently about social and economic problems and the need for social change. He always stood firm for the needs of the elderly, the health service and the poor, and against the unfairness and injustice of the poll tax and all illiberal laws. The golden thread that runs through Donald's life is his abiding commitment to social justice.

Donald will of course be remembered, rightly, for his political integrity. He always stood by his principles and he always stood by his friends. His lifelong courage – standing out, often in a minority, for causes he espoused – deserves to be remembered and celebrated.

Perhaps only someone with his skills and ability to persuade could have moved devolution so rapidly from a commitment in a manifesto in 1997 to a White Paper within weeks, a referendum within months and then on to the creation of a Scottish Parliament within two short years. Combining a grand vision with mastery of the detail, he and the brilliant team he assembled brought about a constitutional transformation – the first democratic Scottish Parliament.

Donald would have been the last to acknowledge the true scale of his achievements. But his massive constitutional achievement will stand the test of any objective historical analysis and debate. Donald did not only study history: he made it.

And he made history more than once. I remember well working in the Garscadden by-election. This was the battleground of the 1970s where the tide was turned against the SNP – and Donald was the leader. By stopping the SNP's forward march, Donald made Labour the Scottish party of the future.

But I know that, successful as the author of the first democratic Scottish Parliament was, Donald would prefer to be remembered for his commitment to social justice – and for the difference his policies for economic and social justice made to people's lives. As First Minister, as Peter Jones writes: 'Social justice was almost invariably mentioned first whenever he listed his priorities for action.'

Indeed, for Donald constitutional reform was never an end in itself but the means to an even greater end: social justice. In fact, his St Andrew's Day lecture in St Andrews in November 1998 set out a vision of devolution 'as the means to a better and fairer society'. Constitutional change was just a stage towards a more equal Scotland, he said. 'The next decade must not be one long embittering fight over further constitutional change; for me the question now is what we do with our Parliament not what we do to it . . . The great challenge for Scottish Parliamentarians is to build an inclusive Scotland.'

Put even more eloquently in his speech at the official opening of the Scottish Parliament, where he traced the Scottish tradition of support for social justice: 'A Scottish Parliament. Not an end: a means to greater ends. And those too are part of our mace. Woven into its symbolic thistles are these four words: "Wisdom. Justice. Compassion. Integrity". Burns would have understood that . . . At the heart of [his] song ["Is there for Honest Poverty", colloquially known as "A Man's a Man for a' that"] is a very Scottish conviction: that honesty and simple dignity are priceless virtues, not imparted by rank or birth or privilege but part of the soul.'

Even before that inauguration day, he had set out in a speech in his own constituency his own personal view of Labour's social justice offer to the people of Scotland as 'a lifetime of opportunity'.

'Scotland is a country where equality of opportunity and social justice are central to our sense of self,' he said, speaking in Knightswood Community Education Centre in September 1998. 'Traditional Scottish values are the foundations on which Scottish New Labour will build . . . the Labour Party which I joined as a youngster was committed to the fight against poverty. I recall with affection the previous generation of radical Scots who helped transform Scotland on the basis of this belief. I believe in those values but each generation must find its own way in the circumstances of its own time, to turn these values into achievements . . . education lies at the heart of our vision for Scotland's future . . . my personal pledge is to restore Scottish education to a position of international renown . . . educational excellence built around opportunities for all must be Scotland's trademark in the first years of the new millennium. That should be the achievement of the first Scottish Labour administration at Holyrood. Ours is no narrow definition of education, our targets stretch into the lives of people of all ages.'

His complaint was that, 'Over the Tory years there was a growing gap between those who had and those who had not. Children saw their life chances damaged and destroyed as whole families were trapped at the wrong end of an unequal society; even life expectancy was for too many cruelly and indeed literally restricted. The Labour Party was brought into being to redress the balance and to fight poverty and inequality. That is still our cause and our commitment.'

He wanted to 'make lifelong learning a passion for our people . . . strategies for social inclusion to fit together with our welfare to work, health, housing and new deal policies to reduce poverty in Scotland's communities'.

And when he introduced the first programme of legislation for the Scottish Parliament, there was one essential element above all others: 'I give a high priority to the social justice agenda.' And once again using his own constituency as his reference point, he said, 'I represent real extremes in terms of prosperity, opportunity and life chances, and I am always conscious of that. What must be done . . . is to attack [poverty] on all fronts.'

What did his social justice agenda mean in practice? It meant, he said, that, 'We cannot accept a Scotland where 4,000 children leave school each year without formal qualifications . . . where one-third of Scottish households have below half the average UK income . . . where one-quarter of our housing stock suffers from dampness or condensation.

'We can,' he said, 'use the power of government . . . to connect, persuade, cajole, encourage, preach and lead to change that.

'We can,' he said, 'and we shall.'

And he did – because what motivated him all through his political life was his own simple and unshakeable belief that poverty was wrong.

Donald refused to accept that the people of Drumchapel, or of any community, should have diminished dreams or lesser lives simply because of where they were born.

No child should be 'born to fail,' he said and he never wavered.

To be 'born on the wrong side of the social arithmetic', as he put it, was an unfairness.

'Righting the social arithmetic' was his life's work.

What made Donald the campaigner for social justice he became lies deep in his roots and thinking.

A natural reserve about things personal meant that while Donald liked to gossip about everything and anything, he was reluctant to reveal much about his own personal influences. 'He was most definitely a Lowland

Scot who felt uncomfortable with public displays of emotion,' Jimmy Gordon writes.

But almost certainly his elderly parents – and their strong commitment to ethics and social responsibility – influenced his own sense of what was just and unjust. This led him, as Fiona Ross writes, to treat everyone equally, generous to all, subservient to no one. 'Donald . . . was just as happy having a conversation with the cleaning lady as he was talking to a head of state,' she writes.

Undoubtedly, too, his youthful experience of the social problems of Glasgow encouraged his commitment to Labour. He would have liked to write a biography of Thomas Chalmers, the Scottish social reformer, and he had an abiding interest in the work of Gladstone, another social reformer. But the principal inspiration for his commitment to social justice came from the work of Richard Tawney – whose books like *Equality* and *The Acquisitive Society* were a precursor to Crosland's *The Future of Socialism*. But his commitment to social justice, as his speeches showed, also drew strength from his understanding of Scottish communitarian traditions and his interest in Scots law and social work. 'His sense of the distinctiveness of Scottish culture was reinforced by his respect for, and knowledge of, Scotland's Presbyterian traditions,' writes Jimmy Gordon. But that history was the history of progress towards social justice and not about kings and queens. As his boyhood friend Charlie Allan writes: 'He had intended to read history [at university] but he had been put right off by the first lecture. In that, the professor had said that to understand European history you had to know about an important family. He then wrote the word HABSBURG in block capitals on the board . . . Donald couldn't see how this course was going to teach him much.'

When in St Andrews in 1998, he explained the basis of his commitment, speaking – as he was to do at the opening of the Scottish Parliament – of enduring Scottish values of community: 'We have claimed a community ethic, we have consistently rejected the political expression of a dogma which asserts the narrow interests of the individual over community values. We still live in a world where the rewards are ill divided . . . The challenge is clear. Too many have been excluded. Big numbers trip lightly off the tongue. Every component digit is a trust betrayed, an opportunity denied, a promise broken . . . In Glasgow, 31,000 unemployed, 250,000 children in workless houses, 400 youngsters leaving school without even one standard grade, life expectancy in Drumchapel seven years less for women and ten years less for men than in comfortable next door Bearsden. I want a Scotland which will fight social exclusion, I want an Executive which promotes prosperity and uses that wealth to fight poverty . . . the vision is a lifetime of opportunity for all Scottish families. The new government of Scotland must pledge itself to the making of the new Scotland.'

That commitment was honoured when he became First Minister. One of his first acts in the new Scottish Executive was the creation of a Social Exclusion Network, chaired by Lord Sewel, its role to coordinate all the work of different departments with responsibilities for social affairs. Indeed, his consultation paper on social exclusion said, 'Tackling the problem of social exclusion is our number one social policy priority.' This network later evolved into the Social Inclusion Network, with many outside experts in social policy and poverty campaigners contributing to the strategy, including the shift in emphasis from tackling social exclusion to promoting social inclusion. As First Minister, Donald later championed a new social justice strategy and an annual social justice report that called for higher investment in education; the transfer of council homes into community ownership; land reform; and just before he died he was instrumental in approving the innovations of free local bus travel for pensioners and the installation of central heating in homes without it.

And Donald always drew inspiration from what was happening near to home in his own constituency. As First Minister, his administration's first report on social justice was launched in Drumchapel. He spoke of a 'Scotland where everyone matters' and he invited Alistair Darling, the United Kingdom minister, to the launch so he could also make a statement that poverty was a British-wide phenomenon, as big a concern in Derby and Darlington as in Drumchapel. Though a strong devolutionist, he always supported a United Kingdom and he remained suspicious of exclusively Scotland-only solutions.

Donald always saw the importance of social justice and economic efficiency advancing together – and this shared agenda is often written about. Indeed, as First Minister he initiated the first Ministry for Enterprise and Lifelong Learning. But the Donald I knew was less interested in the mechanics of macro-economic or supply side policies: economics were a means to an end and he was far more interested in social justice.

So when people say that what was special about Donald was his decency, they tell far less than half the story. His decency is legendary. But what was special about Donald as a politician was that, consistently and tirelessly, he pursued the logic of his decency and worked for a just and more equal society. And because people knew he cared, they trusted him as a politician. And so we can understand why, in an age when people often cross the street to avoid a politician, people would cross the street to meet and talk to Donald. Right through his extraordinary life, Donald reached out to people and in turn people reached out and trusted him. And this was Donald's gift – to establish not only a unique bond of trust with people but also a common cause with them. People came to believe not only in what he did but also in what he stood for: the cause of social justice – the rock upon which his lifetime of public service was built.

And so his achievement is much more than a parliament, much more than the sum of his social reforms: it is that he ennobled the very idea of service and, by his pursuit of a just society, gave moral purpose to our public life. Five years after he died, Donald's ideals, his vision of a just society, challenge us even more strongly. In his final major speech to the Labour Party conference only a few weeks before he died, Donald said, 'One thing I can promise absolutely and without qualification is that the Labour Party in Scotland will hold to its principles . . . for a vision of a just society, a movement fighting for right – and joining in those great causes with colleagues from every part of the United Kingdom.'

Though Donald has gone from us, his cause endures. Let his inspiration continue to lead us forward.

As Scottish Labour Leader

Murray Elder

It is not easy in a short essay to try to define all the qualities that made Donald Dewar the Labour politician he was. I hope by covering a few of the most important events in his political career to draw out something of the substance of the man.

Donald Campbell Dewar was leader of the Labour Party in Scotland in all but name from 1983 to 2000 – save for a four-year gap between 1993 and 1997. He was the dominating figure in Scottish politics from the point when he became shadow Secretary of State for Scotland in 1983 until his death in 2000. His positioning of the party was exceptional, not least because he always knew what the bottom line was and how far he could go without compromising his principles. Above all, he was a Labour man, one who believed in the United Kingdom and also in social justice. And his belief in devolution was driven by all three.

His commitment to the cause of devolution was there from the beginning. At university in Glasgow, and later as MP for Aberdeen South from 1966 to 1970, he championed the cause. However fair it might be to say of some other Labour politicians (although it has been exaggerated) that they only became believers in devolution in the 1970s because the SNP was a threat to their ambitions, it was simply not true of Donald. Donald always believed in devolution.

That commitment to home rule was matched only by his devotion to the Labour Party in Scotland. His long membership of the Scottish Executive Committee of the party as a representative of the constituency section, when he was not in Parliament, is testament to that commitment. Throughout, he remained a rational voice in the Scottish Labour Party, particularly when, in the early 1980s, so many others were taking a very different line. Unlike others, he never thought of leaving the party. He fought for his beliefs – and the Labour Party and Scotland were better for it.

Donald became shadow Secretary of State for Scotland at a very difficult period for Labour in the run-up to the 1983 election. In the immediate aftermath of that massive defeat, his focus on devolution was a means of keeping the Labour Party in Scotland active, offering hope for the years that followed.

The nationalist accusation that Scotland could vote Labour forever but never get a Labour government at Westminster had to be challenged. And challenge it Donald did – with determination and drive. One of the first concrete results was a Labour Party Green Paper on Scotland – setting out Labour's devolution scheme. It was based on the Scotland Act, which had fallen with the 1979 referendum. It was certainly not a substantial document but the basic tenets of the devolution settlement (in terms of what was devolved and what retained) were to remain much the same until the actual White Paper was produced 16 years later.

The Green Paper gave Labour in Scotland something to rally round at a time when the party was deeply demoralised. But Donald continued to worry about the reasons behind the failure of the 1979 referendum: specifically the perception that the scheme was for Labour Scotland, dominated by the central belt, and that the first-past-the-post electoral system guaranteed permanent Labour control. He always knew that these issues had to be tackled head on if a further defeat was to be avoided. Not immediately but in due course. Crossing bridges before they were reached was not Donald's style.

The attempt to keep the political argument focused on the devolution issue became all the more difficult after a second desperate defeat in the 1987 general election. It was a United Kingdom defeat lightened only by the exceptional performance of Labour in Scotland, where the party made half of its total gains. That Labour success, amid the gloom of defeat, was in part due to campaigning against the soon-to-be-introduced poll tax. The poll tax became the dominant issue of the following years. For Labour in Scotland, the issue was not whether it should be opposed but the form that opposition should take.

There was a huge amount of pressure from within the party and from elsewhere for a non-payment campaign. Donald took the campaign as far as he was prepared to but was always determined to ensure that the party did not endorse illegality. All sorts of curious campaigns resulted – 'return to sender', when people were asked simply to send back their bills, was one protest. Others tried to refuse payment of the poll tax but to pay the same amount to their council so that services would not be affected.

Matters were always going to have to come to a head and a special conference – the chosen means of public display of disunity deployed by the Labour Party at the time – was duly called. Defeat would have had appalling consequences for the party and for Donald. A huge amount of work was done in the old-fashioned tradition of party conferences to prevent that. And a number of colleagues, some on the left – who saw how disastrous a road illegality would be for Labour – supported Donald, enabling him to see off the danger.

But in a sense, opposition to the poll tax was a diversion. The national question had not gone away. After the 1987 election, the momentum to find a fresh consensus to deliver devolution increased. The excellence of the Labour performance in the face of such a major United Kingdom defeat meant that, briefly, the issue of whether Labour could ever win again in the United Kingdom became the defining question.

The Scottish Constitutional Convention was proposed and the issue became whether or not Labour would join. The worries Donald had about the perception of a Scottish Parliament as a central-belt Labour council writ large remained, as did the need to widen the appeal of the prospective Scottish Parliament. That meant getting a consensus not just for the idea of devolution but also for a specific scheme. To achieve that, all sides would have to make sacrifices. It was always likely that a form of proportional representation would be necessary if the Liberal Democrats were to be involved. But participation by the other parties in Scotland was not a given.

Donald wisely decided that the benefits outweighed the risks of not taking part. By September 1998, with the poll tax decision behind him, he decided that Labour participation in the convention process should go ahead. I was in hospital, post heart transplant, and he came to visit me to discuss it. We agreed that whatever the risks, it was the best way forward.

I remember him saying that it would be like riding on the back of a tiger but that we would have to rely on our ability to be able to think faster than our opponents to make it work. What he would look for was a suitable opportunity to announce it.

Unfortunately, that opportunity arose only a few days later when John Smith had his first heart attack. Donald agreed to take over a speaking engagement at Stirling University and the decision was announced. This was all before the result later that year at the Govan by-election when Jim Sillars won the seat for the SNP.

Donald was criticised for his description of Labour's defeat at Govan as a 'flash flood', although the more excitable commentators, who criticised him so much in the aftermath of the Govan defeat, were less inclined to give him any credit when less than a year later, in May 1989, Labour convincingly won the Glasgow Central by-election. Donald was not unmindful of the SNP threat but he had seen several such Nationalist surges and subsequent retreats over the years. Perhaps critics forgot that when he won his own by-election in 1978 in Glasgow Garscadden, it was at a time when the SNP held all the local council seats in the constituency and he had been given little hope of success. Determination, commitment and sheer hard work nevertheless had won Donald a famous victory.

Negotiations about the Scottish Constitutional Convention really got underway early in 1989 and a huge amount of attention focused on the attitude of the SNP. Donald always knew that the risk was that their presence in the negotiations might make a consensus agreement impossible. More importantly, he always saw that if Labour was to govern in the new Scottish Parliament, with a more proportional system, then Labour's likeliest coalition partners were the Liberal Democrats.

For very different reasons, both the Tories and the SNP refused to join and paid a price for declining to participate in what was a genuine attempt at consensus, which was what the people of Scotland clearly wanted. Had either joined in the Convention it would have been a somewhat different scheme; perhaps it would have had to be Labour who broke off negotiations. But Labour was never put to that test.

Donald's belief was always that to get agreement in the Labour Party for a more proportional system for elections it was necessary to have agreement on the rest of the package. If the Labour Party felt that it was achieving its goals, the proportional representation pill would be easier to swallow. And it was a bitter pill, because Labour was giving up the system that virtually guaranteed it control of Scottish politics. Donald's view – and ultimately the party's – was that the short-term pain was necessary to reach the ultimate prize. When Neil Kinnock set up the Plant Commission to look at proportional representation, it was in part to create enough room for manoeuvre within the Labour Party for the Scottish party to take that decision. There was, as it turned out, rather a long way to go before a final agreement was reached – with further concessions on proportional representation – but by the 1992 election the framework of the Convention scheme was in place.

Donald, as shadow Secretary of State for Scotland when Neil Kinnock was leader, always had to accept that the party leader was lukewarm at best on devolution – indeed, he had always been opposed to the equivalent for Wales. Later, Donald also had to accommodate the views of another Labour leader. Tony Blair was far from being an instinctive devolutionist but the 'unfinished business' legacy of John Smith, public expectation and the long-established commitment of Gordon Brown, Donald and others made it impossible to dilute the policy.

But two years earlier in the wake of the 1992 election John Smith had become Labour leader and Donald had no need to argue devolution's case with the leadership. This was a factor in the change in Donald's political role that followed. Donald had been a close friend of John since their Glasgow University days in the 1950s. Smith had come later to devolution than Donald but, after the experience of the Devolution Bill in the 1970s, had become wholly committed.

As soon as the results of the Shadow Cabinet elections were known, John suggested that Donald should leave the position of shadow Secretary of State for Scotland. It was never his intention to offer the Scottish Secretary's job to anyone else in power but he felt that Donald had been so long in the cauldron of Scottish politics that a break would do him good and there were other jobs in which he would thrive. It was also the case that for the first time there was another Scot in the Shadow Cabinet who might fill the Scottish Secretary role, given that Robin and Gordon were established elsewhere.

John's first offer, and his preference for Donald, was defence. To those who only know the myth of Donald never having been abroad that might seem odd. He had in fact at various times travelled widely in Europe. And he was the only person I have known who was in Berlin and heard John Fitzgerald Kennedy make his famous speech there.

Donald took the view that the shadow social security portfolio was what he wanted and John accepted that. Indeed, one of the key initiatives of John Smith's leadership was the setting up of the Social Justice Commission. This was a job of enormous importance to Smith and to Dewar. Donald not surprisingly immersed himself in the detail, once remarking that the biggest difference from his past job was that his press cuttings – he was an assiduous collector of press cuttings – started to turn pink, as the quantity of technical articles from the *Financial Times* rocketed.

Although that period, and the spell as Tony Blair's Chief Whip later, removed him from the front line in Scottish politics, in many ways Donald never left. And it came as no surprise to anyone – and a huge delight to him – when following Labour's victory in the 1997 general election, he duly became Secretary of State for Scotland.

Donald's and the government's immediate Scottish priority was devolution. He was accused by his detractors of 'hitting the ground strolling'. But that charge was made largely because of the comparison with the immediacy of the announcement from Gordon Brown of independence for the Bank of England. There was no comparable radical initiative that could be taken north of the border with such impact.

But behind the scenes, the speed with which the Referendum Bill was agreed (two weeks) and the highly complex Devolution White Paper written, agreed through Cabinet Committee and published, was astonishing. Although the best team within the Scottish Office had been appointed to assist – and there were some really outstanding civil servants involved – there was still a great deal of work to be done. When the first full draft was produced, it was completely restructured by Donald and his special advisers, to the consternation of the officials. But this was his legislation more than theirs. And it was not as though there had not been enough trial runs in the Labour Party over the previous years to demonstrate what was required.

The Cabinet Committee on devolution met regularly and Donald predictably underplayed what he had achieved. He used to return from the meetings with a tale full of woe and failure. We would then go through the points that had been on the agenda that mattered and it would turn out that he had won on all of them, with only the most minor of amendments.

The truth was Donald got the White Paper he wanted. Thereafter, the strategy was pretty simple. The White Paper would be agreed as quickly as possible. There was a long-standing belief among Scottish Office officials that the longer something lay in Whitehall the greater the changes that would be demanded. Speed was of the essence, therefore, to get the legislation through the process unscathed. And although the referendum commitment was devised, in part, to deal with the perceived difficulties of getting the legislation through Parliament, it ended up being at least as useful as a means of ensuring that Whitehall departments didn't have second thoughts about what had been agreed when the draft legislation was being considered. The fact that the White Paper was government policy, subsequently endorsed by the Scottish people through a referendum and which now required the Scotland Act to put it into effect, became a sort of mantra.

So much has been written about devolution that at times the scale and direction of policy Donald tackled in other areas is often overlooked. In education, there was a huge amount to do to create a learning environment fit for the twenty-first century. Some of the first priorities were extending nursery provision; early intervention at primary school to ensure basic skills; and a new commitment to further education and lifelong learning. The changes in student finance were intended to end the rationing of student places and to make places available to all who had the necessary skills.

These were not changes for change's sake but because Donald knew they had to be made. Once again, he took the bit between his teeth and drove forward a reforming agenda.

Land reform also reflects how seriously Donald took his responsibilities to govern beyond the fiefdom of the central belt of Scotland. He was careful when launching the plan – which culminated in the provision of the community right to buy – not to oversell it. Money would be there but not enough to finance purchases, only to kick-start the process. And that is what has happened. Following the landmark community purchases of Knoydart and Eigg, five years on a revitalisation of the Highlands that few would have thought possible is now taking place thanks to this groundbreaking legislation. I believe it was one of the most farsighted policies. And it was certainly radical. Donald would have been delighted to see how much it has acted as a catalyst in getting people in the Highlands to look at land use in innovative ways and to develop the potential that was always there but had remained dormant for generations.

These two examples – there are others – show Donald's commitment to radical and pioneering legislation which will leave its mark positively for generations to come. In the meantime, Donald was also formally elected as Scottish Labour leader in 1998 (technically leader of the parliamentary group at Holyrood) in preparation for the forthcoming Scottish Parliament elections in 1999.

Following Labour's victory in those elections, with Labour the largest party but without an overall majority, negotiations with the Liberal Democrats began in earnest. Donald's strength in the negotiation process was that he always knew how far he was prepared to go. He was determined to try to avoid a minority government but not at any price.

The coalition negotiations ranged over all policy areas and, as is well known, they almost faltered over student fees. Donald was concerned that statements made by the Liberal Democrat leadership had given them too little room for manoeuvre in the negotiations and so it almost proved. Donald even prepared a statement for circumstances where agreement could not be reached, which indicated that he had decided that the only thing left to do was go it alone. The Labour negotiating team agreed that statement in principle. But at the last minute agreement was reached and the partnership was launched.

Donald Dewar did not shirk from taking hard policy decisions. Unlike some other politicians he was not fixated with the need for the short-term gain of positive newspaper headlines. The section 28 debate is testimony to that. The debate may have been badly timed, and may have resulted in a more difficult campaign than had been anticipated, but Donald, a social liberal all his days, never doubted that it was the right thing to do – and the Scottish Parliament the right place to do it.

When he addressed his final United Kingdom party conference in 2000, he said, with evident pride, 'We faced unprecedented pressures – a well-funded campaign, hostility built sometimes on malice, more often built on unjustified fears and sometimes built on deep-dyed prejudice. We argued that the law discriminated, that tolerance was an essential virtue in our society, that our children were protected by the vigilance of teachers and by the caring involvement of parents. We stood firm in the blizzard. We won. In Scotland we did not keep the clause; section 28 is no more.'

But what conclusions might be drawn about the way he would have continued as First Minister had his tenure not been so untimely and abruptly ended? Donald Dewar was a strategist who knew what the right thing to do was. I do not believe that he would have introduced free personal care for the elderly, because he thought there were better ways to help pensioners. He believed that the proposals for free care were misguided and the drive to introduce them took place only following his death.

He would not have supported difficult legislation being sent south to be passed on a Sewel motion at Westminster. I think he would have seen that with a Scottish Parliament, there was a much-diminished need for a Secretary of State for Scotland, perhaps no need at all. But he would have worried about the distance between civil servants north and south of the border, which is in danger of isolating the Scottish Executive from Westminster initiatives and thinking. Donald, I'm sure, would also have thought through how far the coalition should be driven by minority partners, sometimes at the expense of the major partner.

Over the last twenty years I have had the privilege to work for two major Labour figures – John Smith and Donald Dewar. They were two of the most 'unspinnable' politicians you could imagine. It was a great strength. What you saw was what you got. Perhaps not unsurprisingly, as a result, they were also two of the most trusted and admired. Both died far too young.

In his last speech to a Labour conference in Bournemouth before his death, Donald said more than I can in this essay about what drove him. 'One thing I can promise, absolutely and without qualification, is that the Labour Party in Scotland will hold to its principles and its promises. We are prepared to be radical. We will always be a party on the attack, innovating, standing for liberties, for change, for a vision of a just society – a movement fighting for right and joining in those great causes with colleagues from every part of the United Kingdom.' I believe Donald would have stuck to those principles and he would have known when to say his goodbyes and turn to the rest of his life – and the rich cultural hinterland that made him the man that he was.

It's sad that the retirement that he deserved was to be denied him but behind him he left a rich political legacy. It is one that will guarantee his place in the political history of Scotland but, more importantly, it means that modern Scotland is a better place thanks to his efforts. He might have found it difficult to admit that but he should surely have been justly proud.

His Finest Hour

Carol Craig

It is humbling to consider that most people's existence on earth disappears, almost without trace, within a couple of generations and their presence lives on only on tombstones or unnamed faces in crumbling photograph albums. This is not the fate of Donald Campbell Dewar. In Scotland, his name and legacy will endure and he will be remembered not just for his personal qualities as a human being but also for his achievements as a politician.

So what kind of politician was Donald Dewar? In some quarters, he was denounced as a hypocrite or a careerist. In others, as a dreary conservative and a political lightweight. My own view is that he was the right man in the right place at the right time – that as a politician he had exactly the temperament and the skills needed to deliver a Scottish Parliament and an iconic building.

Over the course of the past 20 years, I've heard various cynics express the view that Donald Dewar could have joined any political party. Indeed, some even tell a story, no doubt apocryphal, that Donald Dewar, John Smith, Menzies Campbell and John MacKay sat round as students at Glasgow University discussing which party would offer them the best opportunity to become MPs.

As someone from a thoroughly petit-bourgeois background, Donald was bound to attract such allegations. There was nothing working class about Donald and so no automatic presumption that the Labour Party was his rightful domain. Donald had the air of a public schoolboy about him. In a city where for generations poverty had stunted the height of its citizens, even his stature gave away his comfortable middle-class genes. But if we leave aside this narrow class-based view of political allegiance and delve deeper into values, it is easy to see why the Labour Party was for Donald a spiritual home from home.

In what many regard as the most insightful book ever published on the Labour Party, Henry Drucker writes not just about the ideology of the party, as enshrined in various doctrines but also about its ethos – 'traditions, beliefs, characteristics, procedures and feelings which help to animate the members of the party'.[1] And Drucker argues these must be traced to the experience of working people. He subsequently argues that in the Labour Party 'doing well and acquiring a "Tory like" style of living is resented more than corruption'.[2]

In my book, *The Scots' Crisis of Confidence*, I argue that outside the tiny Scottish aristocracy in Scotland there is a veneration of simplicity and ordinary ways. Anything that smacks of upper-class culture or pretension is suspect. This levelling-down influence results from a confluence of the democratic traditions of the Church, the Burns cult and Labour-movement values, and is further strengthened by the notion that a liking for high culture is essentially 'English'. Donald did not come from a working-class, Labour-movement background but the values passed on from his Scottish middle-class family were still in harmony with this predominant aspect of Labour Party ethos.

Donald had a reputation for being an intellectual snob and there may be some truth in this. But he was not a social snob. Indeed, he was one of the least pretentious people I've ever met. I doubt Donald ever 'flaunted' anything in his life or had any notion to keep up with the Joneses. Sure, he loved the Scottish Colourist school of art, possessing both a Cadell and a Peploe, but Donald genuinely loved such items for their intrinsic beauty rather than their monetary value or capacity to impress.

So Donald was no interloper into the Labour Party. He shared their values. Of course, he was no red-blooded 'Clause 4' socialist and never pretended to be. But again, as Drucker points out, the Labour Party has always been ambivalent in its attitude to radical political action. As he argues, traditionally it was essentially an 'opposition party', much more able to unite and argue cogently for what it didn't like than to put forward a coherent programme. What's more, the party has always been a 'broad church' – a loose coalition of differing political views. Donald was firmly in the Crosland wing of the party, which defined its commitment to ordinary working-class people not through programmes to nationalise the means of production but by trying to achieve 'social equality' and a more 'classless society'. Greater educational opportunities, better housing, more accessible health care and a bit of judicious redistribution of wealth were the kinds of goals which animated Donald and his 'social justice' agenda.

But I believe that there was another reason why Donald felt at ease in the Labour Party and it relates to the style of politics encouraged by the participation of the trade union movement. As Drucker points out:

> Labour is more closely tied to its trade unionists than any other major party in any major country. They set the tone of its thought. The experience of trade unionists does not lend itself to extreme demands. The business of a union is to get the best possible arrangement for its members. This raises shrewd and sagacious men to the fore, men who are tough negotiators. It makes leaders of men who can judge what capital can pay. This is an attitude of mind, which says, 'We will make these levers work for us.' It is an attitude that knows the power of loyalty and makes for caution.[3]

As a former lawyer, Donald had no previous experience of union membership. He did not belong to their ranks but, nonetheless, in terms of temperament, Donald was extremely comfortable with such a pragmatic, incremental approach to politics, as it was similar to his own.

Such a political style may deliver tangible results but it is unlikely to set the heather, or anything else, alight. Indeed, it's rather plodding and boring and unlikely to attract much attention let alone gain widespread respect. And yet here we are writing a whole book of essays in his memory. Why?

The answer is simple: Donald's personality and style of political leadership were exactly what was needed to bring about the devolution settlement. Indeed, I do not think there was another political figure in Scotland who could have pulled it off. However, I think it is also true to say that once the Parliament was firmly underway Donald did not make a great First Minister for Scotland. To understand why, we need to know something about different styles of political leadership.

As individuals, we are unique and have certain characteristics that distinguish us from one another but, nonetheless, it is still possible to discern similar types of people. The same is true of political leaders. There are various ways to define different types of leadership styles. The following is a four-point classification scheme I find useful.[4]

The first types in this scheme are called *idealists*, as they combine visionary ideals, to be realised in a future world, with a strong focus on developing people and building relationships. Leaders of this type have exceptional people skills and an ability to inspire others with their vision. Nelson Mandela and Mahatma Gandhi displayed this leadership style at its best. Adolf Hitler was also an idealist – a powerful reminder that ideals are not always life affirming or benign. Tony Blair has the hallmarks of an idealist leader but his inclusion here also illustrates how in the modern world a leader's ideals can seem lightweight and pedestrian. Blair is also a good example of how the ability to persuade and charm can backfire and appear manipulative.

Then there are the *rationals*. These leaders also have large visionary goals, which they pursue with great energy, but they are more logical, if not mechanistic, in their dealings with people. Despite large differences in political ideals and personality, Gordon Brown and Margaret Thatcher could, nonetheless, be classified as 'rational' leadership types. As is the case with the idealists, the values and principles underlying this leadership style depend on the vision.

The third type of leaders can be described as *governors*. These are people who live in the here and now and are not constantly pulled towards the possibilities of an abstract, visionary future. They see it as their job to maintain order, control and stability. They can be traditionalists, as was John Major with his emphasis on 'back to basics' and 'family values', or simply strong organisational types, like Jack McConnell with his emphasis on effective delivery – 'doing less better'.

The fourth type of leaders can be described as *operators*. This name does not imply any fundamental lack of principle and I've chosen this word as it helps to convey that, above all else, what makes such leadership types tick is the desire to pull political levers for pragmatic gains. Of the four leadership styles this is the one which is most difficult to pin down, as such leaders enjoy being flexible and responsive and are not particularly motivated by predetermined ideas. Unlike the idealists and the rationals, they are not abstract thinkers intent on pursuing a vision of a possible

Donald as a child, wearing
the kilt. (SMG archive)

Donald as a young man. (SMG archive)

Donald at Glasgow University, 1961–2, third from the right in the front row, John Smith is second from the left in the front row and Menzies Campbell is in the middle row fourth from right. Jimmy Gordon (contributor) is in the middle row second from right and Neil MacCormick (contributor) is back row second from right. Glasgow University Board photograph. (SMG archive)

Donald with his wife, Alison, daughter, Marion, and son, Iain, when MP for Aberdeen South. (Press Association)

Donald in the studio during his stint as a part-time Radio Clyde current affairs presenter in the 1970s. He was also working as a solicitor.
(Donald Dewar Archive)

Donald celebrating with his supporters after winning the Glasgow Garscadden by-election, 13 April 1978. It was seen as turning the high tide of nationalism. (Press Association)

Donald in May 1978 as the newly elected MP for Glasgow Garscadden campaigning for Hamilton by-election candidate George Robertson. Donald seen here relaxing with the candidate (pictured centre) and Gavin Strang. (SMG archive)

Mayday 1980 – Donald celebrates by giving a friendly pull to the six victorious Labour candidates (Tom Lenehan, Madge O'Neill, Charles Davison, Maria Fyfe, John Kernaghan and David Wiseman) in his Garscadden constituency in the District Council elections. (SMG archive)

Donald's love of sport was legendary, his sporting prowess more mundane! Here seen as part of 1985 Scottish Parliamentary Labour Party five-a-side team. Left to right: Tam Dalyell, Dennis Canavan, Donald, Michael Martin and Willie McKelvey. (SMG archive)

June 1987 – most of Labour's 50 MPs elected for Scotland on the steps of Keir Hardie House, the Labour Party's Scottish HQ. This was midway through Donald's long service as Labour shadow Scottish Secretary from 1983 to 1992. (Donald Dewar Archive)

Donald with the Rt Hon. Malcolm Rifkind MP, then Secretary of State for Scotland, and Hector Munro MP in the background, at a press conference on 22 December 1988 in the wake of the Lockerbie disaster. (TSPL)

Donald with long-term colleague and friend the Rt Hon. Roy Hattersley MP, then Deputy Leader of the Labour Party, in Roy's office. (Donald Dewar Archive)

Donald in Stirling with Parliamentary colleagues launching Labour's 1992 election campaign in Scotland. Left to right: Robin Cook, Gordon Brown, Kate Phillips (Labour's candidate in Stirling), Donald and John Smith. (TSPL)

future. They are feet-on-the-ground pragmatists. Unlike governors, they are not sticklers for rules, regulations or tried and tested ways of doing things. Operators particularly enjoy 'working the system' to advance their goals and they can be risk takers as well as good negotiators. Across organisations, this type of leadership style comes into its own in a crisis, as these types can work speedily and with great flair when up against the wire. Indeed, they often need external pressure to perform well and without it can become easily distracted or even indolent. Undoubtedly, Sir Winston Churchill was this type of leader. I suspect that Kenneth Clarke as a political leader also fell into this category.

So where would Donald fit into such a classification? I knew Donald for over 20 years and had plenty of opportunity to observe him at first hand. One of the most obvious features about Donald was that he was not an abstract visionary thinker; he was a lover and respecter of the known rather than the unknown. Burns's line 'facts are chiels that winnae ding' could have been Donald's mantra. Since this is not how I see the world, I was often aware in conversation with Donald that we just weren't on the same wavelength. For example, we both shared a real interest in the Scottish Enlightenment but whereas I wanted to discuss generally the broad current of Enlightenment thought or how we might use these ideas today to reshape modern Scotland, Donald was mainly interested in the historical figures and their times. Donald is often seen as an intellectual – a bookish and intelligent man. There is no doubt that he was exceptionally well read but his was more the intelligence of the scholar or academic critic than the intelligence of an original and innovative thinker such as Gordon Brown.

Donald was not a visionary type but he was champion of one big idea: that Scotland needed its own devolved parliament. But even then his commitment did not come from some abstract idea of how the future could be different. No, it was Donald's love of Scottish history that led him to believe that a Parliament in Edinburgh was a natural extension of Scotland's past. This was evident in the speech Donald gave at the Parliament's opening ceremony in July 1999. Indeed, the most telling line – 'a moment anchored in our history' – is even used as the title of the speech. What's more, in this speech Donald makes much more reference to Scotland's past than its future. Of course, he has a few lines about looking forward to future debates but much more of the speech is about past battles, Sir Walter Scott, Robert Burns, 'the speak of the Mearns' and the 'shout of the welder in the great shipyards'.

People who worked closely with Donald when he was First Minister were aware, and often rather dispirited by the fact, that he wasn't 'an ideas person'. A year or so before Donald's death, I was seated at dinner beside a very senior civil servant in the Scottish Executive who worked closely with Donald and much to my surprise he spent most of the evening confiding in me that he couldn't believe that Donald was neither good at coming up with ideas himself nor very interested in other people's. 'What does he want to do with these powers now he has them?' he kept asking. And, of course, as someone who studied politics in the 1970s, I was aware of the irony of the situation: during Labour's administration from 1974 to 1979, it was taken as read that it was the conservative Civil Service who acted as a constant check on Labour's reforming zeal. Yet here was a senior mandarin criticising a Labour politician for not wanting to do enough with his political power.

However, it must also be pointed out that Donald at least had the wit, or the self-awareness of his own limitations, to know that he needed some ideas people in his inner circle. This is no doubt why he worked closely with Wendy Alexander for years, as Wendy, as anyone who spends time with her will know, has more ideas in one day than most ordinary people have in a lifetime.

So Donald was no visionary political leader. Neither was he a governor type. In fact, I would go so far as to say that Donald was one of the most disorganised people I've ever met. He often told the story against himself that when he was an MP the police thought his office had been burgled and ransacked, and he had, shamefacedly, to admit that it always looked like that. His car was always a mess. Vote Labour stickers would be on the windows months after elections.

Donald's appearance made him look rather conventional. He often wore a staid grey, albeit crumpled, suit and tie. His concession to weekends was to wear a slipover and a pair of plimsolls. But this appearance belied the fact that there was nothing formal or stuffy about him. I remember taking him to meet my sister, who lived in his constituency, as she had an issue she wanted to discuss. She was rather apprehensive about meeting this famous figure and couldn't believe that within half an hour he was lounging on her floor beside the fire eating chocolate biscuits and chortling. Remember, this is also the man who at the state opening of the new Scottish Parliament walked beside the Queen with his hands in his pockets.

Donald was not a rules and regulations man; as a political leader he was an operator. As a lawyer, he knew the importance of doing things properly and undoubtedly he also had a lawyer's eye for detail and even took a hand in drafting the Scotland Act. But this attention to the use of language and seeing an issue from every angle is different from a desire to become involved in operational matters. Both leadership and personal styles inclined him not to be overly concerned about overseeing the running of an organisation and this no doubt backfired with the commissioning of the new Parliament building – a theme I'll return to. Donald's attention was firmly on solving problems and making decisions, particularly once they became urgent. And for the most fruitful part of Donald's political leadership that meant how he was going to bring about a parliament for Scotland.

Now the Scottish Parliament is in its second term it is very easy for us to forget what an achievement it was for Donald Dewar, as a senior figure in the Scottish Labour Party, to bring it about. As a new leader of the Labour Party, Tony Blair was sceptical about the desire for devolution in Scotland and worried about the lack of a proper political mandate. It was Blair who triggered the process that ultimately forced a referendum on the Scottish Labour Party. Once Labour was elected in 1997, there was much for the new Labour administration to do and it would have been easy for the commitment to devolution to slide down the priority list. The person who managed to keep the Labour Party, at all levels, focused and moving forward on its commitment to devolution was Donald. And this was true even when he wasn't shadow Secretary of State for Scotland – a role that was taken up during some of these critical years by George Robertson. It was Donald who 'wheeled and dealed', first in getting the Scottish Labour Party to accept Blair's demand for a referendum and ultimately with his colleagues at Westminster to make sure that the Scotland Bill got the parliamentary time and support it needed to get on the statute book. Donald's time spent as Chief Whip stood him in good stead and he was well connected at Westminster. But it also took a certain personality and set of skills of a type which Donald had in spades. Even Donald's political opponents paid tribute to the fact that he was a man of principle and integrity. Margo MacDonald, for example, called him 'a man of probity'. You could trust him. He also had the ability to forge good, long-lasting relationships. He was flexible and knew how to come and go with people. He knew his subject inside out. What's more, he concentrated on the task at hand rather than being sidetracked by all sorts of big ideas.

Donald's style of flexible pragmatism also allowed him to take Labour into the Scottish Constitutional Convention. Indeed, he apparently relished the novelty and ultimate unpredictability of this step. Murray Elder elsewhere in this volume recalls how Donald likened joining the Convention to 'riding on the back of a tiger'. He also recalls that Donald liked the inherent risk and the fact that he and his colleagues 'would have to rely on . . . [their] ability to be able to think faster than . . . [their] opponents to make it work'.

It was this flexibility in approach that also allowed Donald to cooperate so effectively with other parties in the campaign that led up to the referendum in 1998. More ideologically driven politicians would not have been able to do that.

Even one of Donald's arch political rivals, Alex Salmond, admits that the referendum campaign itself was won largely as a result of Donald's personal style – that many of the votes were cast because of Donald's personal credibility and the respect that people had for him. And it is important to remember that the success of this campaign was not just in getting people to support the biggest change to the British constitution for hundreds of years but also to support the possibility that they might have to pay more tax for the privilege of having this new institution.

Donald clearly saw his devolution remit as extending beyond the constitutional settlement. He was very keen to be involved in the creation of the physical manifestation of this new institution – the Parliament building. Abstract thinkers, or those more focused on the types of activities and ideas a new legislature could pursue (the idealists and the rationals), could easily have played down the significance of a building. They would have been inclined to argue that it was the nature of the debate in the new Parliament and its subsequent ideas which mattered more. In other words, a more visionary leader, concerned about what a Parliament could be doing, might have been inclined to have just fitted in with the arrangements already in place (the Old Royal High School Building) or devolved the decision to the members of the new Parliament. But Donald, as a concrete thinker (if you'll excuse the pun), was aware of the importance of physical place and the message that a building would send to the world. As one of the members of the Designer Selection Panel explained to the Fraser Inquiry, Donald Dewar was so attracted to the idea of commissioning the visionary architect Enric Miralles because 'his heart was in developing a contemporary icon. He wanted to make a landmark building that would identify that particular moment in Scotland's history.'[5] Donald was also aware that in commissioning a new building he 'had a mandate to act as the most important patron of architecture of government for 300 years'.[6] So, even in the building of the new Parliament building we see Donald animated by a strong sense of history.

Reading the Fraser Inquiry Report it is easy to see the various elements of Donald's personality and style of political leadership coming to the fore. Donald was distinctly unimpressed by lots of new ideas but he was able to put his heart and soul into the few things he did care passionately about. What's more, in the right circumstances he was prepared to take risks. And we can see this passionate, risk-taking side of Donald's personality in the commissioning of the Parliament building. He was extremely hands on in the early discussions about location, how the architect would be chosen and the actual design concept. What is also clear is that he and other members of the Design Panel were aware that they were embarking on a process, and choosing an architect, that entailed considerable risk. Clearly they felt it was better to do this than commission a 'bog-standard building on a greenfield site'. Despite all the difficulties and the spiralling cost, I've little doubt that in time Scots will come to love their Parliament building and will believe that Donald Dewar and the Design Panel took the right decision.

But in the Fraser Inquiry Report we can also see at work the downside of Donald's approach. Once the decisions had been reached about location and design concept, Donald's interest seemed to wane. Lord Fraser is clear that he does not think that Donald Dewar, as First Minister, concealed anything from members of the Scottish Parliament about costs and so forth. He also thinks that various people in the Scottish Executive concealed important facts from the First Minister. However, Lord Fraser is still somewhat critical of Donald Dewar for not asking enough questions about how the project was going. In other words, Donald as leader did not adequately oversee the ensuing building project or check that systems were in place. He left that to others, partly because he had other things to occupy him and partly because this was not the type of activity that Donald liked. As I explained earlier, this type of detailed management was not one of Donald's strengths.

Reading the Fraser Inquiry Report it is also possible to discern how two distinct elements in Donald's personality led to some of the ensuing fiasco.

Donald, as I argued earlier, was a fairly typical Scot in that he liked simplicity and disliked conspicuous consumption. He would have found it impossible to justify allocating £430 million of public money to a new Scottish Parliament building. But as someone who loved beautiful things and had a sense of the historic importance of the new parliament, he was not prepared either to adapt an existing building or to commission 'a shed', as Kirsty Wark put it. So what was the progeny of this tension? A huge ambition for an iconic building, designed by an unmanageable Spanish architect, on a difficult site alongside an opposing commitment to work prudently within a tight budget and tight timescale. Lord Fraser himself is conscious of the absurdity of such clashing goals and at the end of his introduction to the report quotes a handwritten note from 1999 by one of the consultants which states: 'Nobody tells Enric to think about economy with any seriousness.' Lord Fraser even adds, 'Little in this Report improves on that early astute observation.'[7]

I've little doubt that history will be kind to Donald Dewar; that as every decade passes Scots may become even more aware of his legacy to the nation. But this legacy consists of the devolution settlement and the iconic Parliament building – not what else he did as a politician or as First Minister. Certainly Donald believed in cabinet government. He was very supportive of those in his team – particularly the women he had brought on. But he was always unimpressed by airy-fairy new ideas and would have acted as a brake on those with reforming zeal. And in the early days of the new Parliament it was particularly important that it took some bold steps to show that it was indeed worth adding a new and expensive tier of government. Scotland also needed a leader to open up new and innovative thinking – to break the logjam of backward-looking views and lift the dead hand of old attitudes. Donald was himself so steeped in the past he could never have been such a leader. What's more, Donald's tendency to avoid conflict and procrastinate about day-to-day decisions would have allowed the machine to run itself.

To be his best, Donald needed the pressure of an immediate, all-consuming goal. He needed to use his considerable skills of negotiation and bridge building. He needed room for manoeuvre and to take risks. Just as Winston Churchill was able to lead in war but not in peace, Donald was able to excel in the time leading up to the Scottish Parliament, in its 'handselling', as he described it, and not so much in his role as First Minister of a fully functioning parliament.

Some may think this is a rather harsh conclusion but it's not. It's realistic. It naturally flows from the fact that as individuals we all have strengths and weaknesses. No one is good at everything. Visionary politicians would not have the pragmatism and flexibility to build bridges and work the system like Donald. Neither could types who are good at detailed administration. In Scotland, we are fortunate that making devolution reality was Donald Dewar's finest hour.

As Parliamentarian

Roy Hattersley

Two days after John Smith died, I sent a note to Donald Dewar. It was the only time, throughout our long friendship, that I wrote to him. I saw him on most days of the parliamentary year. But I knew that the message I had for him that day – if spoken rather than written – would deeply embarrass us both.

The letter began with a simple, and I fear hackneyed, message of sympathy. Donald was more affected by John's death than anyone outside the immediate Smith family but he stayed silent and solitary in his sorrow. Condolences are always hard to express. And Donald was the most emotionally fastidious man I ever knew. So the paragraph of comfort was particularly difficult to write.

I worked on several drafts before I felt moderately satisfied that I had struck the right note. Then – relieved that my original intention had been more or less achieved – I felt a sudden compulsion to add another sentence. I wrote it without pause, hesitation or doubt. 'In a sensible political system which values ability more than image, you would be front runner in the leadership election which is to come.' There was no thought of flattery relieving the pain of loss. I believed what I wrote then and I believe it, equally strongly, now.

Donald Dewar must have suspected that he would be remembered by history as the Scottish politician whose historic achievement was to lead

Scotland towards the creation of an Edinburgh Parliament and there is no doubt that the epitaph satisfied him. Indeed, he would have been rightly proud of it. He was Scottish by birth, education and, above all, by inclination.

Visits to the Lanark Mills, the Burrell Collection, Keir Hardie's birthplace and the Memorial Gates of Glasgow University convinced me that his Scottish convictions were sincere and all consuming. That made him exactly the right man to be Scotland's first First Minister. But he had the qualities – intellect and integrity, courage and conviction – which would have qualified him to lead the whole United Kingdom.

Scotland so absorbed his closing years that it is easy to forget the judgement of his closest friend in 1992. John Smith made Donald Dewar Labour's shadow Secretary of State for Social Security – confident that he was the man to wrestle with politics' most complicated conundrum. Pensions policy – then, as now, the riddle that nobody could solve – had to be based on a complicated combination of judgements that range from the ethical to the actuarial. Individual inclinations have to be balanced against the common good. Hypotheses have to be constructed about the longevity of generations not yet born.

It would be wrong to pretend that Donald Dewar set about his task with gay abandon. Gay abandon was not his style. But he did enjoy the sweat of wrestling with near imponderable equations. Ideas interested him. There were moments of frustrated depression when he feared that he could not solve a still unsolved problem. But there can be absolutely no doubt that, had Donald lived and the Labour leader had kept his nose to the pensions' grindstone, both the party and the nation would have made more progress towards the solution to what still seems an intractable dilemma.

After John's death, Donald exchanged the social security portfolio for responsibilities that I urged him to reject. Indeed there is, in the Donald Dewar Memorial Library in the Holyrood Parliament building, one of my books open at the incriminating title page. My inscription reads: 'To Donald Dewar on the day when I hope he has enough sense not to become an Opposition Chief Whip'. Foolishly, I thought that he was totally unsuited to the job. He proved to have the ideal temperament and technique for shepherding (and tethering) Labour MPs from all over Great Britain.

In modern politics, whips are rarely persons of great intellectual distinction. During my 33 years in the House of Commons, only one – Ted Short, back in 1964 – was even interested in ideas. Only one, that is, besides Donald Dewar.

Usually Chief Whips concern themselves with good order and discipline – which they enforce with threats, promises and appeals to atavistic loyalty. They boast about caring more for organisation than policy and take pride in maintaining their party's majority for whatever business happens to be in front of the House of Commons that day. Their motto begins 'Don't bother me with the merits . . .' Donald – although better organised politically than domestically – operated quite differently. He subdued revolts with reasoned argument and persuaded rebels to support the party line by explaining the merits of the leadership's case.

During his time as Chief Whip, Donald stayed with me for Christmas. On a long Boxing Day morning walk, he talked of the pleasure he found in mastering the details of policies that were new to him and getting to know young members who had been strangers. They were United Kingdom policies and members from England and Wales as well as Scotland.

That was no great surprise. In the days of Labour's madness, when some of us were struggling to drag the party back into the mainstream of national politics, few people worked harder for sanity than Donald Dewar. On the last day of the 1981 Labour conference, we travelled together from Brighton and spoke at a meeting in Lewisham Town Hall. Donald spoke like a British politician on issues which affected all of Great Britain – the foolishness of even contemplating leaving what was then the European Community, the economic illiteracy of the call for mass nationalisation and the futility of militancy for militancy's sake. He spoke like what he was – a man who could have fitted with distinction any Cabinet post he was given.

Before Scottish devolution – his overriding ambition and supreme achievement – he would, I believe, have been happy to serve for a time at the Scottish Office and then move on. Passionate though he was for the creation of Scotland's own parliament, his support for the Union was absolute and unflinching. We were together at the official opening of Keir Hardie's birthplace and as we walked through Cumnock after the ceremony, I noticed the market cross which was erected to celebrate the Hanoverian victory in the 1745 uprising. 'Not a Jacobite town,' I said. Donald explained, fiercely, that there were few Jacobite villages in all of

Scotland. And went on to explain the importance of devolution within the United Kingdom.

All that being said, there is no doubt that Donald Dewar was often thought of as an exclusively Scottish politician. The mistake was the result of more than his accent and his collection of Scottish water colourists. He had a brief excursion along the fringes of British politics when he became parliamentary private secretary to Tony Crosland at the Board of Trade. Crosland and Dewar did not get on or, to be more exact, Dewar did not get on with Crosland. Tony was my hero as well as my friend. But I understand exactly why some of his habits irritated his PPS. During the last conversation that Donald and I had – over dinner at the last Labour Party conference before he died – I made one of my many unsuccessful attempts to convince him that he was mistaken. He replied, 'Crosland kept trying to persuade me that various trade unionists had brilliant intellects when we both knew that was rubbish.'

Donald Dewar was impatient with what he regarded as nonsense – an attribute that did not endear him to metropolitan journalists. But the mistaken assumption that he was only Scottish had a deeper cause. In London, he was often a solitary figure, working hard on his brief and, when the Commons business was over, rushing out to Hampstead to the flat he rented from Michael Foot. English members and English journalists saw too little of him. In Scotland, surrounded by friends, he came to life. Donald Dewar was the quintessential Scotsman but he was a Scotsman who could, and might, have occupied any of the great offices of state in the United Kingdom Parliament.

Donald and Devolution

Donald could extract gloom from any situation. So great was Donald's predisposition for misery, he insisted on writing the speech I would make if I was to lose the Monklands East by-election caused by the death of his great friend John Smith. We won, and with only Donald's speech in my bag, on the advice of my agent, I made the same speech but smiled! Only once could he find nothing to complain about: the day the Scotland Bill was published – even he was hard pressed to find a suitable put-down!

Rt Hon. Helen Liddell – colleague and friend

Donald was deeply loyal to his friends. As one such friend, and a fellow combatant in the Labour trench wars of the 1980s, I had good reason to know. I vividly remember the week we announced the devolution referendum. Everyone now knows it was an inspired idea, cementing permanently the devolution settlement. Then, the unavoidable surprise blew away common sense. It was a torrid and bleak moment and Donald was a rock for me when the storm hit. His support then – and his closeness in the peak of our political life – will be my lasting memory of a good man.

Lord George Robertson – colleague and friend

The opening of the Parliament was no typical day . . . Donald was posted missing after meeting the Queen. I tracked him down, grinning on hands and knees, playing games with children in the Parliament lobby. Much later, I remember his loud guffawing when we quizzed his views on rock music. He was backstage and about to introduce Garbage to an audience of thousands. He carried it off like a rock critic. That was 'the Boss', he just knew things. Long and punishing working days simply felt shorter with his conversation as company.

Billy McLaren – Diary Secretary

A Worthy Opponent

Malcolm Rifkind

Donald Dewar had been due to come to my home for lunch the Sunday after he died. We were not close friends but he had expressed an interest in the history and architecture of Inveresk, the village in East Lothian where we lived. When I invited him, he had responded enthusiastically. He was, of course, First Minister at the time but it was a mark of the man that he could always find time for his other interests. Politics was his first but not his only love.

I had known Donald for many years, as Scotland is a family as well as a country. Even political opponents often get to know and like each other away from the political battle. We had a further link through the legal profession and through Ross Harper, who employed Donald, during the lean years, in his law firm and, occasionally, instructed me in criminal and civil cases.

Donald had had a stint as MP for Aberdeen South before I was first elected to the House of Commons. He was, therefore, senior to me both in years and in parliamentary experience. It must have been frustrating for him to return to the Commons just as his party was about to begin 18 long years in the political wilderness throughout the Thatcher and Major years.

I was a beneficiary of that period: a junior minister in the Scottish Office from 1979 to 1982 and then Secretary of State for Scotland from

1986 to 1990. For much of that time, Donald was my shadow across the dispatch box. He was always eloquent, powerful, witty and articulate. I can never remember him being snide, rude, bombastic or boring.

But he must, often, have been very bored. The role of an opposition may be a vital part of our constitution but it is not very stimulating when it continues over many long years without any predictable end in sight. Abba Eban, the former Israeli Foreign Minister, was once asked the difference between being in government and being in opposition. His reply was succinct and devastating. 'When you are a minister, you wake up in the morning and ask yourself what will you *do* today. When you are in opposition, you wake up in the morning and ask yourself what you will *say* today.'

It was Donald's fate to carry this burden for almost two decades and never to know for certain, until 1997, whether real power would come his way.

What must have made it even more galling than for his English colleagues was that, throughout this time, the Labour Party in Scotland had an overwhelming majority of parliamentary seats and received far more votes than any of its rivals. Despite that, it was, in political terms, impotent either to implement what it wished or to prevent what it disliked. It was this that persuaded some unionist Labour MPs like Robin Cook and Brian Wilson to drop their opposition to devolution. Donald had needed no persuading.

The Thatcher–Major years and the ever-present threat from the SNP helped unite the Labour Party behind the campaign for a Scottish Parliament. However, although the evolution of policy in this area must have taken up much of Donald's time, devolution did not dominate our parliamentary exchanges when I was Secretary of State and he was shadow Secretary.

Most of our clashes were on the issues of the moment that divided the political parties rather than on the need for fundamental constitutional reform. Local government, council-house sales, the poll tax, self-governing schools, Ravenscraig, the Scottish Development Agency, jobs and the NHS were of far more immediate interest to most Scottish Labour MPs and to their constituents than whether Scotland should have a devolved parliament. Even those who were strongly committed knew that it would not happen unless and until there was a change of government.

In most parliamentary sessions, we did not have more than a single debate on devolution either on the floor of the House or in the Scottish Grand Committee. Occasionally, it would be the Labour Party that initiated the debate. As often as not, it was the SNP or the Liberals.

When such opportunities arose, Donald was powerful in his oratory. But it was, for the most part, not an oratory that depended on passion or emotion for its impact. Rather, it was an impressive exercise in cool, well-reasoned argument well laced with wit, irony and occasional sarcasm. It was a style that owed as much to the Glasgow Debating Union as it did to the House of Commons and was all the more effective for it.

He could never resist teasing me for my support for devolution in the 1970s. I had indeed voted Yes in the referendum in 1978. But the failure to persuade even 40 per cent of Scots to vote in favour had convinced me that there was no justification for a constitutional upheaval in the United Kingdom that was opposed by England and Wales and had only lukewarm support in Scotland.

Of course, I was accused by my Labour and SNP opponents of having gone back on my principles but Donald was careful to avoid personal attacks or to impute bad faith. Throughout that time he stood head and shoulders above his colleagues. He was attracted by logic, evidence and argument. He was uninterested in point scoring, insults or abuse.

In that sense, we had more empathy with each other than either of us had with some of our own party colleagues. Donald and I had both been brought up in the university debating tradition (though Edinburgh's was much more genteel and rather tamer than Glasgow's!). We were both trained in the law, which, whatever its other faults, gives you a respect for facts over assertions and a preference for reason over emotion. We both had contempt for the gross exaggeration that disfigures so much political discourse.

These characteristics left us open to the reasonable charge that politics, however, needs passion as well as reason. To which I think both Donald and I would have responded that we had no problem with passion as well as reason. It was passion instead of reason to which we objected.

Throughout those years, the Conservative government was on the defensive in Scotland. It could hardly have been otherwise given our paucity of numbers. We never had more than 22 MPs and after 1987 the number sank to 10. Against us were between 50 and 60 Labour, Scottish Nationalist and Liberal MPs, including such heavy hitters as Robin Cook, Gordon Brown and John Reid as well as Donald as shadow Secretary.

But while the Labour Party beat us on infantry, we had the artillery when it came to voting in the division lobby because of the government's overall majority. On one occasion, I summed up our strength, much to Donald's intense irritation, by recalling a jingoistic ditty of the Victorian era:

Whatever happens we have got
The Gatling gun and they have not.

My observation was entirely correct but was not, I must confess, either diplomatic or conciliatory.

During most of those years, Donald and his colleagues held the political high ground as regards the Scottish public. They could point to the repeated surveys of Scottish opinion, which suggested large majorities in favour of constitutional change. The Scottish media overwhelmingly backed devolution, as did the Churches, the trade unions and most other collective organs of public debate. Only Scottish business and industry was lukewarm and indeed often hostile to devolution but as usual with industrialists they preferred, most of the time, to keep their views to themselves. Indeed, support for the status quo appeared to be almost a holding position while the real debate was between devolution and full independence as favoured by the SNP.

But in two crucial respects Donald had a far more difficult task than the opinion polls or the views of the political establishment would have suggested. While the public, when asked, appeared to be in favour of a Scottish Parliament, they made it clear, in the same surveys, that it was one of their lowest priorities. Constantly, it was health, crime, education or the poll tax that preoccupied most people. Constitutional change might have preoccupied the chattering classes. It did not seem to excite anyone else.

This was reflected at the highest levels of the Labour Party. Donald Dewar often seemed a rather lonely figure not because his colleagues in the Shadow Cabinet disagreed with him but because they could not be bothered to spend much time on the issue. Gordon Brown, Robin Cook and John Reid were far more concerned with trying to demolish Margaret Thatcher or John Major than with the campaign for constitutional reform in Scotland. This was not just because the key to reform lay with winning power at Westminster. It also reflected their own political ambitions. As we saw when the Parliament at Holyrood was created, only Donald made the trek north. Every other of his Cabinet colleagues opted to remain at Westminster.

These matters did not go unnoticed and made Donald's task much more difficult. The reality is that if the Scottish public had demanded devolution during those years it would have been very difficult for any government at Westminster to have refused them.

Imagine if 50,000 Scots had peacefully demonstrated outside St Andrew's House or if 200,000 Scots had marched down Princes Street. If such peaceful and lawful protest had expressed itself, things would have had to begin to move. At the very least, a referendum would have had to be conceded to test the true wishes of the Scottish people. Instead of 50,000 demonstrating outside St Andrew's House, there were half a dozen people who maintained a lonely vigil outside the old Royal High School. The rest of Scotland went on with its life.

I, and my colleagues, constantly drew attention to this. Donald was far too honest to be able to dismiss it out of hand. He was clearly disturbed by it. He pointed out, quite reasonably, that Scots believed in the parliamentary route to constitutional reform and that the Tories should not mistake acquiescence in the status quo for consent. That was true but he could not pretend that Scots were seething with anger at their lot nor that the government was ignoring the clamour of the people.

Of course, both Donald and the Labour Party were nervous about the threat from the SNP. The Nationalists had shown their ability to win Labour seats in Govan and Dundee, constituencies where neither the Tories nor the Liberals had ever been a threat. Many voters were quite willing to vote SNP either to put pressure on the British political parties or simply as an expression of a new assertive Scottish identity. The Labour Party, therefore, felt it had to use a more colourful language and make more strident demands than it would normally have found necessary in order not to be outflanked by the SNP as the champion of Scottish aspirations.

This was the other respect in which Donald had a very difficult task. At a personal level, he found stridency and exaggeration both distasteful as well as of little real value. But some of his colleagues were so nervous about the SNP that they began to use Nationalist language and rhetoric when they opposed the Tories and the government.

This came to a head after the 1987 general election when the

Conservatives won power again but lost more than half of their seats in Scotland, being reduced to a rump of only ten MPs. The day after the general election was one of the most miserable in my political life. We had won but in Scotland we had been humiliated. There was no reason to believe that devolution had been the cause but that did not stop either the Nationalists or some in the Labour Party declaring that we had no mandate to govern in Scotland. The cry of 'No Mandate' became a formidable one and I had to reach a quick decision as to how to respond. I decided that we could not give an inch on this issue without endangering the whole unionist position and the integrity of the United Kingdom.

Donald, I am sure, realised this from the start but some of his colleagues did not realise, or did not care, that they were playing with Nationalist fire. It was quite logical and not unreasonable for the SNP to accuse us of governing Scotland with no mandate. It stood for an end to the Union and if independence had been achieved the only relevant and democratic mandate, thereafter, would have been the votes of the Scottish electorate.

But the Labour and Liberal parties were unionist in that they wished Scotland to remain within the United Kingdom with ultimate sovereignty being retained by Westminster. In such a union, it would obviously be absurd to argue that a British government could only govern in those parts of the Union that had voted for its candidates.

This did not need a degree in rocket science to be understood but some Labour MPs were so fearful of the SNP that they adopted its rhetoric and posturing. Donald was never tempted, so far as I am aware, in this direction. He was a believer in constitutional propriety and disdained showy gestures that were not rooted in serious politics. In this respect, he showed himself to be a statesman as well as a politician.

The implications, if he had decided otherwise, would have been very serious. The House of Commons can only work with the consent of the Opposition and if that consent had been withdrawn there would have been a constitutional crisis.

I suspect that even if Donald had been willing to pander to the Nationalist demands, his colleagues in the Shadow Cabinet, who had mixed feelings about the whole issue of devolution, would not have let him. They would have had no interest in alienating the electorate, particularly in England, and presenting the Labour Party in a quasi-revolutionary mode.

Donald did not bend but nor, at least in public, did he rebuke or warn those of his Scottish colleagues who did. I suppose he may have thought it was safer to allow them to let off a bit of steam but the consequence was that I and other Tory MPs were able to point to the inconsistencies in Labour's position.

I left the Scottish Office in 1990 and, therefore, could only view from the sidelines Donald's relationship with my successors Ian Lang and Michael Forsyth.

Politicians who leave their mark on the times during which they live need not only exceptional ability. They usually need both luck and opportunity. Donald did not have much luck in his political life. He was stuck in opposition for long, unremitting years and was given only occasional exposure to the United Kingdom issues that dominate Westminster. Then, at the height of his power and influence he was cruelly struck down by an early death.

But he was fortunate in having the opportunity to lead Scotland at a crucial time in its history and evolution. Without him, devolution would still have happened and a Scottish Parliament would still have been created. However, it was his skill, temperament and integrity that produced what was close to a national consensus in the delivery of that change.

This was seen in the concession of proportional representation for elections to the Parliament. It surrendered Labour's dominance and forced them to share power. It was not, however, entirely disinterested. Without proportional representation, there was a fear that the Nationalists might, one day, win power on a minority vote and use their position to weaken or destroy the Union.

Some of his other judgments are less easy to defend. The abandonment of the old Royal High School as the site for the Parliament has always puzzled me and can be criticised not only because of the appalling escalation in the cost of the new building at Holyrood.

But statesmen should be judged by the totality of their achievements, even when that includes occasional lapses or errors. Even the critics of devolution recognise that the transition of the United Kingdom from a unitary state that had survived for almost 300 years to a new relationship between England and Scotland was no simple, easy or straightforward matter.

In the event, it has happened without rancour or bitterness. So far there is no evidence that it will lead to the end of the United Kingdom. Indeed, the party that has lost most support has been the SNP. This success has been due mostly to the good sense and mature beliefs of both the Scottish and English people who know that they have far more in common than anything which might ever divide them.

However, individuals can also make a difference to the march of history. Donald Dewar did make a difference and we all salute him and his memory for that.

His Obedient Colleagues[1]

Peter Jones

The boss had discovered that his staff had been on an office outing to the theatre the previous evening. He was intrigued. What had they been to see? There was some embarrassment and shuffling of feet. Eventually, one confessed that they had been to see a play called *Shopping and F*******.

'Oh,' said the boss, considering this. 'And was it any good?'

'Well, actually, no, it wasn't all that good, really.'

'Oh,' said the boss again. 'Too much shopping?'

The exchange would be not all that exceptional in many offices. But in this case, the boss was Donald Dewar, Secretary of State for Scotland, and the staff were his private office civil servants and in most high-ranking politicians' offices, familiarity and banter is frowned upon. Dewar's office, say those who worked for him, was qualitatively different. He treated his staff as a team, as colleagues rather than functionaries. Says one, 'I have rarely met a minister for whom it was a greater pleasure to work, both personally and intellectually.' Another said there were many reasons why a civil servant might work hard for a minister – in order not to be accused of incompetence, or to get promoted well away from them: 'But you worked hard for Donald because you wanted to do a good job for him.'

There was no shortage of hard work required. Donald Dewar was appointed Secretary of State for Scotland among the first tranche of ministerial appointments made on Saturday, 3 May 1997: a sign of the importance Tony Blair attached to getting Labour's manifesto pledge to set up a Scottish Parliament implemented speedily. There was little time to waste. A team of senior civil servants led by Russell Hillhouse and Muir Russell, the outgoing and incoming Permanent Secretaries of the Scottish Office, went to Dover House, the department's London base, to meet Dewar.

The civil servants explained the structures set up within the Scottish and Cabinet Offices to deal with devolution. Unlike the 1970s, when the then Labour government tried to handle its devolution proposals centrally through the Cabinet Office, this time the Scottish Office would be in charge of the Scotland Bill and the Cabinet Office would coordinate the work with the other constitutional changes Labour had promised. The workload – preparing a White Paper, then a Bill and getting it through Parliament – would be heavy and intensive, as any delay could allow Whitehall opponents to be obstructive. A good working relationship between Dewar and the civil servants was therefore essential.

Those who met Dewar that Saturday recall him as looking tired but buoyed by Labour's victory: 'There was this feeling about something that had been 20 years in planning, thinking and persuading about how Scotland should be governed, and now it was about to happen.' A paper on the Devolution Referendum Bill had to go to a Cabinet sub-committee by Tuesday. Then there were proposals for the devolution settlement, which would have to be negotiated with each Whitehall department and then agreed in the Devolution, Scotland, Wales and English Regions Cabinet sub-committee (DSWR).

Dewar and the team agreed they would meet in Scotland on Monday, which was a bank holiday. The Edinburgh-based civil servants said they would go to Glasgow to make it easier for Dewar. 'No,' said Dewar. 'There are more of you, I'll come to Edinburgh.' That he was prepared to put himself out for the officials impressed them a great deal, though, in truth, he was privately keen to savour the inside of a department where he had long been the outsider. They were also impressed by the certainty he brought to what he wanted them to do. One says, 'From the very beginning, we had a sense of his strategic perspective on the whole project. I wouldn't say Donald started off with a detailed pre-judgement on how he wanted the wide range of issues to turn out but he wanted the maximum flexibility for the Scottish Parliament over the maximum range of subject matter, delivered in the shortest possible time.'

The courtesy with which Dewar treated his staff meant that he got a lot from them. 'The relationship,' says one official, 'was not based on shock and awe. Officials everywhere would go that extra mile for him, just because of who he was, his character. That was partly because of the way he dealt with them at meetings. He was what officials really like – courteous, but penetrating and with a clear sense of what he wanted. You could have a debate with him. You could say, "Well, you say that, but have you thought about this?" He would stop and say, "You're right" – or he would say, "No, I don't care, we'll do it this way."'

He treated his staff as human beings, not just as functionaries who were there to fill a role. One civil servant recalls being phoned at home by Dewar for some extra briefing. 'He apologised for ringing me at home. I said no need, that was quite all right. He asked what I was doing. I said I was having supper with my family. He asked me what we were eating. I told him it was a beany cheese crunch. He wanted to know what went into it, how was it cooked, what did it taste like.' The official paused, recollecting the conversation and still marvelling that a Secretary of State would be interested in such domestic details, and added, 'He was always asking me what was I reading and what was I eating.'

This eccentricity, particularly about food, readily endeared Dewar to his officials. Visits to companies often resulted in gifts of pens and produce, which Dewar gave to his staff. An exception was made for a large box of Tunnock's biscuits, which he carefully stowed in his desk. An official recalls Dewar asking him to go to Bute House, his official Edinburgh residence, for a couple of hours of discussion before heading to Waverley Station to catch the night sleeper – Dewar's favourite means of travel between Scotland and London. 'He apologised that there was nothing to eat except cake, chocolate cake and lemon cake. So we ate slices of cake and discussed education policy.' The official eventually moved to other things but was charmed to find that Dewar still remembered him. 'He was on the stairs with a big entourage but he stopped and asked how I was and what I was doing.'

Working for Dewar, however, was not all food and fun. 'He was quite acerbic,' says one official. 'There were people he had to deal with that he was quite negative about.' He made it clear that he wanted changes in the private office that he inherited from his Conservative predecessor, Michael Forsyth. Officials learned that they had to know their stuff. One says that even when Dewar had only time for a quick verbal briefing before a meeting with officials who had been working on the topic for days, 'within ten minutes, he would be bouncing them around the walls with stuff they hadn't thought of'.

He also insisted on clarity. After umpteen drafts, he corrected and rewrote the final version of the Devolution White Paper himself. With Wendy Alexander, special adviser, and an official in attendance, he started at lunchtime on a Thursday and continued until 2 a.m. on the sleeper north, handwriting his preferred words. The White Paper was perhaps the Scottish Office's only bestseller. It won an award from the Plain English society, whose only complaint was about one technical word – vires – which civil servants insisted had to be left in.

The staff greatly admired his intellect. One senior civil servant recalls a particularly tricky point in the Scotland Bill: a question of 'purpose and effect' of decisions where there was debate about whether Westminster or Holyrood had primary power of decision over an issue where both legislatures had some responsibility. An example would be Holyrood using its planning powers to refuse permission for power-line construction in order to frustrate the building of a nuclear power station decided by Westminster using its reserved powers over energy supply. When they required Dewar's approval of an urgently required document on this topic, officials tracked him down to Henry McLeish's wedding.

'We were all crowded round a telephone with Donald at the other end while our lead lawyer went through it. It was the sort of thing where if you blinked, your whole understanding of it disappeared. But he was absolutely on top of it.' Despite much Whitehall pressure, the Scotland Act gives no general power to override Holyrood; instead, there are points in it where override powers can be brought into play by both legislatures. 'Donald came up with some very good ideas on that which helped us work towards solutions,' says an official. Civil Service legend is that, like Lord Palmerston's remark on the Schleswig-Holstein Question, there were only about three people, including Dewar, who fully understood the subtleties and complexities of the issue.

He was at his best with complex issues. 'He liked getting into the meat of an issue and enjoyed debating it with his officials, getting lots of information out of them so he could master a subject very quickly.' Another official adds, 'I don't know that negotiation was Donald's strongest suit. He certainly could when he needed to but he was a great believer in the power of argument. He loved the process of argument, you know – argument, counter-argument and the resolution of a case – that process fascinated him and he was very good at it.'

Yet, according to one who saw the negotiations at the critical DSWR committee, chaired by Lord Derry Irvine, the Lord Chancellor, Dewar wasn't always confident of his ability to sway his colleagues. 'I think he misjudged himself on that. Derry Irvine's handling of the meetings was brisk but not bullying. He sometimes, I thought deliberately, allowed Donald to have a hard time because he knew Donald liked the process of argument. He would give Donald the chance to argue his case; give others the chance to put the contrary argument and would put quite a lot of hard questions himself. But at the end of the day, Donald got out of it pretty much what he wanted. He seemed almost disbelieving on some issues where he wasn't sure he was going to get what he asked for: you know, that slightly quizzical look he would give you.'

Although by the time of the 1997 election there was an impression in Scotland that the devolution settlement agreed by the Scottish Constitutional Convention was set in concrete and just had to be followed through obediently by the government, that was not the case. Much of the argument, for example that the extent of devolution should be defined by stating what was reserved to Westminster rather than by describing what was devolved to Scotland, had to be won again inside government. Some of the new Whitehall ministers were entirely new to the devolution debate and they, and their departments, had to be convinced of the need to give away some of their power.

'Having a very strong advocate in the Secretary of State was very important,' says an official, who points out that although Lord Irvine was broadly positive, he had his own view of what devolution should look like. 'Donald's role is not to be underestimated. His own personal weight and influence, and his capacity for arguing issues through DSWR was very important to delivering policy outcomes, a very strong counterweight to overcoming some of the Whitehall ministers' objections.'

After Dewar died, his private office staff paid tribute to him in the Scottish Executive staff magazine. They wrote:

> We were lucky to work with a unique individual who somehow managed to attract comparisons as diverse as Victor Meldrew and Che Guevara. His conversation was stimulating and often challenging, and he was just as comfortable in offering his

opinions, unasked, to staff in the lifts of St Andrew's House as he was to fellow MSPs in the Chamber.

His views on subjects ranging from his own chances on *Who Wants to be a Millionaire?* (which he rated quite highly provided he could call a friend on the pop music questions) to the singer whom he referred to as 'Broccoli Spears' were always worth hearing. Friendly, generous and appreciative, his customary farewell when he left for the night was 'thank you for all your help', a phrase that never lost its sincerity. We were proud that he called us his colleagues and all of us will sorely miss the Boss.

A Skilful Advocate

Derry Irvine

In 1996 when Donald Dewar was shadow Chief Whip and I shadow Lord Chancellor, Tony Blair asked me to chair a committee to report to him on the proposals for devolution to Scotland. Among those involved were Donald, Gordon Brown, Robin Cook, George Robertson (then shadow Secretary of State for Scotland), Jack Straw and Ann Taylor. It was from this committee, with the full support of Tony Blair, that there emerged the first major departure from the then current proposals – a departure that was set to produce great ructions within the Scottish Labour Party. The previous Labour position was that there would be devolution to Scotland authorised only by a manifesto commitment and a general election victory. No more was needed. The departure was twofold: that the devolution proposals should require pre-legislative endorsement by the Scottish people in a referendum; and that the proposal to give the new Scottish Parliament a power to vary the standard rate of tax, up or down, by three pence in the pound, was to be a distinct question in the referendum. Thus the possibility was opened of different answers to each question.

There were arguments both of principle and pragmatism in favour of this departure. First, devolution was set to be the most fundamental change to the constitutional fabric of the United Kingdom and therefore required a referendum, not least because it was opposed root and branch by the Tories as destructive of the Union. Second, of course no Parliament can bind its successors but prior popular endorsement of a devolution settlement would be a strong basis for making the settlement stick: in practice it would be difficult to reverse it without a referendum producing a contrary result. And in 1996, with four general election defeats behind Labour, there was no expectation of the huge majority that was to come. A pre-legislative popular endorsement would ease the passage of the legislation in a Westminster Parliament where the majority might have been tight. Also, these were days when Labour felt highly vulnerable to its perceived 'tax and spend' image and the Tories were making some headway with their jibe that the three pence proposal was a 'tartan tax'. Hence it had to be neutralised by the pledge of a second distinct referendum question on the issue. Finally, a referendum would diminish the salience of devolution as a general election issue. The Tories believed there was political capital for them in the forthcoming election campaign in opposing devolution and upholding the Union. The referendum decision meant that the Scottish people would take the devolution decision themselves but *after* the election.

Neither Donald nor George Robertson, or indeed myself, were under any illusions that major trouble within the Scottish Labour Party lay ahead, and not least for them. It is also true that both nursed in the first instance substantial misgivings about the departure from previous policy. They, after all, had to face, as I did not, the understandable hostility from within the Scottish Labour movement. There were conspiracy theorists who feared that the decision signalled a weakening of resolve on the principle of devolution. On the contrary, however, it signalled a determination to ensure that devolution stuck. Both Donald and George were persuaded of the merit of this decision and so it proved: in the referendum of September 1997, three-quarters of those who voted backed devolution and two-thirds the power to alter income tax.

This was my first political cooperation with Donald. It was opportune, because Donald was then destined to become Secretary of State for Scotland and I Lord Chancellor and the chairman of the four Cabinet sub-committees responsible for developing and settling policy in the four key areas in the new Labour government's constitutional change programme, of which one was devolution. DSWR – 'Devolution to Scotland, Wales and the English Regions' – was the committee charged to develop and settle policy at Cabinet level for Scotland.

Donald had spent a life immersed in Scottish history, culture and politics. We came to the committee with a shared view that the renaissance in Scotland's sense of its national identity demanded the amplest devolution of legislative authority to a Scottish Parliament consistent with the maintenance of the Union. We also knew that we had to strike when the iron was hot and make it top-priority government business. We also judged that the Tories, who had been annihilated in Scotland in the 1997 election, would remain a spent force there unless and until they could bring themselves to embrace devolution and the new Scottish Parliament. And, finally, we shared the view that the achievement of devolution and a Scottish Parliament was the end of a journey, in the sense that it was *not* a stepping stone to independence: a consequence would be the marginalisation of the SNP.

I look back with awe that continues to this day at the scale of the task we set ourselves – to achieve, within the first parliamentary session, first, agreement within the committee on every essential detail, including the terms of the White Paper; then success in the referendum itself and, lastly, ensuring the passage of well-thought-out legislation through Parliament.

The Civil Service treated the achievement of devolution within this narrow timescale as the first major test of its capacity to deliver a flagship policy of the new government. The Scottish Office was the lead department but the Cabinet Office had ownership of the whole constitutional change programme, of which devolution was a part. The Cabinet Secretary, Sir Robin Butler (now Lord Butler), was determined that the Civil Service impress to the highest standard and it did. He put together for me a team of what I described at the time as among the brightest and best in Whitehall (the Constitution Secretariat) under the demanding leadership of Kenneth Mackenzie. The Scottish Office too was no less pro-active and a similarly high-powered team stood ready to serve Donald. Over eleven weeks and fifteen meetings, mostly each of two hours, DSWR considered thirty-nine papers prepared by the Civil Service and debated by me with them in lengthy pre-DSWR meeting briefing sessions. The issues were legion: had Labour erred in the 1970s when it decided that every legislative power to be devolved to Scotland, and its small print, had to be meticulously specified? The answer was, yes, it had erred. Scotland should essentially have a general power of legislative competence, subject to powers expressly reserved to the centre, for example, defence, foreign affairs, the Constitution and the Crown.

Another was whether the legislation should declare that the sovereignty of the United Kingdom Parliament remained undiminished: that is, what it conferred on Scotland it could revoke – a strictly unnecessary provision since that would have been the position whatever the legislation said. It was also an unpalatable reminder to Scotland thought necessary to assuage English sentiment. And, on top of a multitude of lesser issues, there was the vires dispute resolution machinery between Scotland and Westminster; the West Lothian Question; the role of the devolved administrations in relation to the European Union; the tax-varying power; and the budget issues, to name a few.

DSWR, a committee of Cabinet ministers from across the United Kingdom, was clear from the outset that it was unwilling to rubber stamp the Convention blueprint, *Scotland's Parliament, Scotland's Right*, of 1995. This in no way diminishes the central importance of the achievement of George Robertson in particular and many others in securing agreement on the milestone of the Convention but the reality was that only a Labour victory nationally, and then the United Kingdom government and Parliament, could deliver devolution. Some members of DSWR were underwhelmed by the Scottish project and every detail was rightly debated closely in committee – a seamless translation from Convention to statute certainly there was not.

Of all the Cabinet committees I chaired, it was the most demanding. DSWR wanted to scrutinise and debate everything. It was my duty to ensure it did and Donald was equally clear that this was necessary. DSWR was determined that the Scots could not proceed as though their lucky number had come up and what they wanted they could demand. The pressures thus imposed on Donald were immense.

But Donald and I were equal true believers in devolution. There was a period when it seemed as if Donald was never out of my room to discuss the resolution of pressing issues. We cooperated in perfect amity. Newspaper assertions abounded that, since, over a quarter of a century before, Donald's former wife, Alison, and I had come together, there was a disharmony that impeded the transaction of government business. These assertions were the stuff of pure fiction. We both saw the political wisdom of the whole package being closely scrutinised, then settled and endorsed by a committee of Cabinet ministers from across the United Kingdom. A superior product would emerge, better able to withstand parliamentary scrutiny, as it did. The first elections for the new Parliament were held in

May 1999 and the new Parliament was up and running from 1 July 1999.

For Donald, DSWR was onerous in the extreme. There was constant sniping – entirely legitimate – from those whose enthusiasm for the Scottish project was somewhat behind Donald's. Proportional representation was a case in point. The concern was that to concede PR for Scottish parliamentary elections would create a momentum for PR nationally. Donald stood his ground. As Donald MacCormick has neatly and accurately put it, 'He was convinced that the Scottish nation in all its variety would not embrace a devolution package which entrenched Labour, and thus West of Scotland, dominance.' This was one of many key issues where Donald prevailed in DSWR. His contribution was major and also genial. There was much honey and very little vinegar. Donald put himself on display within the inner workings of government as a consensus politician.

Getting the Act Together

John Sewel

One of the repeated lessons of British policy making is that there is a yawning chasm between a political party's commitment to a particular policy and the implementation of the policy through effective legislation. On more than one occasion, the Labour Party's commitment to taxing the development value of land has been frustrated through an inability to produce effective legislation and, more recently, the virtual collapse of the Child Support Agency bears witness to the difficulty of framing legislation, even when the policy objective enjoys wide bipartisan support. So when the Labour government took office following the 1997 general election, there was no guarantee that the commitment to Scottish devolution would automatically be translated into effective, durable legislation. The need to do so, and to get it right first time, or at least as right as possible, was great. Otherwise, there was the risk that what was envisaged as an enduring settlement would have to be continually reopened in order to rectify legislative deficiencies. By 1997, simply reverting to the previous proposals of 1979 was not an option. Thinking had moved on and the earlier proposals looked decidedly dated. For example, by 1997 it was politically impractical for a continuing Secretary of State for Scotland to perform the quasi-vice-regal role that the earlier Act foresaw.

Major constitutional change, especially when achieved over a period of decades, can never be seen as the product of a single individual. The shape and content of the final outcome represents the contribution of many individuals and the interplay of events. From the election in May 1997, Donald's task was made easier by having at the heart of government an old ally, Gordon Brown, who similarly had a long record as a powerful advocate of devolution. As important, if possibly more unexpected, was Dewar's ability to forge an effective partnership with Derry Irvine. Irvine, as his contribution in this volume attests, not only chaired the Cabinet committee on devolution through which the White Paper and subsequent Bill had to be negotiated, he also enjoyed the confidence of the Prime Minister. He was also determined to leave a legacy as a constitution-reforming Lord Chancellor. The stages from idea to realisation are many and complex. This was certainly the case with devolution but what is beyond doubt is that Dewar's contribution runs as a thread throughout the whole process to the extent that the Scotland Act would not have been the same without him.

Labour's political credibility in Scotland required swift progress immediately after the general election: the more so as the Scottish Conservative Party, having campaigned on an anti-devolution platform, had been entirely vanquished. Any apparent backsliding on the part of Labour would have incurred significant political costs both for the party and the new Secretary of State. The first, and perhaps the most strategically important, task of the entire legislative process was the writing of the White Paper. Not only would the White Paper form the basis upon which Labour would fight the referendum but also as the definitive statement of government policy it would provide an irrefutable, authoritative reference in later discussions with ministerial colleagues on the details of the Bill.

In many respects, the government was fairly well advanced in the preparation of its devolution legislation. The broad outlines had been defined through a prolonged public debate in Scotland, which had then been worked up in greater detail through the work of the Scottish Constitutional Convention and the Constitutional Commission. By the time Dewar walked into St Andrew's House as Secretary of State, not only, as in John Smith's phrase, was devolution the settled will of the Scottish people but in addition the broad outlines of what devolution would look like had been endorsed by a broad swathe of Scottish political and civil opinion leaders.

The Labour victory did not come as a surprise to civil servants in the Scottish Office who had spent some time well before the election making plans on how to implement the new government's flagship policy. A devolution team of senior civil servants had been identified, under the leadership of one of the Scottish Office's highest fliers, and the opportunity had been taken to make informal contact with devolved and non-unitary systems elsewhere. The initial work on policy development had started. Senior civil servants are well trained in taking generalised statements of ministerial policy and translating them into detailed legislative proposals but that was not the situation that existed in relation to devolution. Dewar and his closest political colleagues had a well-developed and clear view on what the White Paper should contain. It was inevitable that the first draft of the Civil Service-produced White Paper fell far short of Dewar's expectations. Both the tone and the detail failed to capture the strong devolution model that Dewar advocated and, as it stood, failed to provide a convincing or attractive prospectus on which to fight a referendum. The Secretary of State intervened with his own particular mix of despair and decisiveness. Over one weekend, Dewar and his two special advisers, Wendy Alexander and Murray Elder, rewrote the White Paper. In the long and sometimes tortuous history of Labour and devolution, that weekend marked one of its most salient episodes. The Dewar draft, although it had still to be negotiated through Derry Irvine's Cabinet committee, set the framework for a strong devolution settlement that went far beyond what were, in comparison, the timid proposals of 1979. For someone who has often been thought of as a cautious politician, when the crucial moment arrived he acted decisively to change the terms of discourse and secure a bold outcome, which in essence would survive all the way through to the final Act.

Speed was essential in agreeing the White Paper, not only because of the need to hold a referendum while the government could still exploit the momentum created by its overwhelming electoral victory in Scotland. Speed was also the most effective weapon with which to defeat any rearguard action on the part of Whitehall departments. Within the Scottish political class, devolution was a familiar concept; the same was not true south of the border. Ministers, and more so mandarins, are adept at shading the details of policy so as to defend the interests and above all the powers of their departments. The obvious tactic was to obtain the agreement of colleagues before the full implications were realised and thereby reduce the scope for any possible subsequent Whitehall fight back.

The proposals contained in the White Paper more than met any expectations that could have reasonably been entertained. Critically, it confirmed the radical change in approach from that adopted in 1978. Rather than having to argue case-by-case and line-by-line the justification for individual areas to be devolved, the White Paper proposed a complete reversal; every area was to be devolved except those that were specifically reserved. Dewar's White Paper triumph lay not only in the comprehensive range of powers and functions that were devolved (or more accurately the limited powers and functions that were reserved); by securing agreement early, he ensured that Whitehall would be on the back foot if, after more reflection and a greater awareness, there were to be any attempt to regain lost ground during the later discussions on the details of the Bill.

One chapter of the White Paper deserves special mention: that dealing with the relationship between Scotland and Europe. From the outset, it had always been assumed that Agriculture and Fisheries, both more important economically and politically in Scotland, would be devolved. The difficulty lay in the fact that in these areas the European Union extensively determined policy. It was the United Kingdom rather than Scotland that was the member state and consequently it was the United Kingdom that was represented at the Council of Ministers. The danger of which Dewar was only too well aware was that Scottish ministers would be exposed as broken-backed. They would have responsibility in Scotland for an area where the key decisions were taken in a forum that was the preserve of a United Kingdom department and a United Kingdom minister. The risk of apparent total marginalisation potentially played into the hands of the Scottish Nationalists, who would be able to mount the argument that only through independence could Scottish interests be defended through a separate seat at the Council of Ministers.

Dewar's challenge was to secure a mechanism through which Scottish ministers could demonstrate that they could credibly protect the interests of Scottish farmers and fishermen. Help came from Robin Cook, who as Foreign Secretary had lead responsibility for relations with the EU, and crucially from Derry Irvine. The Irvine-drafted chapter in the White Paper describing the Scottish Executive's relationship with Europe is a masterpiece of circle squaring. The Scottish minister was to be a member of the United Kingdom team and as such would play a full part in determining the United Kingdom line. Having been part of the policy-deciding process, he would be bound by its eventual outcome. However, where decisions were made by qualified majority voting, it was argued that it was more effective to be part of a member state with a large number of votes than to stand apart with a small and likely inconsequential number of votes.

Dewar's advocacy and Irvine's drafting were tested in the referendum campaign. Although there were misgivings, and indeed outright opposition, within sections of both industries, to the relief of at least one junior minister, neither industry mounted a sustained policy of opposition. So one of the most difficult and potentially most damaging issues was resolved and the incoming rural affairs minister was destined to spend countless hours as a participant in the excruciating and interminable finger-nail pulling process of European decision making.

Two further policy areas had to be resolved before the final package was in place. The driving principle that informed decisions on what should be reserved and what should be devolved was simple. Unless a convincing case could be mounted that required policy to be made at a United Kingdom level then it was devolved, and where possible subject areas were treated as a whole and not part devolved and part reserved.

As health was devolved, it followed that abortion should be also. But abortion raised practical and political problems. At one level, there was a genuine concern that if abortion law differed either side of the border then there was the possibility of an undignified and unedifying prospect of cross-border traffic in women seeking terminations. The political problem had to do with the salience of abortion for the Roman Catholic Church and the correlation between Labour voting and Roman Catholicism, especially in the west of Scotland. If abortion were to be devolved, there was the very real prospect that it would come to be one of the dominant and recurrent issues of the Scottish Parliament, with many Labour MSPs coming under strong and sustained constituency pressure to make the law more restrictive in Scotland than was likely to be the case in England. Dewar canvassed the views of his junior ministerial colleagues in the Scottish Office and decided in favour of reservation – virtually the only example in the allocation of powers where principle gave way to pragmatism, and rightly so.

The final issue raised the complex inter-relationship between the number of Scottish MPs at Westminster, the size of the Scottish Parliament and ultimately the electoral system itself. The electoral system for the Scottish Parliament had been a matter of dispute within the pro-devolution camp before 1979. The Scottish Assembly that would have emerged from that failed piece of legislation was to have been elected on a first-past-the-post basis, with every Westminster constituency returning two members of the Assembly. Not only would such a system entrench Labour's disproportionate dominance in relation to its share of the vote, it also was in straight contradiction to the Liberal Democrat Party's advocacy of the single transferable vote. Furthermore, it had been argued that the failure of the 1979 referendum had in part been the result of the reluctance of the non-Labour voters to support an Assembly which, because of the electoral system, was allegedly to be dominated by Edinburgh lawyers and Glasgow trade unionists.

By the time Dewar transferred his shadow portfolio from Scotland to Social Security, at the time John Smith became leader of the party, he had signed up to an understanding with the Liberal Democrats that the electoral system would be more proportional. When he returned as Secretary of State, the work of the Constitutional Convention and the Constitutional Commission had produced an additional vote system, combining one member per Westminster constituency, plus additional members elected on a regional list basis and allocated to make the overall regional representation more proportional.

The problem lay not with the electoral system's newness or relative complexity but the fact that Westminster constituencies were the building block of the whole system. The decision, taken after the broad structure of the electoral system had been agreed, to remove Scotland's numerical over-representation in the House of Commons had, as a direct consequence, a reduction in the size of the Scottish Parliament. Although there was never any magic number for the size of the Parliament, ministers were in the uncomfortable position of arguing that the size of the Parliament, when first elected, was broadly appropriate for the work it had to do, while at the same time defending a significant reduction in its size over the medium term. Not surprisingly, opposition parties focused on this tension in the government's position and a series of defeats were suffered in the House of Lords.

Dewar's room for manoeuvre was limited, as this was one of the few areas where the Prime Minister asserted himself and insisted on the new policy. The only flexibility available was for Dewar to allow his junior minister in the Lords to indicate that it would be open to the Scottish

Parliament, in the light of experience gained through its new working practices, to make representations to Westminster that the work of the Parliament would be seriously compromised if it had a reduction in membership forced upon it. Although the original size of the Parliament has been retained, it is unlikely Dewar would have foreseen the consequential undermining of what had been a carefully constructed electoral system: an undermining which was to put in reach of the Liberal Democrats their much coveted prize of the single transferable vote and the exposure in Scotland of only Westminster elections having even an element of first-past-the-post.

The circumstances surrounding the parliamentary progress of the Scotland Bill could hardly have been more favourable. The decision to hold the referendum on the White Paper prior to the introduction of the Bill itself proved inspired, with a decisive majority in favour of the principle and a smaller, but nevertheless comfortable, majority in favour of the tax-varying powers. Both through the general election and subsequently by the referendum result, the people of Scotland had unambiguously endorsed the government's scheme. In Parliament, the Conservatives were still visibly demoralised at the scale of their defeat and their total lack of representation in Scotland hardly put them in a position where they could claim to speak for any significant section of Scottish opinion. However, not only was it the state of the principal opposition party that was different from the case in 1979; the governing party itself was united and faced none of the continuing internal revolts that had previously proved so debilitating and ultimately destructive. The impression created at the time, and still evident from a re-reading of Hansard, was of Dewar on top of his form, in command of his brief, rousing his supporters and dismissing interventions with his distinctive brand of withering parliamentary humour.

By the time the Bill reached the Lords, the possibility of the opposition mounting anything like a sustained guerrilla campaign, a state of affairs that had been anticipated with some foreboding prior to the general election, had been eliminated. The government's position was further strengthened as a result of the majority in the main votes in the Commons not having been dependent upon Scottish Labour MPs. Although the Bill spent eighteen days in the Lords – longer than any government Bill since Labour returned to power – and was subject to thirty-six divisions of which five were lost, there was wisely no attempt to inflict major damage.

Both the Liberal Democrats, in anguish, and the Conservatives, in mischievous fun, defeated the government on the question of the shrinking Parliament, where no concession was possible. That apart, the Lords did what it does best, allowing the government to amend and refine its proposed legislation outwith the partisan cockpit of the Commons.

Although the parliamentary opposition may have been quiescent, the same could not be said about the awakening Whitehall warriors. The speed with which the White Paper had been agreed was a major factor in securing Dewar's objectives. As time went on, other ministers and departments began to mount a defensive campaign. It was too late to challenge the architecture of the Bill – the White Paper had seen to that – but as time went on and where the White Paper was not explicit, Dewar had to make deals with Cabinet colleagues. But for the most part the die was cast.

The final major issue that had to be addressed dealt with one of the more arcane areas of the relationship between the Scottish and Westminster parliaments: the question of legislative competence. The principle that whole subjects were to be devolved or reserved left unresolved the difficult problem of how to deal with issues where the exercise of a reserved power could affect policy in a devolved area and vice versa. Although such a debate may seem esoteric, the political implications were real and potentially explosive. Could the Scottish Parliament be in the position where it could use its ancillary powers to frustrate policy in an area that was reserved? In more concrete terms, could the Parliament use its devolved planning powers to prevent the construction of nuclear power stations in Scotland despite the fact that strategic energy policy was reserved? Dewar accepted that in these circumstances and where agreement did not exist between the two Executives, the courts would have to give dominance to the primary purpose.

In the recent history of the Labour Party's advocacy of devolution, many individuals played their part, among the most notable being John Smith, Gordon Brown, George Robertson, George Foulkes and Harry Ewing. But would the Scotland Act have been the same without Donald Dewar? The answer must be no. Dewar was able to secure a model of devolution for Scotland that surprised even his pro-devolution colleagues. He succeeded above all because he had a clear idea of the type of devolution he wanted and was able to carry it through because of his force of argument and mastery of the issues, his standing and authority among his colleagues and his parliamentary dominance. What did it all mean to him and to others? A clue to the former comes in his own aside during the Dover House party held to celebrate the passing of the Bill where he turned to one of his colleagues and observed with uncharacteristic passion, 'We have delivered and whatever happens they can never take that away from us.' As for others, and particularly his colleagues, the scale of his achievement is best captured by his successor as Secretary of State, John Reid, who commented soon after entering Dover House, 'I have been a long-standing supporter of devolution, but I didn't realise that it had gone so far.' It had and there was to be no turning back.

Enduring Foundations

Neil MacCormick

A book to celebrate the achievements of Donald Dewar has much to celebrate. Long after the controversy, and the just criticisms, concerning the process of building the Parliament at Holyrood have faded from memory, the building itself and the embodiment of Scotland's political will that it houses will remain as inspirations to succeeding generations. Dewar's role as the one who commissioned this building, having first piloted through the legislation that made a parliament building necessary, will not be forgotten. A not dissimilar thought to this first occurred to me when I was sitting beneath the magnificent roof-beams of Glasgow Cathedral during his funeral and speculating on the proportion of the gross domestic product of fourteenth-century Scotland its construction must have cost.

From the mid-nineteenth century, many were the attempts to restore the Scottish parliamentary self-government signed away in the Union of 1707. The twentieth century saw a sequence of efforts in that direction, each acquiring a little more momentum than its predecessors. Yet nothing was ever likely to happen until it became a project embraced by a party of government assured also of broad cross-party support. That moment arrived when Donald Dewar took office as Secretary of State for Scotland in the Blair government of 1997.

Two streams of thought converged in the Scottish referendum and the

Scotland Act. One concerned subsidiarity and improved government in the context of a Europe in which the 'regional' level of government was being fortified. The other concerned a kind of 'small-n' civic nationalism, which can be summarised as the belief that a country like Scotland with its ancient sense of nationhood and its many flourishing national institutions ought to have political recognition as such through appropriately democratic institutions.

Opinion among proponents of the latter belief is notoriously split among those who think that only independent statehood is adequate to express the democratic life of the nation, and those who believe that democratic institutions within the framework of a larger state can sufficiently realise the end sought. What was required was a moment in which competing strands of thought could come together rather than let mutual antagonism hold them apart. Statesmanship on all sides was called for and a degree of mutual goodwill often lacking among rival parties. The work that had been done in the Scottish Constitutional Convention foreshadowed much of this: Dewar was willing to forego partisanship, and the willing cooperation offered by the SNP led by Alex Salmond, Allan Macartney and Winnie Ewing made the common drive for a clear referendum majority irresistible.

I am one of many for whom participating in the referendum of 1997 was a memorable and moving experience. For me, it was characterised by quiet and calm resolve among a great diversity of voters, untinged by triumphalism, unshaded by anglophobia or dislike for any other person or people. The sentiments of the moment were entirely positive, of taking responsibility for our own problems and solving them together. The same mood bubbled to the surface again in Edinburgh on 1 July 1999 on the occasion of the formal inauguration of the Scottish Parliament, with the double symbolism of ancient crown and 'A man's a man for a' that'. The rarely heard visionary voice of Donald Dewar rang out in a magnificent speech setting a motif for a new Scotland. No one then imagined he had little more than a year left to live, as they saw him cheerfully engage in the public celebrations to which Edinburgh gave itself over that day.

I have been a member of the SNP for very many years and was president of the Glasgow University Scottish Nationalist Association in the same year as Donald Dewar was chairman of the University Labour Club. He was a couple of years older than me but we both belonged to the same generation of Glasgow University students, so many of whom went on to make a mark in political and public life in Scotland and beyond. Friendships were sustained notwithstanding tenacious and occasionally vituperative political argumentation. Certainly, despite his oft-attested contempt for the politics and politicians of the SNP, he and I remained friends as members of a wider group of what some people have sometimes characterised as a 'Glasgow mafia'.

Perhaps in this context I may be forgiven for indulging in a personal memoir of Donald Dewar as I knew him. He was a devout and vigorous champion of the Labour Party, even through times when in his soul he was far out of sorts with his party's programme. Despite all, he also inspired huge affection and loyalty – love, even – among a large circle of friends, not all of whom were Labour co-partisans of his.

He was famously crabbit and carnaptious (two words of which he much approved). He could be very kind but was also capable of being mean minded and vindictive. He liked social occasions but occasionally sulked his way moodily through evenings of general jollity. He had a sense of irony, without which he would have been less than amused on one occasion when he lingered after a party at the MacCormick residence. An accident involving the spindle of a door handle appeared to have immured him irredeemably in the sitting-room and doomed to miss an important meeting. Even if he were able to effect an undignified exit through the window, the keys of his car were in his jacket in the hall, behind a locked front door. Flora's lock-picking skills were in high demand and did the trick. Throughout, the victim of this misadventure exhibited that rather downbeat humour that was his trademark.

He had family roots in mid-Argyll in which he took genuine pleasure. When John Smith and he won the Scottish Universities' *Scotsman* debating trophy for Glasgow in 1960, the *Lochfyneside Echo* hailed this as a triumph for Ardrishaig and Lochgilphead. He was, in an old-fashioned way, Scottish to the core, having some of the uncompromising outlook of the old United Free Church of which he was determinedly not a member. His grasp of Scottish history and literature and visual arts was enormous, and the habits of scholarship lingered about him. On a holiday visit to the MacCormick retreat at Cairnbaan in 1996, he disclosed that he never read a book without a notebook in hand, making notes about it.

On that occasion, despite a stiff back (the legacy of his long-term spinal problem) he ascended the ancient capital of the Dalriadan Scots at Dunadd and admired the archaeological relics and the view. The rest of us decided to bestow the name 'a Dewar' on any hill in Scotland not exceeding 400 feet in height that was endowed with a good view and historical or archaeological associations. (Ages previously, before the breathalyser was ever heard of, a more youthful Dewar had shared a dram of whisky at the same summit with a handful of university friends and had descended to discover an irate retired lieutenant commander and a member of the local constabulary critically eyeing a car parked at what turned out to have been an ill-chosen spot. On ascertaining the licence holder's name to be 'Donald Campbell Dewar', the bobby administered a mild rebuke and went about more urgent business. The lieutenant commander was less than amused but we youthful revellers went on our way rejoicing.)

University days were not the beginning of my acquaintance with Donald Dewar. From childhood, we shared an aunt, the redoubtable Aunt Eleanor Dewar. She was his father's sister but to the young MacCormicks only a 'courtesy aunt', being a very close friend of my parents, my mother in particular. They were friends from political association as founder members in 1928 of the original National Party of Scotland and then again in 1934 in the newly formed Scottish National Party.

When I came to know Aunt Eleanor, and thus Donald as well (though indirectly to begin with), the Scottish Covenant campaign of 1947–51 was at its height. My father was convener of the Covenant Association, and mother and Aunt Eleanor were among its stalwart workers. Eleanor was in hospital having a gall bladder operation at the time of the removal of the Stone of Destiny from Westminster and the news of it hastened her recovery. Her brother Alistair, Donald's father, was of the same political sympathies, though never a political activist, being a busy consultant dermatologist.

Memory tells me that Donald's earliest political outlook ran much along the lines of support for the Covenant and home rule – nationalism of a kind, if with a small 'n'. Eleanor once quoted to us at a family party around 1952 a lecture given by 13-year-old Donald on holiday with her in the Lochgair Hotel to some English co-residents who had injudiciously aired opinions hostile to the current of home rule opinion then flowing in Scotland.

When he went up to Glasgow University, eager to hone his skills as a debater, he joined the Labour Club. Aunt Eleanor averred that he had swithered between the Scottish Nationalist Association and the Labour

Club, opting for the latter on the ground that Donald MacCormick (later presenter of BBC2's *Newsnight*) had taken up the former. Ironically, he in turn switched allegiance later in his first year, going on, as Dewar had apprehended would happen, to precede him in achieving the presidency of the Labour Club and with it the coveted role of prime minister in a Glasgow University Union parliamentary debate.

Family and political origins do not determine the settled political commitments of thoughtful citizens. Over the years, I watched with respect how Donald Dewar developed his own stance on the social democratic wing of the Labour Party alongside others such as John Smith and Kenneth Munro – while Bob McLaughlan was a relatively early defector to conservatism. Genetics are not politics, nor vice versa. Through parliamentary activity and party and trade union engagement, also while working as a reporter to the children's panel, he came to his own stance in political affairs, always convinced that the success of the Labour Party was essential to any of the progress he believed in. On the occasion of the second ascent of Dunadd, he revealed himself as feeling that the next election would be his last throw and that failure would leave him regretting he had devoted his life to being a parliamentarian only in opposition.

Among the silliest things ever said of him was that he 'hit the ground strolling' when appointed Secretary of State for Scotland in 1997. Rightly, he had no sympathy with the view that frenetic activity, or the appearance of it, was the course of wise policy implementation. Another silly thing was the complaint that when he assumed office as First Minister, the business he took forward was essentially that which he had started while Secretary of State. A belief that a different forum is the appropriate democratic testing ground for the policies of government does not call for changing one's policies in changing the forum. These things seem to me obvious, even from the point of view of a critic and opponent of some of the policies in question.

Dewar the statesman had come a long way from Dewar the student. Yet probably no one ever completely sheds the sympathies of their younger years. When in 1969 Oxford University Press accepted a proposal of mine for a book of essays on 'the Scottish Debate', I turned to Donald for a statement of the Labour position. He was then MP for Aberdeen South and able to write from the government benches in Westminster, while David Steel (MP for Roxburgh, Selkirk and Peebles) laid out his Liberal vision, Esmond Wright (MP for Pollok) the Conservative case and Iain MacCormick (future MP for Argyll) that of the SNP. At that time, while still acknowledging the dynamic potential of a revived domestic politics within Scotland, Donald followed a line developed by John P. Mackintosh in suggesting that projects for home rule should essentially be seen as an upward growth from local government, with enhanced empowerment, rather than a devolution down from the centre. Matters progressed a long way after that. Eventually, he reverted to a more full-blooded view. Partly, I am sure, he had it in mind to 'dish the Nats', but partly, I suspect, he was responding also to an old call from old roots.

The intervening years included electoral defeat in 1970 and the traumatic years of the 1974 parliaments initially seen by Dewar from the wilderness. They included, however, his victory over the SNP's Keith Bovey in the crucial Garscadden by-election of 1978, during which I put my best efforts into trying to deny my old friend his return to Parliament. There followed the rise of the Social Democratic Party, and its eventual fall, followed by the coming together under Sir Robert Grieve of the group that drafted the 'Claim of Right for Scotland', thus triggering a Scottish Constitutional Convention from which, to my great disappointment, the SNP excluded itself.

In the end, the scheme he so determinedly piloted through the Westminster Parliament to become the Scotland Act 1998 turned out to be very much a writing-large of the proposals the Covenant Association of his boyhood allegiance had adopted following a 'Scottish National Assembly' in March 1948, subsequently published as *A Blueprint for Scotland.*[1] Originality is difficult to achieve when it comes to making schemes for parliamentary devolution and the Covenant scheme owed its own debt to Gladstone's and successors' attempts to figure out schemes either for Irish home rule or indeed for 'home rule all round'.

The best of it all, and here the coming together of Liberal Democrats and Labour in the Convention was decisively important, was the decision to build proportional representation into the Scottish Parliament from day one onwards. The mixed system of constituency and list members is not ideal and may in due course be superseded. But the simple democratic justice of giving reasonable and reasonably proportional representation of all substantial shades of political opinion in Scotland makes it inconceivable that Scotland will ever recede into first-past-the-post in the Westminster style. Even for Westminster, the grotesque distribution of seats following the 2005 general election ought surely to mark the beginning of the end of devotion to first-past-the-post.

The emerging quality of a distinctively Scottish democracy is and will continue to be deeply marked by the strategic decisions that were built into the Scotland Act. 'There shall be a Scottish Parliament' was a phrase famously well liked by Donald Dewar. It is a liking many of his compatriots share and will go on sharing.

A Father of the Nation

Ruth Wishart

The television cameras dwelling on the crowded pavements outside Glasgow Cathedral in October 2000 captured many memorable images, none more so, perhaps, than that of two young men in leather jackets silently, almost absent-mindedly, weeping as they listened to the funeral service for Scotland's first First Minister. They were a different generation from the man they mourned and almost certainly had few, if any, interests in common with him. But some impulse had propelled them to participate, however peripherally. Just as some instinct had propelled office and shop workers on to the streets of Glasgow's city centre in their thousands to applaud the cortège as it bore Donald Dewar to the private cremation service following the formal public tributes. Marion and Iain Dewar, his children, later pronounced themselves astonished at the numbers and at their overt distress and evident respect. Living in Brussels and London respectively, they had little inkling of the footprint their father would leave behind on the country where they themselves had lived for a relatively short period.

It was one of the many paradoxical facets of Donald Dewar's character that this sometimes aloof, more than occasionally grumpy, politician had a rare ability to relate to unexpected groups of fellow humans. Nowhere was this more apparent than when the Glasgow Academy old boy attended to business in the constituency originally known as Garscadden, which housed much of the overspill Glasgow housing estate of Drumchapel. It was in precisely those activities where he had seemingly no personal locus that he appeared most genuinely at ease: teasing the bingo-playing granny waiting on that elusive 'wan'; swapping surprisingly accurate sports statistics with the men in the pub; offering rude commentaries on the neighbourhood children to their mothers, remarks which might have provoked outrage and hostility from another source. Some sixth sense evidently persuaded these constituents that the gangling figure in the crumpled suit was basically on their side. Their instincts were sound. Here was a man who could thrill to the successful purchase of a rare book he'd stalked, or wax lyrical over the evocative tones of a gallery exhibition featuring the works of a Scottish artist he particularly admired. Yet a man who could rage passionately – as he once did in our apartment to the bemusement of fellow guests – about the iniquity of a mother on his patch having to fight for the right kind of incontinence pads for a disabled adolescent. Here was one of the few senior Scottish politicians to spend holiday August in Edinburgh so that he might sup deeply of the soul food of the International Festival, its theatre and most particularly its concerts. Yet here too was a man who could bore for Scotland on the minutiae of not just soccer but a raft of more esoteric sports.

When we first knew Donald, I used to think it no more than a trick of the political trade that he would engage my sports cartoonist husband in an energetic replay of the previous weekend's football scoreboard. No more than observing the basic social courtesies. It transpired that politeness – never one of his core virtues – had nothing to do with it. When he moved to a new flat in Glasgow and was convalescing from surgery, the television set his family installed to his specifications had a quite extraordinary array of sports channels. Perhaps his own lack of prowess in any known sporting pursuit fired a vicarious enthusiasm. (There is a picture of him in newspaper archives clad in a soccer strip for a Westminster five-a-side challenge – with Denis Canavan perfectly cast on the left wing – which at once offers visual evidence of a genuine personal commitment to the sport and of a physique never destined to thrill crowds at a Hampden Cup Final.)

Of the many constant threads woven through the tapestry of his political life, few mattered more than the delivery of devolution. And few were to cause him more intermittent despair. There was the memorable weekend in 1974 when the Scottish Executive of the Labour Party concluded that it didn't much fancy devolution after all and had to be reminded by its London-based colleagues that it was actually party policy. (In the days when that mattered!)

Conversely, few issues provided greater personal satisfaction when the dream proved stubbornly resistant to neglect and hostility. As with John Smith before him, Donald never wavered on devolution. His introduction of the Devolution White Paper, first at the dispatch box and later that same day at a special ceremony at Edinburgh Castle, was a highlight that compensated in part for the long inglorious slog in opposition, not even to mention the internecine struggle over devolution in the ranks of his own party. 'There shall be a Scottish Parliament,' he read from the formal text. 'I like that,' he added, grinning broadly, by way of wholly unsurprising admission. It was a soundbite destined for endless replays.

For a man who still bore the scars of the disastrous failure to secure sufficient votes for devolution in 1979, the night of the count in the September 1997 referendum found him pacing the nether regions of the Edinburgh Conference Centre like an expectant father advised that if this much-delayed delivery wasn't successful, the game was up. The relief was palpable as the first result came in positively for both the parliament and the more controversial tax-varying powers. The decision by Tony Blair to add a second question on taxation had caused a massive uproar, not least since George Robertson, when shadow Scottish Secretary, had publicly set his face against one. It was also a low ebb in my friendship with Donald Dewar. After a testy exchange of views on the telephone, he elected to come for Sunday lunch and give me a background briefing. The meal lacked a certain jollity; I remember my husband concluding by the pudding stage that it would be significantly safer to colonise the garden. It was not, after all, a subject about which the pro-devolution lobby was remotely unemotional. Anyone who had lived through the horrors of 1979 and a referendum sabotaged by the George Cunningham 40 per cent rule was liable to be paranoid about risking an action replay of that debacle. Subsequently, of course, the votes second time around held up and that first parliamentary opening on the Mound, shorn of the later cynicism which dogged the formal occupation of the Holyrood building, represented, you suspect, the happiest few hours of Donald Dewar's life.

The day was punctuated by a series of unfamiliar events. One was the delivery of his speech, of which more in a moment. There were many times in his crowded life when he would busk important speeches, sometimes getting away with minimal preparation on the back of a formidable intellect (not to mention a handy envelope), good memory and considerable wit. There were other occasions when he miscalculated. I was working at *The Scotsman* newspaper and, with its then editor, Magnus Linklater, put together a devolution debate with the Scottish party leaders. The event attracted a huge level of interest and had to be moved from the original thought of the McEwan Hall into a packed Usher Hall. Alex Salmond, it was rumoured, had rehearsed at length for this outing. Donald, it became all too clear, had not. As Salmond gained enthusiastic responses from an audience which seemed to house a majority of Nationalists, Donald's features settled into one of his familiar expressions: the look you might strive for had a sudden bad odour escaped from the pavement in front of you. No such risks were taken on 1 July 1999. Not only was the speech elegant and evocative, it was delivered free of characteristic 'umms'. He spoke with clarity, passion and conviction, and duly impressed political friend and foe in equal measure.

It was a good day, which moved seamlessly into a memorable night. Donald, never one of life's natural party animals, seemed determined to leave no celebration untouched by his presence. This was Edinburgh, this was his fiefdom, and so there was no spin-doctor with the power to advise against sharing a stage with a pop group called Garbage. He hit the opera stage and supper party too, and the hootenanny cum ceilidh in the Assembly Rooms. If you've waited four decades for an event, you don't go home early.

There are two questions people always pose in the years since his untimely removal from a fledgling, inexperienced legislature. What would it have been like if he had lived? And what would he have made of subsequent events? Most people would concede that, had he lived through at least one full term of the Scottish Parliament, there would have been a greater coherence and authority. We would, self-evidently, have been spared the messy political demise of his successor. Yet he would not, I'm pretty certain, have had the appetite for a second four-year stint. Anyone who has served as a Shadow Cabinet minister for any length of time will tell you what an unrelenting slog is the life of a politician who has to master complex briefs without the life-support system attendant on actually holding office. That applied in spades to the thankless job of shadow Secretary of State for Scotland, a role that effectively covered three or four different portfolios. He stuck that out, just as he subsequently did the wholly unglamorous roles of shadowing social security and running the whip's office because he had been promised the top Scottish job when and if Labour came to power. Secretary of State for Scotland was, unusually for a Scottish politician, the only post he ever really coveted. Latterly, becoming First Minister added extra icing.

It also, in some ways, narrowed his social horizons. As a single man, Donald had operated around a circle of friends and safe houses from whom and which he derived sustenance both psychological and gastronomic. Inevitably, office places tensions and logistical problems in the path of continuing these friendships as before.

The constraints operated on both sides. In the village that is Scotland, he was acutely aware that if he accepted, for example, two corporate tickets to a concert and turned up with anyone female under 90, the media would leap with Olympian ease to the wrong conclusions. Meta, now Baroness Ramsay, once joined Jimmy and Anne Gordon and Donald on a brief holiday to the Northern Isles. By the time she returned, at least one tabloid had concluded that two students who had been to university together 40 years before had somehow belatedly discovered they were romantic soulmates. Equally, those of us who broke bread with Donald on a regular basis would now pause before calling him up with a social invitation. You didn't want to intrude. You didn't want it to be thought your motivation was suspect. Yet it was easier for journalists than other friends. Journalists seen in earnest conversation with a minister are hardly a phenomenon.

He did earnest conversation well. There is one Italian restaurant in Glasgow that used to feature strolling players. I well remember his irritation at the intimate attention of the mandolin player to our table as he was in full flow about employment legislation.

But he did fun, too. A dinner party with Donald on board was never short of laughter, usually on the back of a wickedly accurate observation about a colleague. It was a tendency to waspishness rather than malice and always leavened by wit. Above all, he did loyalty. Sometimes to the detriment of common sense, often to his own disadvantage.

He was, when you think of it, very Scottish in both vices and virtues. Prickly, impatient, quick witted, complex, steadfast.

Because of what he was, many dozens of important people gathered to mourn him in October 2000. Because of who he was, because of what he represented in the national psyche, many thousands of his ordinary countrymen and women felt impelled to join their ranks.

Donald and Scotland

In an age where the public can be cynical about politics, Donald stood out. He transcended party politics, winning the respect and affection of those of all political persuasion and none. I remember the last time I was with him in Scotland. As we left a lunch, we went over to the sizeable crowd which had gathered. What left its mark on me was the genuine warmth of his reception and his own surprise and embarrassment that so many people wanted to shake his hand. It was typical of the bond between Donald and the people of Scotland. Even when times were difficult, they recognised that he was always fighting for them. They responded, as did his colleagues and many friends, to his integrity, wisdom and modesty but perhaps most of all, to his decency.

Rt Hon. Tony Blair MP – Prime Minister

He appeared to some as a dour humourless Scot. Yet he was outgoing, energetic, friendly and positively effervescent. He was a fascinating cocktail of joy and doom. Ebullient on the day, he was always cautious if not downright dismal about the future. The glass was not even close to being half-empty. Yet his friendship once given was true and unerring.

Ross Harper – legal partner, political opponent and friend

He was refreshingly reluctant to get into a flap about trivial media scare stories – he'd seen it all before. His spontaneous wit in discussion (even when things weren't going well) was a constant delight. And his eyes always lit up when food appeared at meetings – 'Let there be scones!' he once said – and he ended up eating at least six.

Sir Russell Hillhouse – former Permanent Secretary, Scottish Office

A Coalition Partner

Jim Wallace

I have a vivid memory of the Cabinet meeting in Bute House on 10 October 2000. It was the last time I saw Donald Dewar alive. He asked me to explain a legal issue arising out of a paper I'd presented on the EU Charter of Fundamental Rights. When I finished, he rolled his eyes ceilingwards – a sign of evident incomprehension. He then asked the Lord Advocate to see if he could explain the point any better. *His* attempt was similarly dismissed.

On returning to St Andrew's House later that day, I was advised by the doorman that doctors were with the First Minister. An ambulance was expected soon. I went to my office and was told that he'd felt unwell after a fall. Given his recent major surgery, no chances were being taken. As a doctor and some of his private office were in with him, I decided not to go in and add to the enquirers after his health. Oh so sadly, I was never to see him again.

Some of the political analysis after his death speculated on whether the still fledgling Labour–Liberal Democrat coalition could survive given the theory that the long-standing friendship between Donald and me was pivotal to its success. In fact, although Donald and I had been acquaintances for the best part of 20 years, the political and personal relationship, so remarked upon, only really started after Labour's 1997 election success and only matured during the months of partnership government.

I first recall being introduced to Donald in Glasgow Sheriff Court in or about 1980. We were both lawyers and he was aware that I had political interests – but I was a Liberal!

Donald was already a well-established politician. He became shadow Secretary of State for Scotland in 1983, the year I was first elected to Parliament. He was a social animal and good company, and we enjoyed the friendly acquaintance of Scots MPs who had other friends in common. We also shared the experiences of debates on the Rate Support Grant Order, the Scottish Grand Committee and occasionally the Thursday night sleeper back to Scotland.

In 1991, there was outrage in my constituency when social workers removed seven children from their homes. Donald, with his own professional experience of the children's hearing system, was only too willing to talk through the issues with me.

In the late 1980s, the Scottish Constitutional Convention had been established. Although I played a full part in its deliberations, it was the then Scottish Liberal Democrat leader Malcolm Bruce who engaged in most of the direct negotiations with Donald and the Labour Party. And when I became Scottish party leader in 1992, Donald was given remission from shadowing the Scottish Office and took on responsibilities for social security and, latterly, as opposition Chief Whip – a role in which he struck up a very good working relationship with my own party's whip and fellow Scots MP Archy Kirkwood.

So it was not until after the 1997 election, when Donald became Secretary of State for Scotland with the mission of delivering devolution, that any real political engagement between us took place.

Shortly after his appointment, I was invited to go and see him at Dover House. Given our two parties' involvement in the Constitutional Convention, he wanted to make it clear that Labour intended to legislate using the Convention blueprint, including proportional representation. He obviously wanted our cooperation and indicated that he would always be willing to speak. Indeed, as the date for publication of the White Paper approached, we had further discussions and he was able to assure me that two Liberal Democrat proposals knocked back in the Convention – reducing the number of Scottish MPs at Westminster and making the presumption that all subjects would be devolved, unless expressly reserved – would feature in the White Paper.

It was at that first meeting when he said to me, 'I suspect we're going to find ourselves working together quite a bit.' The significance of his words was not lost on me, although I was very conscious that nothing could ever be taken for granted – and he knew that as much as I did.

We worked and campaigned together in the 1997 referendum. Subsequently, he ensured I was kept abreast of developments on the progress of the Bill. And there were disagreements, especially on the extent of the reserved powers. We wished to remove the reservation on abortion but Donald defended the Cabinet line vigorously. He later admitted to me that he was relieved my homework was incomplete. I hadn't found his speech during the passage of the 1978 Act when he too had argued strongly for abortion to be within the Scottish Parliament's competence.

During this period, other parliamentary business was going ahead. The cooperation which existed in trying to secure the establishment of the Scottish Parliament did not extend to other areas of policy. We challenged the government hard on issues such as their spending plans and particularly on the introduction of tuition fees for students. I sometimes got the feeling that because the Liberal Democrats were 'in the tent' as far as taking forward the Parliament was concerned Donald thought we should suspend the natural right and instinct of an opposition party to oppose. He certainly could be tetchy if attacked too much.

However, one particular occasion comes to mind when we were on opposing sides of an amendment. The Church of Scotland had expressed concerns that the Human Rights Bill could compromise its constitutional independence guaranteed by its 1921 Act. The debate gave Donald the opportunity to indulge his fascination for history, as the finer points of the Kirk's status were examined, and his sheer delight and skill in the cut and thrust of that debate made it an occasion when I felt privileged just to be taking part.

Once the Scotland Bill was enacted, the focus very much turned to the Scottish elections, fixed for 6 May 1999. And the results were very much as expected. Labour clearly had the most seats but fell well short of the majority that would have been theirs if we had used the first-past-the-post system.

Throughout, the Liberal Democrat position had been that we would talk to the largest party to see if we could come to some agreement. Whilst Donald had clearly foreseen the likelihood of coalition, I'm not sure how much thought he'd given to its actual detailed operation.

On the afternoon of 7 May, he phoned me and offered a coalition with two Liberal Democrat ministers holding full Cabinet positions. Little or nothing was said about policy. The impression I formed was that we were being made a genuine offer but it was basically for two Liberal Democrats to join a Labour Cabinet. I indicated that there would need to be an agreed policy basis before we would join any government.

We agreed to meet at Bute House later during the weekend to assess what progress we could possibly make. When the two of us met, he had prepared four sides of A4 on what a programme for government might look like. The draft Liberal Democrat policy statement for the negotiations ran to 28 pages. In the event, we agreed that if coalition government was going to work, we would require a quite detailed understanding of what we were each committing ourselves to.

The negotiations between the two parties started on the Sunday evening, on the fifth floor of the new parliamentary headquarters on George IV Bridge. It was a place with which we were to become quite familiar over the next three days. Our talks were interspersed with screams from down below – we later discovered we were on the route of one of Edinburgh Old Town's renowned ghost tours! I vividly remember Donald's look of horror each time the cries rang out.

To assist the overall process, we had arranged for two party groups to go through our manifestos subject by subject, identify areas of agreement and place in square brackets the areas of divergence that the negotiating teams would then seek to resolve. On one occasion, Donald made some very deprecatory remarks about one bracketed policy idea, which he dismissed as 'Liberal nonsense'. He had to be told that that particular policy originated in Labour's manifesto. And he laughed wholeheartedly.

By the Wednesday evening, I believed we had reached an impasse. The sticking point was over the future of tuition fees. I went to see Donald alone to say that we had tried. We had given it our best shots – all manner of formulae had been considered – but we hadn't succeeded. The subsequent breakthrough came about through two Scottish leaders looking into the abyss and going over the ground again to see if a way forward could be found. In the event, we agreed to set up a committee of inquiry, and Donald was prepared to accept that the tuition fee issue would not command collective responsibility, so that we could be free to argue our respective cases to the inquiry.

The logjam was broken and we had the basis for an agreement that ultimately would lead to the abolition of tuition fees for Scottish students.

Although numerous t's still needed crossing and i's dotted, there was sufficient agreement to allow Liberal Democrat MSPs to vote for Donald when the election for First Minister took place the following day. My parliamentary team and a party caucus later approved the agreement and Donald and I duly signed the partnership agreement in the National Museum of Scotland on the morning of 14 May. It was the start of a valued personal partnership.

It was only in the latter stages of the negotiations that Donald and I ever discussed Cabinet posts, although there was a tacit understanding that if a coalition was to work, I would have to be Deputy First Minister. We agreed I should take on the newly created justice portfolio. At the time, it seemed natural given my legal background. In retrospect, it carried more significance than I then realised. Given subsequent Labour positions at Westminster and Holyrood on crime and law and order, the appointment of a Liberal Democrat as Justice Minister surely says something about Donald. The man who was in Parliament at the time of the 1968 Social Work (Scotland) Act and who had been a reporter to the children's panel himself seemed comfortable with a Justice Minister who had liberal instincts.

Moreover, he specifically gave me responsibility for introducing a robust freedom of information regime. He surely knew that I would want to go further than the Westminster package. A number of seminar-type meetings followed, as he tested the proposals I was putting forward. I well remember an interview on the first anniversary of the election when Donald cited a more robust position on freedom of information – along with the abolition of tuition fees – as key examples of success in our first year and where we had trodden a different path from London. (Later, he would add the abolition of section 2A to that list. During the storms which attended that decision, Donald steadfastly supported the abolition of this particularly pernicious piece of discriminatory legislation, showing a very real commitment to the social liberal tradition in the Labour Party.)

His willingness to let me pursue a liberal agenda in the Justice Department undoubtedly strengthened the rapport between us and the respect I had for him. But there were other key features of these months in government that helped to strengthen our working relationship.

Donald had a very genuine belief in cabinet government. Very early on, he indicated his disappointment with the perfunctory nature of discussions around the United Kingdom Cabinet table and his wish to see more open discussion around the Scottish Cabinet table. This led to good debate, which rarely ever split on party lines, and allowed individual ministers an opportunity to offer views which Donald rigorously tested and challenged from the chair. This was his natural style and I'm sure it would have been the same if he had led a Labour-only Cabinet. But in the context of a coalition, it ensured that the views of Ross Finnie and myself were considered alongside everyone else's, thus limiting the possibility of tribalism.

He also made me feel I had his trust and confidence. During the Easter 2000 recess, I was in St Andrew's House and was asked if I would go and have a private word with Donald. He told me about his health difficulties, that he would be going into hospital for tests and most likely, thereafter, for heart surgery. He could be away from his duties for three months and he expected me to look after the shop in his absence. I immediately recognised the significance of what he was saying and not least that I, a Liberal Democrat, would have to lead, temporarily, an administration with a large Labour majority. I recall saying, 'I don't remember this being in the script, when I joined up.' Donald's brief reply was, 'Deputies deputise.'

Three or four weeks later, Donald took me aside and said that he'd been given a date for his operation and would be going into hospital on the following Sunday. His parting words to me were, 'Enjoy yourself.' In retrospect, I enjoyed myself, as much as a paid-up Scots Presbyterian is allowed to – something, I know, Donald would understand. And I like to think that I merited the confidence that Donald had placed in me. After his return to work, it was pretty much business as before and I recall how we worked together to find ways of defusing potential traps set by the opposition to try and divide the coalition partners.

Our personal partnership in government ended on 11 October 2000 but I believe that the continuing political partnership, which saw us through to the 2003 election and was renewed thereafter, was made possible by Donald's contribution during these first months of devolution. Donald was a Labour Party man through and through. He was devoted to the party he worked for all his life. But he did not have a narrow tribal approach to politics. It is to his credit, and that of the Labour Party, that the Constitutional Convention commitment to proportional representation was honoured by a government with a majority to do the opposite. It is a rare event in politics that a party willingly gives up a ready advantage for power.

Donald knew, however, that the new politics would only achieve its potential if the Parliament were given time to find its roots, and that meant embracing coalition government. I still don't think he had appreciated the extent to which a detailed policy agreement would be required but when he did recognise it, he strove to make it work. Although I have worked amicably and constructively with his two successors, I do believe that it required someone of Donald's long standing in his party, his receptiveness to change and his vision to ensure that our partnership government was established on firm foundations.

The Modernising Radical

Peter Jones

Journalism, it is sometimes said, is history's first draft. But the first draft of Donald Dewar's political history turns out to be pitched in absurdly wide terms. While he was First Minister, the press verdict, from the right-wing anti-devolution *Daily Mail* to the Labour-supporting pro-devolution *Daily Record*, ranged from 'deeply disappointing' to 'shambolic incompetence'. After his death, the same newspapers lauded him as 'a Great Scot . . . for whom we have much to be grateful'.[1] Other newspapers wrote similarly.

Clearly, the obituary editorials were based on the simple fact that Dewar fought for, and then established, the Scottish Parliament, the biggest constitutional change Scotland has known since 1707. The pre-obituary comment, however, was based entirely on what he did after becoming First Minister in May 1999. The record here is not an unalloyed triumph but it has some surprises given his reputation as a cautious and rather traditional right winger. From the legislative record, three Dewars emerge. One – the champion of social justice – is unsurprising. But Dewar the radical? And Dewar the moderniser?

Social justice was almost invariably mentioned first whenever he listed his priorities for action. Two decades of representing Glasgow Garscadden (later Anniesland), one of the poorest constituencies in Britain, is sufficient explanation. 'I give a high priority to the social justice agenda,'

Donald on 24 July 1997, the evening of the launch of *Scotland's Parliament* the Devolution White Paper in hand, arriving at Edinburgh Castle with Baroness Elizabeth Smith. (Dan Tuffs/Scottish Viewpoint)

Donald and the Rt Hon. Tony Blair MP, Prime Minister, on 12 September 1997, the morning after the Devolution Referendum victory, celebrating the decisive Yes, Yes vote. (Colin McPherson/Scottish Viewpoint)

Donald and the Rt
Hon. Gordon
Brown MP
campaigning in
Argyle St, Glasgow,
during the 1999
Scottish Parliament
election, with Frank
McAveety, then City
Council leader, in
the background.
(SMG Archive)

May 1999 – Donald leads the newly elected Labour group of MSPs up the
Mound to the first meeting of the new Scottish Parliament.
David Whitton is in the foreground. (TSPL)

Scotland's new Cabinet meets for the first time at Bute House, Edinburgh. Left to right: Tom McCabe, Muir Russell, Donald, Jim Wallace, Lord Hardie QC, Susan Deacon, Ross Finnie, Wendy Alexander, Sam Galbraith, Henry McLeish, Jack McConnell and Sarah Boyack. (SMG archive)

1 July 1999 – Donald and Sir David Steel, Presiding Officer, accompany Her Majesty the Queen out onto the streets of Edinburgh following the official opening of the Scottish Parliament. (Press Association)

Donald in 1999 with one of his young constituents. Within six months of becoming First Minister, he launched an annual *Social Justice Report for Scotland: A Scotland Where Everyone Matters*. (TSPL)

Donald reached out to people and typically they reached out to him. He is pictured here as Secretary of State for Scotland talking with Agnes Davis, a long-standing Labour Party member at a Scottish Labour conference.
(Paul Dodds/
Scottish Viewpoint)

Donald in contemplation in the Secretary of State's, and then the First
Minister's, magnificent art deco office in St Andrew's House. However, Donald's
favourite government office was in Meridien Court, Cadogan St, Glasgow.
(Paul Dodds/Scottish Viewpoint)

Donald discussing the design of the Scottish Parliament building at Holyrood
with the architect, Enric Miralles. (TSPL)

Donald talking to Hillary Clinton at the White House whilst attending a
Presidential Dinner during a visit to the USA in March 1999.
(Donald Dewar Archive)

Donald disliked some of the consequences of high office, including having to
take a keener interest in his appearance than came naturally!
(Adam Elder/*Scotland on Sunday*)

Donald receiving the Royal Warrant from Her Majesty the Queen at Holyrood as she formally appointed him First Minister in May 1999. Donald, somewhat to his surprise, found the Queen remarkably good company, sharing as they did a dry, even irreverent sense of humour and a keen appreciation of history. (TSPL)

Donald emerging from the Royal Infirmary, Glasgow, following his successful heart operation in May 2000. (TSPL)

On 11 September 2000, a month to the day before his death, Donald looks pensive and tired on the opening day of the TUC conference at Glasgow's Scottish Exhibition and Conference Centre.
(Press Association)

Donald was gregarious but he also valued the rare bonus of solitude. Here pictured visiting the Commando Memorial at Spean Bridge.
(Adam Elder/*Scotland on Sunday*)

he said when introducing the first legislative programme in the new Scottish Parliament. 'I represent real extremes in terms of prosperity, opportunity and life chances, and I am always conscious of that. What must be done . . . is to attack on all fronts.'[2] He explained what those fronts were. 'As a Parliament, we cannot accept a Scotland where 4,000 children leave school each year without formal qualifications, where heart disease and cancer have given us a mortality rate among the worst in Europe, where one-third of Scottish households have below half the average United Kingdom income, and where one-quarter of our housing stock suffers from dampness or condensation.'[3]

Once the Herculean task of the devolution referendum and White Paper was out of the way, Dewar and his ministers found more time for this agenda. It was no easy task, for Labour's election pledges meant that Dewar's administration, and the rest of the government, was constrained to work for the first two years within the existing spending programme bequeathed by the defeated Conservative government. Chancellor Gordon Brown's July 1997 budget raised some extra money but gave no room for big spending commitments. Dewar opted to put most of the money he gained from this into education and health. But an additional £106 million for health, for example, still meant that cutbacks had to be made, according to Sam Galbraith, his Health Minister.[4]

Thus the first big announcement on social justice seemed pretty small beer – £23 million to enable schools to provide additional out-of-hours teaching for struggling children. Of bigger importance was a decision to set up a social exclusion network within the Scottish Office chaired by one of his junior ministers, Lord Sewel. It would coordinate social exclusion work by departments covering health, education, housing, social work and crime, and signalled the cross-cutting way he wanted officialdom to work.[5]

In February 1998, he published a consultation paper on the topic, stressing: 'Tackling the problem of social exclusion is our number one social policy priority in Scotland.'[6] Of the four priority areas, education and housing were those where he had most power to make a difference. According to Galbraith, his closest ministerial colleague at the Scottish Office and the Scottish Executive, 'Donald had a special interest in education. He still had that old Scottish Presbyterian belief that a good education is a necessary condition for individual improvement.'[7]

An early innovation was the introduction of classroom assistants but

Dewar was aware that more teachers and better buildings were not enough. Social problems in disadvantaged areas could pose almost insuperable barriers to some children. In 1998, new community schools, later called integrated community schools, a reform thought long overdue by many educationalists, were introduced.[8] This initiative brought social workers, community education workers and health professionals to work with teachers to help children and their families to get more out of schooling. This radical change in thinking has been slow to develop but a 2004 evaluation found it had clear potential: 'Whilst, as yet, there has been little effect on overall levels of attainment in schools, there was clear evidence that the broader achievements of some pupils had improved, as had some aspects of health and personal development.'[9]

Once in the Scottish Parliament, Dewar quickly used his new legislative freedom to keep up the pace of educational reform. The Standards in Scotland's Schools Etc. Bill was, according to Galbraith, almost entirely Dewar's creation: 'In the schools system, you have complacency at the top and an acceptance of failure at the bottom. He wanted to give head teachers and inspectors powers to look at failing schools and to do something about them.'[10] The Bill brought the idea of children's rights to schooling into Scottish education law for the first time, an attempt to reinforce trends towards a much more individualised approach to teaching. It was also a subtle way of eroding the power of the Educational Institute of Scotland, the big teaching union which Dewar increasingly came to regard as hindering, rather than helping, progress.

Dewar was also determined to make an impact on housing. Glasgow City Council's 90,000 municipal homes were in a shocking state: estimated in 1998 to need £3 billion spent on them. The council stock was estimated to be worth minus £200 million (a figure which proved an underestimate after more detailed survey work). Dewar, however, was privately impressed by the big improvements achieved when ownership of chunks of estates was transferred to tenant-managed housing associations, which, with some subsidy, were able to borrow private money for repairs and refurbishment.

These schemes were the model for what became the biggest revolution in social housing since the Housing Acts of 1919 and 1924 created council housing. Key to making it work was persuading Glasgow City Council to relinquish control of what, to many councillors, was their power base and reason for being in power. That was solved by a straightforward bribe – the government took over the council's £900 million housing debt, which was consuming 40p of every £1 of rent collected.[11] The carrot for tenants was lower rents and better homes. They took the deal.

Dewar said, 'I can think of no more radical and fundamental reform than the proposals on community ownership in housing. We will tackle the debt problem and create room for investment in the housing stock, which has been crumbling and is hardly viable in many areas. We will also put the tenants and their elected representatives at the very heart of the management of that housing stock.'[12] With this one act, Dewar closed the book on 80 years of traditional Glasgow municipal socialism. Seen as a betrayal by some in the Labour Party, it was in reality an overdue end of a failure and perhaps the beginning of a community socialism more true to the workers' housing dreams of Red Clydesider John Wheatley.

That alone could justify describing Dewar as a radical but his determination to secure land reform ensures it. Reforming the law on land ownership to tilt the balance of power away from landowners, especially in the Highlands and Islands, towards crofters, tenants and communities had gradually become part of Labour Party policy. This was in large part due to the campaigning efforts of Brian Wilson, who became a minister in Dewar's Scottish Office team. Yet it still seems a little odd that Dewar should have moved ahead so swiftly with land reform, setting up a working group in October 1997 to examine the issue. After all, it affected a minority of Scots and even fewer Labour voters. Galbraith explains, 'Donald came at land reform as dealing with another form of exclusion. He saw it as correcting a great social injustice.'

Dewar described the January 1999 report of the Land Reform Policy Group as proposing the 'most far-reaching reform ever of Scotland's system of land ownership'. The report set out powers to assess the public interest in major property sales in remote areas, rights for communities to buy land when it came on the market, powers to use compulsory purchase in the public interest to prevent evasion of a community right to buy and abolition of the remaining vestiges of feudal ownership. Dewar added, 'We also propose reform of crofting: to give all crofting communities a right to acquire their land at any time; remove barriers to the creation of new crofts; allow for the possibility of extending crofting tenure to new areas within the Highlands and Islands and simplify the regulatory burden of crofting legislation.'[13]

163

Coupled with legislation to allow a public right of access to land, the legislation eventually passed by the Scottish Parliament was indeed radical. Though Dewar died over two years before it was enacted in January 2003, the relative ease of early community purchases of land, such as the island of Gigha, was due to his work. Particularly significant was securing the agreement of Chris Smith, then the Secretary of State for Culture, Media and Sport, to allow a different use of New Opportunities Fund lottery money in Scotland, enabling grants to assist community land purchases.

If these two acts – reform of urban housing and rural land ownership – justify the description of Dewar as a radical, they also go some way to justify the further label as a moderniser. It was never a label applied to him in his lifetime, mainly because of his oft-cited disdain for spin-doctoring and image management and his attachment to crumpled suits. This disdain did not prevent him, albeit after relentless nagging by party colleagues, from consulting Barbara Follett, New Labour's image guru. She was responsible for Dewar switching to more modern-looking rimless spectacles and wearing more fashionable ties. She gave him three ties, the image-improving powers of which he then tested to destruction.[14]

Yet the words modernisation and innovation crop up frequently in his speeches about the Scottish Parliament. This attitude emerges most clearly in Dewar's remarks about how the new Parliament would operate. Again, he was contemporarily portrayed as an archetypal Westminster man, seen as thoroughly at home there. He did indeed relish the intellectual life and debate of the House of Commons but he had little time for its antique procedures. He knew that the proportional electoral system would very likely produce a coalition government and that the referendum result had suggested a public desire for a different style of government: challenges which he also seemed to relish.

In a 1997 lecture, he said, 'One of the most significant innovations will be the additional members system we are proposing for elections. It will simply not be possible to participate within the Parliament without giving due consideration to building coalitions of interest, as the chances of any one party holding power will be greatly diminished. That in itself will mean a sea change in the way we conduct our political business. The tactics of parties will have to be rethought.'[15]

Introducing the new coalition government's programme in 1999, he said, 'Today's politics in Scotland should not be dominated by the nineteenth-century maxim that oppositions oppose everything and propose nothing. The government's programme contains ambitions that are shared by many members; there should be scope for working together, across the party divide, to deliver them. If that were to happen, it would do much to justify the votes so generously and determinedly cast in the referendum that created the Parliament.'[16]

He also approved, even though it would be inconvenient, of the much greater transparency and openness of the new parliament. Members of the Scottish Parliament would have much more power to scrutinise Scottish Executive spending than MPs had to examine Whitehall spending. 'Here,' he told newly elected MSPs, 'there will be machinery for scrutiny in the Finance Committee and relevant ministers can be interviewed – that is a nice, neutral term – so that this Parliament can keep closely in touch with what is happening on financial matters and the allocation of monies. I say with heartfelt sincerity that there will be times when the Administration will curse all this scrutiny, but it is right that this machinery is put in place.'[17]

These three facets of his thinking – social justice, radical reform, modernisation – have been presented in isolation. To Dewar, however, they were all part and parcel of the same thing – a political outlook that made him less excited by ideology than by practical solutions that would make things better for the people he served. In a St Andrew's Day speech in 1998, he argued it was time to put aside constitutional debate. He said, 'Modernisation matters now. There is no time to waste. But there are those who would waste it. We have been trying to reform our school examination system since Howie delivered his report in 1992 and there are still politicians today who will argue for further delay. There is the challenge of land reform. We are committed to give a legal right to those who live and work the land to bid if that land comes on the market. We are using the New Opportunities Fund to back social progress but there are still many who obstruct and complain. The need to banish the blight that has affected our housing stock is pressing – the failures of the past are there for all to see. We have set out suggestions for dealing with the debt, providing new ways to manage housing based on community ownership. And yet we meet too often the false charge of privatisation from those apparently ready to live with the errors of the past. The biggest hospital-building programme in the history of NHS is derided because it uses private partnership cash. I tell you again, the test of a political system is its practical effect on the lives of human beings. The new Edinburgh Royal

Infirmary has been discussed for over 30 years. We are going to deliver it. That is what matters.'[18]

Why then, given the anxiety to press on and deal with Scotland's big problems, did the year that Dewar had as First Minister result in such a negative media verdict? Why, when he had a clear vision, was his administration's programme characterised as dull and lacking in vision?[19]

First, his relationship with the media deteriorated rapidly after he became Scottish Secretary. This was because, almost alone amongst the new government ministers, he did not indulge in spin-doctoring techniques of leaking, pre-announcements and re-announcements. He believed that announcements were one-time events and the protocols of informing Parliament first should be observed.[20] Thus, although the pace of Scottish Office activity preparing for devolution in the first few months was frenetic, nothing of the internal negotiation and debate within government emerged publicly. Moreover, Dewar had been away from the Scottish Office brief since 1992 and had no carefully worked-out timetable for implementing manifesto changes to health, education, etc. Nevertheless, a mere 12 days after the election, *The Scotsman* complained that whereas the new government had 'hit the ground sprinting', the Scottish Office was 'strolling'.[21]

Second, in the absence of programmed activity, events and even non-events rushed to fill the vacuum. Sleaze allegations about the Labour Party in Glasgow erupted weeks after the election. The referendum campaign launch was disrupted by the suicide of Paisley Labour MP Gordon McMaster and an implication that he had been driven to it by murky local politics. A row blew up about the failure to give actor Sean Connery a knighthood. By far the worst problem was a request by the Northern Ireland Secretary, Mo Mowlem, at the prodding of Ulster loyalists, to transfer a Scottish prisoner, Jason Campbell, to an Ulster jail as part of the peace process. Henry McLeish, the Scottish Home Affairs Minister, unthinkingly agreed. Once the press found out that Campbell was in no way a political prisoner but was the vicious killer of a Celtic football fan, a furore erupted.[22] Dewar sorted it out but was hugely embarrassed that the row dragged in the Prime Minister and his staff, using up political capital he needed for impending devolution Bill debates in the Commons.[23] But he felt much more keenly the anguish caused to the family of Campbell's victim, to the extent that he handwrote and rewrote, and had hand-delivered, a two-page letter of apology to the family.[24]

Under pressure from colleagues and Downing Street to improve the Scottish Office media operation, Dewar forced the resignation of Liz Drummond, head of the Scottish Office press office, and brought in David Whitton, a television and print journalist, as a media special adviser. But the catalogue of calamity continued once the new Parliament was elected.

First there came a rumpus, largely created by the print media, about the sittings of the Parliament and MSPs' expenses, interpreted by tabloid newspapers as the Parliament 'voting itself huge salaries, allowances, a three-day week with short hours, 17 weeks' holiday a year and a medal'.[25] None of that was Dewar's doing but it meant that the First Minister and his team would have to do a spectacularly good job to overcome public scepticism.

Unfortunately, problem followed problem until it appeared Dewar and his team were in constant crisis. A smart lawyer found a legal loophole which looked like compelling the release of Noel Ruddle, an abnormally aggressive patient, from the State Hospital at Carstairs. Emergency legislation was needed to close the loophole (August 1999). A newspaper reported that lobbyists with strong Labour party links were claiming to have undue influence with Labour ministers, particularly Jack McConnell, the Finance Minister: the so-called Lobbygate affair (September 1999). Dewar's quite proper response that the Parliament's Standards Committee should investigate provoked an almighty semi-public row with John Reid, then the Scottish Secretary of State, whose son Kevin was one of the lobbyists (October 1999). John Rafferty, Dewar's chief of staff, had to resign for wrongly telling reporters that Susan Deacon, the Health Minister, was under police protection after receiving death threats (December 1999). Another adviser resigned after being charged with a drink-driving offence (January 2000). Andrew Hardie, the Lord Advocate, promoted himself to be a judge before new rules were brought in to stop such self-promotion (February 2000). Ian Welsh, Labour MSP for Ayr, resigned, saying there was not enough interesting work to do, causing a by-election which Labour lost (March 2000). Wrangles over the health budget between Susan Deacon, Health Minister, and Jack McConnell, Finance Minister, caused semi-public Cabinet in-fighting while Dewar was convalescing after his heart operation (July 2000). Protests at fuel tax rates by hauliers blockading refineries threatened to bring the country to a halt (September 2000). Wrong

Higher Grade exam results were sent out by the Scottish Qualifications Agency, causing weeks of uncertainty to prospective university students (August–September 2000).

Viewing this catalogue of calamity, it is easy to see why the media found it much more exciting than Dewar's legislative programme. There were indeed two other big headaches. One was the Holyrood building project, the escalating costs of which provoked endless controversy. The second was a decision to abolish a legal provision, known as section 2A, which forbade the promotion of homosexuality in schools. This was signalled by the Scottish Executive in September 1999. A consultation exercise found broad support, soundings taken with the churches indicated no great opposition and a formal decision to legislate was announced by October by Wendy Alexander, Communities Minister.[26]

In January 2000, however, opposition began to appear. The *Daily Record*, then edited by Martin Clarke, a former *Daily Mail* journalist who was struggling to reverse declining sales, started to campaign against the repeal of section 2A. Cardinal Tom Winning, Archbishop of Glasgow, joined in. Much more unexpectedly, Brian Souter, a wealthy bus company owner and an evangelical Christian, funded a big opposition campaign, including a postal referendum in which a third of Scottish voters participated, 87 per cent of them voting to retain the clause.[27] The campaign was an enormous controversy, with accusations that the Executive was paving the way for gay sex lessons, and claims of lies and deceit being flung in all directions.

Dewar stuck to his guns. He was a social liberal who believed, he told the Parliament, that section 2A 'singles out a minority in our community for stigma, isolation and fear' and was incompatible with a society in which 'people can live together freely in a spirit of solidarity, tolerance and respect'.[28] Since this is also the wording of the reformed Clause IV of Labour Party constitution, he was proud to tell the United Kingdom Labour Party conference later that year, 'We stood firm in the blizzard. We won. In Scotland, we did not keep the clause, section 28 is no more.'[29]

These are not the actions or words of a ditherer, as Dewar was sometimes labelled . . . In some ways, the words 'solidarity, respect and tolerance' go a long way to explain Dewar's own character. Galbraith says, 'People talk about trust in politicians and how that matters a great deal. I think respect matters more and Donald had respect. People from right across Scottish society respected him.' That, he maintains, is because

Dewar's basic decency was obvious. And yet, it was also a flaw which undermined his leadership. Galbraith explains, 'I think, in his leadership, he relied on his decency, respect and his intellect. That works well with people who have decency, respect and intellect. But when you get amongst hooligans, it is no use.'[30]

The problems with Dewar's style of government became obvious after he became First Minister. External events, such as the Ruddle affair and the fuel crisis, he could deal with and were in fact resolved fairly quickly. But events originating from inside government were poorly handled.

That is in part because the change in style and machinery of government which was needed in moving from the old to the new regime, in which Dewar effectively became prime minister of Scotland, was not properly appreciated by Dewar or by the Civil Service. Dewar as Secretary of State for Scotland had five junior ministers and two law officers, plus two pieces of legislation a year at most to pass through a Parliament where the government had a huge majority and was subject to relatively weak scrutiny mechanisms. Dewar as First Minister had a much tougher task. His Executive was a coalition with a small majority, reliant on a group of MSPs mostly new to regimes of Executive-supporting disciplines and subject to much greater degrees of scrutiny and constraints. It was also expected to pilot about ten pieces of legislation a year with ministers mostly new to elected office. Symptomatic of the lack of thought given to this new governing environment was civil servants' total surprise that Dewar appointed ten Cabinet ministers and eleven deputy ministers. The bureaucracy had been expecting eight or nine ministers in all.[31] There was thus a frantic rush to find offices and private secretaries for the new team. Since a capable private office is critical to ministerial success, inexperienced ministers and inexperienced staff gave the new team insecure foundations.

That meant all the more need for a strong First Minister's office. Some provision had been made to increase the number of special advisers from the three that Dewar had as Scottish Secretary. 'We had looked at what was around the Prime Minister in Number 10 and, to some extent, that was reflected here,' a civil servant said. 'But you are probably right that we, ministers and officials, underestimated just how much capacity you need at the centre around the First Minister.' There was also little of the glue that ensures collective discipline in policy-making. Another civil servant commented, 'I don't think [Dewar] gave sufficient thought to leading a team of ministers. You have to give thought to each member of the team, their job description, what is expected of them and how they know whether they are doing well or badly.'[32]

Dewar had to be persuaded that he needed a strong policy unit. Against his own judgement, he was persuaded that Lord Elder, a long-time confidante, was not the right man to head the team. At others' urgings, principally Wendy Alexander, John Rafferty was employed as head of this office and Philip Chalmers was brought in to strengthen media presentation. In the event, the unit's personalities, ten at its largest, never gelled into a team. Neither were they given clear direction. One remarked later, 'I don't think Donald had any idea what to do with any of us.'[33] Rafferty and Chalmers were not replaced after they resigned, perhaps because political opponents and the media had begun portraying any additional cost as executive extravagance.

The lack of a strong central political machine had several consequences. First, Dewar's own political vision and goals, though they seem remarkably clear in hindsight, were never all that clearly expressed when he was in office. It is a modern media paradox that the more sophisticated the media becomes, the simpler and more often repeated have to be the messages that politicians give the media. Dewar was, however, a man of eloquence rather than soundbites.

Second, there was inadequate capacity to take control of events and deal with them before they turned into a crisis. That meant that Dewar often had to take charge. For example, Dewar and I were due to have dinner one evening in February. I turned up at St Andrew's House and was ushered up to his office, where Dewar apologised and explained he had to call off. '*The Scotsman*,' he said, 'has got hold of the fact that Andrew Hardie [the Executive's senior law officer] is going to the bench [appointing himself to be a judge] and I'm damned if I'm going to let them have an exclusive. So I had better stay and deal with it.'[34]

Unfortunately, as crisis after problem after event turned up, the more depleted became his stock of political authority amongst Labour MSPs. In April 2000, the Executive ran into difficulties over Socialist MSP Tommy Sheridan's private member's bill to abolish warrant sales and poindings. Though there was general agreement that this degrading form of debt recovery should be abolished, the Executive's problem was that no alternative was being proposed. Dewar, whose heart problems were now being investigated by his doctors, was at a meeting of the Scottish

Parliamentary Labour Group to explain the problems and possible solutions.

It turned out that the Executive had been caught napping and had no clear strategy. Mike Watson, a Labour MSP, recorded: 'The First Minister is widely respected, and usually his contributions at SPLP meetings are heard in silence. On this occasion, and despite his return from hospital, there was audible disbelief at what we were being told. Why had none of this been foreseen?'[35]

In the end, the Executive was forced by the Parliament to climb down, illustrating the consequences of the lack of foresight that ought to come from a functioning First Minister's policy unit. On this occasion, Dewar's authority was not enough to deal with the problem. The same decline in authority was all too apparent by the summer of 2000. His control over ministers, loose to begin with, virtually disappeared. Ministers were always aware it was probable he would relinquish office by the 2003 elections when he would have been 65 years old. His heart operation made that a near certainty. So preparing for the contest to succeed him became more important to some – Henry McLeish, Jack McConnell and Susan Deacon were the main contenders – than maintaining collective purpose and responsibility. Unattributable briefings suggesting in various coded terms that it was time for Dewar to step aside, and usually sourced to ministers, started to appear in newspapers.

In July 2000, an almighty row between McConnell and Deacon burst into the public domain. McConnell announced that he planned to divert £34 million of a £134 million health underspend into reserves, forestry and Historic Scotland. Deacon was livid. The row dragged on for several days until Sunday newspapers were briefed by Deacon's allies that all the £134 million would indeed be spent on health, though McConnell's camp briefed that £34 million would be kept in a special reserve, thus allowing both sides to claim victory.[36]

Reading the mayhem, the convalescing Dewar was horrified. He asked Tom McCabe, business manager, to put a stop to it. McCabe told an SPLP meeting that Dewar was 'incandescent with rage' and that if the in-fighting did not stop, ministers would be sacked. Though McCabe was tactically correct, Dewar had issued no such threat. Ruthless sackings were not his style. At various times, he was urged by Cabinet colleagues and by Downing Street to sack McLeish and McConnell. Partly because he hated confrontation and partly because he feared even bigger rows would ensue, he loyally stuck by them. That loyalty, however, was hardly returned.

This picture of an ailing Dewar struggling to keep a disintegrating administration together seems a poor epitaph. The true test of a political career, however, is to ask what will endure. The various events which precipitated headline-dominating crises showed up flaws in his political leadership but they were, in the main, just events. They may have temporarily deflected Dewar and sapped his energy but they did not fundamentally alter his programme of government. No one now seriously argues for the reintroduction of section 2A. The tide of protest at the rocketing costs of the Holyrood building has ebbed, leaving a continuing debate focused more on its architectural merits. That it is there at all and that it contains a functioning democratic legislature is, of course, Dewar's lasting monument. His legacy, however, is broader than that. Two landmarks from his governance stand out: a revolution in urban social housing and a revolution in rural land ownership. For someone who would have thought it hilarious to be described as a revolutionary, they are not just impressive achievements but enduring practical outcomes of a lifelong campaign for devolution.

Cabinet Voices

*Henry McLeish, Jack McConnell,
Sarah Boyack, Susan Deacon,
Sam Galbraith and Tom McCabe*

Donald and History — *Henry McLeish*

History shows that it is given to few politicians to fulfil their destiny. Donald Dewar was without doubt one such politician – and, as with his physical stature, he will stand head and shoulders above others in posterity.

Although we are in the early and formative years following the successful establishment of the Scottish Parliament, it is worthwhile to reflect on how and why home rule for Scotland was achieved. Historical analysis and the reading of parliamentary reports cannot give the full picture of how one man's sharp intelligence, political skill and sheer grinding hard work helped to make Scotland's dream a reality.

In 1997, when Labour came to power for the first time in 18 years, our party was in a state of euphoria. We needed time to assume our new responsibilities and become accustomed to our new status as the party of government. It would have been easy to lose focus but Donald would not be diverted from the commitments we had made. Throughout that summer, he got down to work to deliver on the promises we had made to Scotland to finally deliver on the home rule campaign that had spanned nearly a century.

In doing so, he was responsible for the production of what was generally acknowledged to be one of the most significant White Papers ever presented to the Westminster Parliament and to the Scottish people. The Devolution White Paper, *Scotland's Parliament*, spelled out with clarity and conviction exactly how we would deliver devolution to Scotland, with all the technicalities and procedure for setting up a Scottish Parliament. Many were surprised at how robust it was in relation to Scottish aspirations.

Because of that, and Donald's advocacy, the White Paper proved popular and largely received cross-party support. The White Paper, the Scotland Act and driving through the devolution programme were, in my view, Donald's finest moments.

Despite Labour's clear commitment to devolution, there were some in our new government and Parliament for whom it was a grudging concession. Donald had to struggle with the big beasts of the political jungle at Westminster and powerful figures within our own party. Yet throughout the weekly battles within the Cabinet sub-committee called 'DSWR', the White Paper emerged unscathed and was massively and triumphantly endorsed in the referendum. That, to me, was Donald's true legacy: history's verdict will be that Scotland's hopes and future were enshrined in and ensured by that White Paper. Donald was our nation's trustee and he did not fail his native land.

Donald had another great concept: the Scottish Parliament building at Holyrood. I disagreed with him at the time because I thought there were more urgent priorities but he had faith in the project and he also had the far-sightedness and the tenacity to see it through. Sadly, he died without seeing it completed but there is no doubt that the Holyrood Parliament building will be a source of great pride for our country. It is one of the iconic parliament buildings in the world, not only in architecture and design but also as a statement about modern Scotland.

Donald Dewar's political career stretched over four decades but he was never in government until 1997. In his relatively short period in power, he left a lasting mark and he will be remembered as one of Scotland's outstanding statesmen. It is a profound tragedy that he was not allowed to see the fruits of his labours. In his oft-quoted comment as he read the opening sentence of the Scotland Act: 'There shall be a Scottish Parliament.' He immediately added, 'I like that!' His real monument is that future generations will look at both Scotland's form of government and its unique home and they, too, will say, 'I like that . . . '

Reflections — *Jack McConnell*

The Scotland Act detailed the structures of devolution but gave little guidance on what to expect as a new minister in Scotland's first Cabinet.

When I was asked to Bute House shortly after the election, I expected a role in Rural and Environmental Affairs. I'd spoken on these issues during the election campaign but Donald was later to explain to the Queen that he appointed me as Finance Minister because I had been a maths teacher and he had assumed that I could count. Whether he went through similar appraisals for all of his ministerial appointments, I'll never know.

Whatever the case, the end result was that we gathered in Cabinet, enthusiasm in abundance, some egos often on display and with any Westminster experience counting for very little. In our new devolved Scotland, we were all novices alike.

The one steadying influence in those early, often chaotic, days was Donald.

In the years since his death, many have shared their memories of individual meetings, conversations or decisions. But it is the totality and sincerity of Donald's leadership that I remember the most.

His work rate was impressive, and he expected the same from his ministers. He inspired a fierce loyalty but he remained loyal to his team, too. He could have ruthlessly asserted the authority he had through his position as First Minister or as the 'Father of Devolution'; but, instead, he would endlessly discuss the options and the implications of new legislation, policy or resource allocations. And, unlike others, Donald didn't judge an idea by its source. New thinking was debated on its merits alone.

He demonstrated many of his finest qualities in the first few months of devolution when a complaint about lobbying had been made against me. I knew that a harsh word from Donald, or even a hint of ambiguity in his support, and my fledgling Cabinet career would be over. I also knew that some people were advising him to cut me adrift. Instead, he took me aside, pledged his full backing and gave me good advice.

The complaint against me was dismissed and in the process I had gained an insight into Donald's honesty, loyalty and ability to rise above the political fray on matters of principle.

Looking back, the ministers in Scotland's first Cabinet made some right decisions and some wrong decisions. But in the way that he chaired meetings, engaged in relaxed conversation with us and by just being around, Donald was encouraging better decision making.

We probably didn't realise it at the time, some even resisted it, but slowly and with subtlety in all that he did and the example he set, Donald was influencing us and shaping us.

There may not have been a blueprint for the post-devolution Cabinet, but there was an architect.

The New Landscape — *Sarah Boyack*

Three hundred words on working with Donald Dewar in the first Scottish Cabinet seemed an easy commitment to make. But actually writing those words takes me back to the summer when he was clearly very ill and pulled back into the maelstrom of Scottish politics and government far too soon. His operation had clearly made him step back and look at what we were all doing and think about spending more time with his family and the new grandchild he loved. His death was such a waste and I think partly a comment on the punishing and unrelenting nature of the job he had been doing.

His legacy was to oversee the establishment of our new democratic institution and to make the transition relatively smooth. The 1997 proposals were so much more radical than the more tentative version which fell with the Labour government in 1979. He kept faith with the work done by the Scottish Constitutional Convention in the run-up to the election of the Labour government in 1997 and delivered his White Paper unscathed.

He surprised many by selecting a relatively young and untested team for his first Cabinet, with only a few 'old hands' who had made the transition from Westminster. But he valued professional experience beyond the political system and was keen that the Parliament was not just the old Scottish Office with a new logo. He gave us remarkable support, often telling us to use our judgement, although he was not slow to provide a critique of a proposal if it had not been thoroughly thought out.

Cabinet meetings reflected our collective ambitions to deal not just with our own individual responsibilities but to work across departmental boundaries on issues such as social justice and sustainable development. Looking back, the first few months were a constant ferment. The old system struggled to support and cope with the new levels of interest and political scrutiny that followed the establishment of the Parliament. The old cosy ways were blown away with the election in 1999 and the first legislative programme generated huge debate. The consensus of the Constitutional Convention was replaced by harder debates and arguments about priorities and investment. It was Donald's job to make sure that the transition worked for the long term.

Donald also ensured that Labour's parliamentary team was not just the usual suspects and he stood firm to deliver the strong women's representation that we now almost take for granted. There must have been many times when dropping our commitment to gender equality or abandoning our agreement to a fairer, more proportional voting system would have made his life much easier. But Donald wanted our new Parliament to live up to our aspirations for better governance and the delivery of more just decisions.

He also understood that the Scottish Labour Party had to embrace the new political landscape that devolution opened up. Transparency and increased scrutiny did not make life easier but he was prepared to take tough decisions that were not populist – if he believed they were the right thing to do.

Donald, the Radical — *Susan Deacon*

Donald Dewar's administration was, I believe, the most radical we have seen to date. This was a reflection of Donald's ambitions for devolution and for Scotland. He was always clear, as he said at the official opening in July 1999, that the Scottish Parliament is not an end, it is a means to greater ends.

Donald was often criticised for paying insufficient attention to the tools of modern politics – and perhaps rightly so. But I for one found it refreshing that he did not simply view an issue through the prism of tactics or presentation. He was always more interested in a principled solution than a political fix.

During the exceptionally heated debate around the repeal of section 2A, while others focused on how this or that would play in the headlines or with the voters, I recall Donald often saying, quite simply, that the section was 'an unjust piece of law'. For him, that was reason enough to repeal.

Donald neither rewarded nor expected blind loyalty. Rather, he valued hard work and commitment, and was open to different viewpoints, so long as you could defend your position with sufficient 'intellectual rigour'. I was pleasantly surprised by the autonomy he afforded his Cabinet ministers – even those of us who were 'new kids on the block'. He also fostered a degree of debate and discussion around the Cabinet table that, to my knowledge, has not been matched since.

That was not to say he did not keep a watchful eye over our work. He was available for advice and support where it was sought and, from time to time, would invite you to his office to discuss or to justify a particular course of action. I recall one particular decision I planned to take which I knew would not naturally find favour with him. After a long 'one-to-one' – where my logic was tested to destruction – he said simply, 'Well, I'm not sure if it's the decision I would have made but I can see you've thought it through carefully and so you'll have my full support.' True to his word, and despite his reservations, he backed me to the hilt.

Some People Love Meetings — *Sam Galbraith*

Some people just love meetings: they are part of the political process and usually a substitute for work and making decisions. I am not one of these people. Meetings, including Cabinet meetings, are a bore and get in the way of doing things.

Scottish Executive Cabinet meetings were different and were so because of one man: Donald Dewar. I loved to watch him operate. He dominated the meetings: his knowledge, his analysis and his sheer intellect made him the towering figure in all our discussions. Cabinet was for most of the time a happy and collegiate place where we all worked well together.

Donald led by respect; even his enemies respected him. He would help the weak, work with the strong and ignore those with other agendas. He would sit above us like an old-fashioned schoolmaster reproachfully watching over his errant pupils, all of whom thought they were the ultimate politician (most politicians do).

He would watch with a passive calmness as Henry huffed and puffed, unable to hide his bitterness at not being Deputy First Minister and indeed First Minister. He smiled at Jack's tantrums over his lack of publicity. Jack believed that wherever he went there ought to be huge flag-waving crowds accompanied by the media singing his praises. Fat chance! And he greatly appreciated the support and contributions from Jim Wallace and Ross Finnie.

It was Isaac Newton who said he had seen further than his forefathers because he had stood on the shoulders of giants. All of us in his Cabinet were greatly privileged because we too stood on the shoulders of a giant: Donald Dewar. I hope we saw and continue to see further than our forefathers.

A Sense of Scotland — *Tom McCabe*

For what wasn't to be the last time, Donald Dewar caught me by surprise when, not more than two days after the first elections to the new Scottish Parliament, he phoned to offer me a place in his new Cabinet team. It was from this perspective that I was able to begin to appreciate fully his true character and abilities.

Though an essentially private and reserved individual, Donald held a remarkably strong awareness and perspective of the tremendously important phase in our history that he had led us into, and the anxiety over how this would develop never left him. That this great and broad awareness did exist was to be properly confirmed to me in the first few months of the Parliament.

I repeatedly saw him agonise over the early direction of our new Parliament and, using that marvellous intellect to rationalise all that was happening around us, he would again settle in his mind that this institution, which he had done so much to create, would indeed be the catalyst for Scotland to reach its untapped potential.

I well remember walking with him from the Scottish Parliament's first home in the Church of Scotland's Assembly Halls on the Mound after another of our early and typically tempestuous debates in which he had weathered opposition criticism and, not for the first time, won the argument.

He suddenly stopped and turned to me saying, 'You know, Tom, we've just debated in our own Parliament, we're here in the wonderful surroundings of our flourishing capital city and we're surrounded by visitors who want to come to Scotland to enjoy our culture, architecture and history.' 'How lucky are we,' he asked, 'to be the people who are at the centre of all this?'

This short but clear memory serves to indicate Donald's remarkable understanding of his own involvement in Scotland's history. He knew just how fortunate he was to be executing with such expertise a role in our country's progress, a role that it is all but impossible to underestimate, and I fully understand how fortunate I am to have worked so closely with such a man.

Real Devolution: In Housing

Duncan Maclennan

David Hume argued that the actions of individuals are driven by both passion and reason. There is now wide recognition that policies, to work, to deliver their intent, cannot solely be driven by passions and politics but that they must also embody evidence and reason. For more than half of the twentieth century, the squalid state of housing endured by as many as half of Glaswegians provoked the strongest of passions in those with a concern for social justice. Slums, overcrowding, squalid and mean streets impacted the health and well-being of adults and the opportunities and pathways of their children.

From the visionary Wheatley Acts of the 1920s onwards, Labour led the push for municipal public housing in the city and other parties followed. By the 1960s, the city of Glasgow was, with the exception of Hong Kong, the largest public landlord outside the Soviet bloc and almost two-thirds of Glaswegians lived in some form of public housing. This massive effort, which absorbed £7 billion (2001 prices) of government investment in the period 1953 to 1983, housed the population better but only in the short term. It also put in place a system of management that failed to maintain quality and create variety even prior to the Conservative cuts of the 1980s, albeit these cuts prevented solutions being implemented and reinforced concentrations of deprivation.

In consequence, Glasgow's public housing did not mesh well with the

180

economic, demographic and lifestyle shifts of the last 30 years, such as the penchant for home ownership or even the desire for tenant and community control. It created some high-quality neighbourhoods in the oldest areas of public housing but also left the city scarred with the construction of large estates (and more than 300 tower blocks) with little variety, poor design and low amenity.

Public housing had entered the soul of the Labour Party in the city and became a central pillar of Scottish socialism. But by the 1980s, the housing system had failed Glaswegians as state planning has the masses of Eastern Europe. By the late 1970s, the council owned some 8,000 unlettable homes and most were quickly demolished.

Glasgow housing policy was long on spent passion and short on reason. It was a system with little influence of heart, or indeed head. There was, in the halcyon days of the 1960s, no tenant voice, no community involvement. The council controlled housing and used it to shape its short-term political prospects through heavily politicised allocation, rent and maintenance policies. Andrew O'Hagan's novel *Our Fathers* conveys the spirit of these times as well as any social science research document.

Through the 1970s, in contrast, locally based, community-driven not-for-profit (NFPs) housing associations and cooperatives had led the renovation of older Glasgow. Arguably, they had made the greatest difference to city quality of any policy sector in the 25 years prior to devolution. After 1988, Conservative housing policies pushed for the expansion of these cooperatives and associations into taking ownership parts of rundown estates. Between 1988 and 2003, the City of Glasgow transferred some 17,000 units to such cooperatives and associations. Although the leader of the council was subsequently to claim, risibly, that associations had cherry-picked stock, these transfers almost invariably comprised the properties in the worst condition and in the poorest and most remote locations. Associations also built or renovated some 25,000 homes in older, private areas so that there was, by United Kingdom standards, a vigorous and successful NFP sector operating in the city.

The real challenge of the Glasgow context in the middle of May 1999 was that although there were thriving NFP and low-cost home ownership sectors in the city, the municipal housing sector was in cumulative crisis. The council had already raised rents to the highest levels in Scotland, for a demonstrably poor-quality product. Households were leaving to go to other landlords, to home ownership and to other places. For decades, the city had repaid little of the outstanding debt on its housing stock. With half of high rents devoted to repaying debt, the consequent squeeze on maintenance and management costs sharply curtailed the service quality for tenants. Then, inevitably, vacancies and demolitions rose. Demolition removed giro drops and drug dens but it did not remove the substantial debt outstanding for the now demolished assets. As the lucky, usually more affluent, tenants left, the shrinking number of those remaining had to share the unchanged total debt costs. This then set in train the next round of exits.

High rents, poor services, poor-quality and unpopular homes, with a likely repair bill in the region of £4 billion to £5 billion, constituted Glasgow City Council's legacy for the new Parliament. The stock, constructed at a cost of billions, had, according to the initial estimates of consultants, a value of £118 million and by the time more detailed studies were undertaken the real value of that municipal inheritance was an estimated minus £600 million to £700 million.

Prior to 1999, the transfer of Glasgow's poorest homes to NFPs involved Scottish Homes not only paying positive prices for redundant assets but also then incurring rehabilitation bills of £50,000 to £70,000 per unit. For much of the decade, Glasgow (with 14 per cent of Scotland's population) had absorbed around 40 per cent of the Scottish Homes budget. It was manifestly clear that the Glasgow housing quality crisis could not have been dealt with via this route unless there was a 20-year programme with doubled Scottish housing policy expenditure. And that was simply a theoretical calculation, as it is likely that quality decline and abandonment would have grown cumulatively. Trickle transfer, which was advocated by many Scottish Nationalists and some housing commentators, was simply either not fast enough or too expensive for the Scottish budget to sustain.

Creating Change

The notion that Glasgow City Council might transfer its stock evolved in the 1980s. Stock-transfer opponents had always, incorrectly, seen it as emerging out of the policies of Scottish Homes. In fact, the Grieve Inquiry of 1983 had reached the conclusion that the city needed to transfer at least 40 per cent of its homes. In 1989, the board of Scottish Homes decided to transfer Scottish Homes' own public stock, including about 16,000 units in Glasgow. Although the decision may have been consistent with

182

Conservative beliefs at the time, the board initiated transfer policies because it believed that since its primary role was to promote local and community ownership of homes it was absurd that it should sit in Edinburgh as landlord for stock spread from Campbeltown to Wick. Moreover, the revenues from disposal to these non-market providers would help provide decent homes for households on waiting lists and on poor estates. The Labour supporters on Scottish Homes Board, and there were at least three in the period concerned, all supported that policy and were right to do so. For them, stock transfer was never privatisation but rather an efficient route to creating a more European and community-led style of social housing and subsequent evaluations of tenant and staff outcomes confirm that proposition.

By 1999, Glasgow City Council had decided that it would bow to incentives and pressure from the Scottish Office, which Donald led, to transfer its housing stock. However, the initial transfer proposal contained little about real system change and community control and was largely a rebadging of the existing council service. There was no system change, no devolution to communities envisaged and certainly no intent to engage with or use the talents of the existing, growing and popular NFP sector.

As the Parliament formed, the real challenge was no longer whether or not the council would vote for change. Rather, it was whether tenants would support the shift, whether the banks would fund the likely programmes, and the extent to which the outcomes would make the Glasgow housing system diverse and contestable. If the policy initiative had failed, it would have derailed the main thrust of Scottish housing policy; it would have left the Parliament facing an impossibly large bill to put Glasgow's housing back in shape and it would have led to a reduction in Labour's vote in the city. Opponents of stock transfer may care to note that the party's share of the vote increased in Glasgow more than nationally during the 2003 Scottish elections.

The equivalent initiative in England, in size and complexity, was the proposal to transfer Birmingham's 80,000 council homes to a trust. That proposal failed and was rejected by tenants in a roughly 60–40 split, the mirror image of the Glasgow outcome. Creating community ownership was a good example of where devolution to Holyrood and the leadership of Donald Dewar produced better policy proposals and more creative outcomes than south of the border (and that conclusion was shared by the team that completed the inquiry into Birmingham's housing in the wake of their failed vote).

How did Donald and devolution make a difference? There has been a tendency to cast Donald as the clever, reasoning First Minister with the implication that perhaps passion and delivery were not his hallmarks. He knew the municipal versus community debates (beloved of some new Labour intellectuals) but they rarely featured in our discussions of 1999 and 2000. Nor, albeit that he was evidently, often visibly, scunnered by the intrigues and incompetence of the city Labour Party, was he inclined to attack old municipalism. Rather, Donald simply wanted to change Glasgow's housing system.

He was well aware of the awfulness of housing provision and housing services in his constituency and how, after almost a century of active municipal housing, his constituents were still trapped in cruel habitations. He liked the association sector, because in the housing cooperative areas of Drumchapel he had worked with the local community to begin to change their places for the better. Even prior to 1997 he was prepared to defend Scottish Homes' outcomes from COSLA critics. Practical interest in delivering social justice rather than 'new ideas for new times' drove his interest. Fundamentals, not fashions, were his concern.

His contributions to the process of change were invaluable. It was particularly important that Donald unleashed his Minister for Communities to give, for a year at least, her fairly undivided attention to shaping a better proposal and arguing a wider case for change. Donald really enabled Wendy Alexander to shape ideas that mattered.

Donald's direct involvement was in the crunch points that would occur in the process between the Executive and Glasgow City Council or the STUC. He trusted his ministers, advisers and officials to make progress without his constant intervention. When the Executive rejected the council's 'trust' proposal and created a partnership to develop the notion of the Glasgow Housing Association, Donald made clear his resolve to the leader of the council (for whom he had some personal regard). And it was Donald's support that gave encouragement to significant senior officials from outside the Glasgow council sector to play a role in developing the GHA: for instance, Bob Allan (the former Chief Executive of Clackmannan), who did so much to make the early proposals of interest to tenants.

The housing-association model attracted antipathy from leading councillors and their officials. Yet, when negotiations between the council and the Executive became dysfunctional, Donald had an uncanny knack of recognising when the issues were real or just bruised egos. If it were the latter, there would be a short discussion or a longer phone call always containing irrefutable arguments for better behaviour. This typically worked.

Creating the change did not simply involve using influence within the Labour Party. Donald always listened to the advice received from the able civil servants who supported the process. My experience was that we sat in discussions with civil servants as equals and for Donald what mattered was the strength of the argument rather than its provenance. This led to good relations between advisers and civil servants involved in the Glasgow process. After Donald died, there was a tendency for some senior civil servants to try to begin to fill the role of special adviser, simply because there were too few special advisers to serve individual ministers adequately. The Scottish press should look further afield to see what support ministers really need to be effective.

Delivering a step change in investment and control required both a financially viable proposal supported by private lenders' and, of course, tenants' approval. Donald launched the GHA proposal in early April 2000 at the Royal Concert Hall. As we left the arena, Donald confided to me that the good reception (for his excellent speech) was all very well but that it would take at least two miracles for the proposal to succeed: the tenants would have to vote for it and the banks would have to agree to fund it. (I was, in general, usually more optimistic than Donald but on this occasion I felt that two miracles might have been an underestimate.)

In terms of making these miracles work, Donald allowed the proposal to develop a public-finance argument for short-term extra support to achieve longer-term spending economies. However, the ultimately critical financial aspects of the proposal, namely the agreement of the Chancellor of the Exchequer to write off Glasgow's billion-pound housing debt and so give real support and new autonomy to some of the United Kingdom's poorest households, was largely the work of Wendy Alexander. Donald's role was critical in discussions, separately, with the Chief Executives of the Royal Bank and the Bank of Scotland. They could see how the project could work and, in turn, Donald took comfort from their interest. This was no mean achievement with £4 billion of borrowing and £700 million of peak debt in question. Would it happen now?

Donald's understanding of Glasgow, all its networks and its people in the poorest communities, was also critical in giving reassurance to tenants that they were being offered something real and better and different. Citizens and community groups in Glasgow had a high regard for Donald but they also really liked him. At the end of January 2000, Donald reappeared in Meridian Court from a bruising and bilious morning encounter with the more conservative and illiberal Scottish press fired up by the debate on the repeal of section 2A. He was tired, already ill, of course, and deeply despondent about how to make progress in terms of new politics. Later that afternoon he went, still tired, to the Mitchell Library to address an anniversary event of the housing association sector in the city. He was given a standing ovation as he entered the hall and when he left. He spoke with passion and with all his reason, too. He changed people's minds; he gave them a bigger vision of what they could do. When it came to the tenant ballot, in which the council and its staff frequently behaved uncooperatively, it was these activists, these people who had changed their communities, these people who had been labelled as cherry pickers, these people who had been harried as privatisers by the SSP, these hearts and minds, that persuaded council tenants that they could do the same, too. A lot of the Yes ballot was a vote for Donald, by then deceased.

Continuing Commitments

Donald's leadership, allied to Wendy Alexander's vision and relentless energy, contributed directly to the Yes vote and the commitment of the financial institutions to support the Glasgow Housing Association. They created the potential to change Glasgow's housing systems and outcomes for the better. The delivery of that change has been in the hands of their successors. After Donald's death, and with ministerial changes, there was some significant dilution in the final form agreed for GHA. For instance, it has always made little sense to me that in a project seeking variety and choice that GHA was given a new development programme and the sense of contestability was further eroded by bringing the DLO back into the organisation. That said, subsequent ministers battled relentlessly to keep the project on track and Margaret Curran's Glasgow nous and community commitment were essential to the final completion of the process.

The GHA currently has an outstanding leader with aims to deliver the community-based system that Donald and others envisaged. But GHA now operates in an environment where the Executive bureaucracy seems to be little interested in what changing tenure involves; they really focus on stock transfer rather than creating real community ownership. Communities Scotland, I believe, has failed to be the innovative and influential housing change agent that Scottish Homes was. Scotland's housing and neighbourhood renewal policy innovation capacity has slumped alarmingly in the years post-devolution. Equally, there is now much ambiguity as to whether the community and local devolution aspects of stock transfer lie at the heart of the Executive's housing policy or whether they are seen as simply an evil necessity enforced by spending rules.

We lost the man, we may have momentarily lost the vision but we have not yet lost GHA. Drumchapel is demonstrably better than it was a decade ago. There was reason in the passion.

And Holyrood

Bernard Ponsonby

His heart was in developing a contemporary icon. He wanted to make a landmark building that would identify that particular moment in Scotland's history. – Joan O'Connor, Member, Designer Selection Panel.

When Donald Dewar died on 11 October 2000, it was difficult to offer a considered judgement on his achievements as a politician in government. For one, he had only served in high office for a little over three years. Much of that time had been taken up with establishing the Scottish Parliament. Death was to rob him of the opportunity of changing the nation in a way consistent with his long-held political values.

And yet at the time of his death his reputation was in danger of being battered beyond repair. The issue that led to this was the fiasco of the Holyrood building project. His opponents accused him of vanity in making the site-selection process a matter of personal rather than collective political choice. He stood accused of misleading Parliament and the public and of doing a botched job that undermined the very institutions he had spent a lifetime trying to create.

My interest in the Holyrood building stems from reporting nightly on the proceedings of the Fraser Inquiry on behalf of Scottish Television. The observations in this essay do not seek to explore what Dewar's motivations might have been in taking the decisions he arrived at. Nor do they offer any judgements on the architectural merits of Holyrood. Rather, it critically assesses his role in the fiasco by drawing conclusions from an abundance of published evidence.

Donald Dewar saw the building of Scotland's Parliament as part of the process of devolution. And he seems equally clear that the task fell to him to drive the process forward. The then Permanent Secretary Sir Russell Hillhouse claimed that the Secretary of State for Scotland saw it as his duty to 'endow' devolution with a really good building, fit for the purpose of shaping the new Scotland.

There had been a working assumption on the part of just about everyone that the Calton Hill complex of the Old Royal High School and St Andrew's House would provide the home for the first Scottish Parliament in 300 years. The site was redolent of a debate that dominated Scottish politics in the latter half of the twentieth century. It is testimony to how little thinking went on in pre-devolved Scotland about the shape of post-devolved Scotland that no one seriously asked the question: can this site deliver what is required?

Dewar did pose this question to his officials when he paid a visit to the site on 30 May 1997, just weeks after the Labour landslide. From that meeting it was clear that civil servants would have to explore the possibility of other sites. By the time the Devolution White Paper was published on 24 July 1997, the 'serious disadvantages' of the Calton Hill site were openly referred to. And yet at that point no one seriously thought the Parliament would go anywhere other than Calton Hill.

The more immediate task for Dewar was not site selection but what to say about the cost of the new Parliament building. The White Paper talked of figures ranging from between £10 million and £40 million. With hindsight, it was a mistake to put such a broad range of figures in the White Paper. The £40 million figure was to be a millstone that would launch a thousand negative headlines in the subsequent years.

Indeed, he seemed overly sensitive to keeping everything within a tight budget. Given the status of a national legislature, he could have been tempted to ditch the Scottish reputation for tightfistedness and simply made the argument that it would have to cost a substantial sum if it were to properly reflect the aspirations the people had for the new institution.

Site-Selection Process

By August of 1997, a long list of sites had been drawn up by Edinburgh City Council. Ironically, it contained the Holyrood site but it was dismissed as being too constrained. Two months later, the ever-cautious Secretary of State for Scotland accepted the advice of officials and postponed a decision on site selection until the end of the year. This would allow for design feasibility, environmental and traffic studies to be completed.

Three locations emerged from the site-selection process: the Calton Hill complex, a site adjacent to Victoria Quay in Leith and one at Morrison Street, Haymarket, in the west end of Edinburgh.

On 8 December, it was announced that Holyrood was being added to the shortlist of sites, after a chartered surveyor informed the Scottish Office that Scottish and Newcastle Brewers were willing to sell. So, was the whole process fixed? Rigged in favour of Holyrood as has been suggested? Was Dewar by this time working to the ABC principle (Anywhere But Calton Hill) in an attempt to drive the institution away from this 'nationalist shibboleth'?

The evidence doesn't support the conspiracy. The feasibility study on Holyrood was certainly commissioned quickly but as Lord Fraser was subsequently to judge 'it was only marginally less detailed and of no significant qualitative difference from the studies for the other site options'.

Indeed, when all four sites were being considered, Dewar's Private Secretary Ken Thomson observed that he was 'genuinely' torn between Calton Hill and Holyrood. Figures were put on all four sites, with Holyrood emerging as the cheapest option and Calton Hill the most expensive. Alex Salmond is absolutely right to point out that these figures were not produced from a level playing field. But there is no evidence that Dewar instructed his officials to provide figures to make Holyrood a fait accompli.

There were practical as well as iconic reasons why Dewar at this time would have steered away from Calton Hill. The Old Royal High School was exactly that. Its listed status compromised opportunities for a complete overhaul. Likewise, neighbouring old St Andrew's House was also listed. In practice, the Calton Hill site by then under consideration would have required straddling the two listed buildings, with old St Andrew's House, in all probability, becoming a building shared between the legislative and the executive arms of government, something that Dewar was keen to avoid.

Holyrood was unveiled as the chosen site on 9 January 1998. The decision enraged the SNP, who felt that the referendum consensus had needlessly been shattered. Undoubtedly, Dewar as Secretary of State had the right to take the decision. He was correct in his view that to leave the eventual site to the new Parliament would have produced a row befitting the worst excesses of the politics of the old Scotland. For one, the SNP would not have gone to anywhere other than Calton Hill.

Much of the criticism of Dewar at this time centred on allegations that his judgements were impulsive and driven by vanity and not objective reasoning. Those close to him may well have wished that at times his judgements had been made impulsively. The truth of the matter is that he was simply someone who refused to make decisions without first of all exhausting all the alternatives and interrogating all arguments.

It has been suggested that there was a link between the Holyrood site and cost increases. However, as John Spencely, who conducted an independent probe into the Holyrood fiasco, observed, none of the subsequent cost overruns was directly attributable to Holyrood as a site.

Designer Competition

Seventy architectural practices returned pre-qualification questionnaires en route to the appointment of an architect for this most historic of projects. A panel had been appointed, chaired by Mr Dewar, to oversee the competition that would lead to the selection of a designer.

The winners of that competition were announced on 22 June 1998. The Catalan architect Enric Miralles in partnership with Edinburgh-based RMJM were declared the winners. The process that led to their appointment is still at the time of writing the subject of controversy, with the European Commission effectively charging the United Kingdom government with a breach of procurement rules.

It is little wonder that Europe has demanded answers. At this point in the Holyrood story, a recurring theme gets into full gear. Dewar was consistently let down by officials who displayed a truly breathtaking mix of ignorance, incompetence and arrogance. Little wonder that Lord Fraser in his inquiry report says of one aspect of the designer selection process 'it appears to me to have been sloppy, unprofessional and fraught with danger'.

Lord Fraser's report into Holyrood was an exercise in safe politics. Although generally sound and logical, he bottled making sterner judgements which are merited by the available evidence. One of these relates to the breach in EU rules in terms of the appointment of the architects.

Dewar relied heavily on the advice of Dr John Gibbons. He acted not only as secretariat to the designer selection panel but also as an expert member of it. Didn't it strike anyone that this might involve a conflict of interest? Indeed, Dr Gibbons was central in driving a flawed process. Miralles was initially ranked 44th out of 70 for entirely sound reasons to do with the size of his practice and his relative experience. Yet he was put on a long list of 20 practices at the suggestion of Dr Gibbons. Miralles made it to the final 12. RMJM did not. And yet it appears the shotgun wedding of Miralles and RMJM was in part at Dr Gibbons' instigation. To make matters worse officials visited some practices that were on the long list of 12 but not others. EU law dictates a transparency and equality of approach, which does not seem to be evident here.

Another potentially botched job, which interests the European Commission and may yet end up in the civil courts in Scotland, concerns the appointment of Bovis as construction managers for Holyrood. Much of this sorry episode was acted out away from Dewar's desk. Bovis won a contract despite submitting the highest tender. They were put back on to a shortlist and allowed to vary their tender, an opportunity denied to another firm. Indeed, McAlpine, who had submitted the lowest bid, were not afforded the opportunity of a debrief, which arguably they were entitled to as a matter of law as well as courtesy.

The Bovis controversy was the catalyst that led to the resignation of Mr Bill Armstrong as the first project manager. Armstrong's departure was only reported to Dewar when the issue was the subject of media comment. Also hidden from Dewar was Armstrong's parting shot to project sponsor Mrs Barbara Doig. It is worth quoting from because it is an incredibly insightful epistle to have been written in late 1998. He laments that 'a stand must be taken to bring Miralles to heel or to accept his inadequacies. He does not believe he has any. The programme will drift, the cost will increase, the design team will make claims, the contractors will make claims and the project will become a disaster.'

Cost Overruns

When Holyrood was unveiled as the site of Scotland's new Parliament, Dewar gave more definitive costings. The budget would be £50 million but that excluded site acquisition, VAT and fees. The decision to separate construction costs from overall budget has to be viewed as a bad political call by Mr Dewar. First, it would allow a hostile media as well as political opponents to talk about the £50 million figure as a budget rather than a construction cost. It may have been a wicked misrepresentation on their part to deliberately represent a construction cost as an agreed budget but it was entirely predictable that they would. Indeed, when the figure of £50 million was put in the public domain it was already known that the 'add ons' would take the budget to over £80 million. It would have been good politics to talk about the higher rather than the lower figure.

Dewar's Role

Separating construction costs from overall budget was a presentational misjudgement by Dewar that is easy to criticise with the benefit of hindsight. What we also know is that there were policy decisions taken on this project that were disastrous and yet were not taken by him. The behaviour of civil servants in this regard is nothing short of scandalous. But for the Fraser Inquiry their incompetence might have been buried in dusty files in the corridors of officialdom for a period of 30 years.

The key to explaining why the project got out of hand relates to the decision to opt for a procurement method known as construction management. The key benefit of using this approach is that buildings with tight timescales can be erected quickly. Construction work starts before finished designs are in place. The construction manager (Bovis) timetables works packages to deliver a building within a tight timescale. But construction management, if mismanaged, can spectacularly backfire. If the architect is temperamental (and he was), if the client changes (and it did), if changes to finished designs are ordered (and they were), a roller-coaster of spiralling costs is one of a number of inevitabilities.

For such a fundamental decision, ministerial approval should have been sought. And despite early agreement that the pros and cons of different construction methods should be placed before Donald Dewar, they never were. The design team, made up of civil servants and construction professionals, pressed ahead with construction management in July 1998. Mr Dewar was left in the position where he was the client for a building being constructed using a controversial method he knew nothing about and did not sanction.

Lord Fraser's judgement on this matter is short and very much to the point. 'It beggars belief that ministers were not asked to approve the proposal to adopt construction management.' It would be absurd to suggest that civil servants simply decided to bypass the Secretary of State as a matter of design. But it speaks volumes for their incompetence that not one of them thought to run it by the boss. Did Dewar come to regret not having a plan in place to shake up the mandarins who would be charged with delivering public policy?

The other, and politically more serious, issue where he was misled relates to the spiralling costs of the Parliament. The Civil Service exercise in denying the obvious and telling the boss only what they thought the boss wanted to hear led to an inadvertent but systematic deception of Parliament and the public over the true cost of the Parliament building.

On 17 June 1999, in an emotionally charged debate in the Parliament's temporary home on the Mound, an 'under fire' First Minister, just a matter of months into the job, misled Parliament. His civil servants told him that by this date construction costs stood at £62 million. This is a figure Mr Dewar held to in the debate. It was worse than hopelessly optimistic. It was hopelessly wrong.

The Holyrood cost consultants Davis, Langdon and Everest (DLE) had told civil servants that the true figure at the time of the debate stood at £89 million. Civil servants believed that £27 million could be assessed as risk and could therefore be 'managed out' of the budget. It was a defence relied upon by project sponsor Mrs Barbara Doig and by the then Permanent Secretary Sir Muir Russell. It beggars belief that mandarins thought that £27 million could be managed away when the cost consultants and construction managers were saying quite categorically that it could not. Perhaps Mrs Doig and Sir Muir should have fired DLE and Bovis, since the logic of their position was that they could manage away costs that professionals could not.

The following year when John Spencely published his independent report into the state of the project he put the construction cost at this time at £89 million. On reading the report, Dewar realised he had misled Parliament the previous June. He contemplated resignation. That is hardly surprising. Dewar's instincts would have been to shoulder the blame personally. There was no greater crime in his book than a government minister arguing a position based on lies.

The charge of the Conservatives and the SNP is that the project was a mess at handover and that the cost overruns were due to decisions taken by Donald Dewar in the early days of the project. The project was indeed a mess at handover but the cost overruns principally related to the cack-handed way construction management was being mismanaged.

There is legitimate criticism of Donald Dewar to be made. The £40 million figure should have been removed from the Devolution White Paper. The presentational decision to talk of construction costs and not a full budget was also a mistake. He was central to the appointment of an architect who, it could be argued, was more a hindrance than help.

But on the big political charges history will judge him not guilty, as indeed Lord Fraser has done. Alex Salmond has always been clear not to hang the misdemeanours of civil servants around Mr Dewar's neck and for that he is to be commended. It is also quite legitimate of Mr Salmond to criticise the politicisation of the site process. In a sense, it would be a dereliction of duty on his part not to criticise that. That being said, Mr Dewar was quite within his right to press ahead as he saw fit.

If all of this reads a bit too enthusiastically like a 'defence of Donald' contribution perhaps I should own up to a number of things. I first met Donald Dewar in 1981. By the time of his death, I had interviewed him on hundreds of occasions. Most of those exchanges were business-like, many were robust and on at least a couple of occasions very bad tempered. He was not a friend of mine. Nor was I a friend of his. Our relationship was professional. He probably found me at times exasperating, a thought that leaves me entirely comfortable.

I did, however, have great admiration for him. His intellectual range was colossal. His basic belief in social justice was unshakable and genuinely heartfelt in a man who was frequently a 'cold fish'.

It is a great pity that he was lost to Scotland at a relatively young age. Devolution has struggled to give a radical cutting edge purpose to government. And yes, he struggled too. But with his capacity for hard work and determination to do the right thing by the right people, he might just have been a very unusual kind of hero had he lived.

History's Judgement[1]

Tom Devine

The title of this essay may seem somewhat pretentious. No full or measured judgement on Donald Dewar's life and achievement will be possible for some years. The perspective of time and distance is needed for more impartiality and balance, while the vital private and administrative documentation which is the very stuff of the historian's trade are not yet available for scrutiny in a systematic fashion.

That said, however, I have little doubt that this volume will be of real value to future scholars. It contains the views, often frankly expressed, of some of Donald Dewar's closest friends, political associates and Civil Service colleagues. The book will be essential reading, for instance, for those who wish to understand the rocky road to devolution and the establishment of the new Scottish Parliament: the single most important constitutional change in the relations between the nations of the British Isles since the emergence of the Irish Free State in 1922. Two of Dewar's closest advisers on the framing of the Scotland Act, Wendy Alexander and Murray Elder, feature in the collection, as do John Sewel, Derry Irvine and Jim Wallace, all of whom were at the heart of the devolution process and the development of coalition government in the Scottish Parliament and Executive thereafter. Further, the essays by the journalist Peter Jones contain off-the-record comments from senior civil servants who worked closely with Dewar in that crucial period between his appointment as

Secretary of State for Scotland in 1997 and the formal opening by the Queen of the Parliament in July 1999.

These essays and others contain invaluable material which casts new light on that critical phase in Scottish political history, though the book cannot be the last word in the subject for the reasons given above. However, it does extend knowledge of the Dewar years much further than the often pietistic and platitudinous obituaries which appeared after his premature and untimely death in 2000. Then there was much talk of the 'Father of the Nation' and the man above all others who had finally achieved devolved government for Scotland. But both in the press and the wider media there was previously little specific evidence or detail to support these assertions or shed much light on what had actually gone on behind the scenes during the complex process of constructing an epoch-making set of constitutional reforms. For the first time, some at least of this story has been revealed in earlier essays. The purpose here is to examine this evidence from the perspective of the academic historian. In particular, the central objective is to reassess the contribution Donald Dewar made to the achievement of devolution: how far was his role exaggerated in the inevitable national outpouring of grief which followed his sudden death? To what extent can we be specific about the role he played given the number of other significant figures deeply involved in the process? Where sits the role of the individual in this context of wider long-term historical forces?

It is in this last respect that the book is at its weakest. Predictably, perhaps, given the focus on Dewar himself, there is a tendency to see the road to devolution as one constructed in the late 1990s and built on the interplay of leading personalities wheeling and dealing in committee. As I shall stress later, this aspect of the process was indeed crucial but it is only part of the story. To understand Dewar's role properly we need to see it in context and against a longer historical time span. His achievement depended ultimately on the changes which had occurred in Scottish society and Scottish relations with the Westminster government since the failed devolution referendum of 1979.

Then some suspected that a piece of inadequate legislation had been cobbled together in a cynical and expedient attempt to see off a resurgent SNP. Others, however, viewed the result as an abysmal failure of nerve by the Scots and a comprehensive refutation of the claim that there existed any deep-seated national demand for a Scottish Parliament. In his celebrated cartoon in the *Glasgow Herald*, James Turnbull brilliantly captured the mood of national recrimination when he drew a lion representing Scotland refusing to leave its cage even though the door had been flung open. The caption read simply, 'I'm feart'.

The contrast between the late 1990s and the debacle of 1979 could not have been more stark or dramatic. The divided nation of the 1970s was replaced by one where a strong consensus for devolution was firmly in place across virtually the whole of Scotland. This was the new context in which leading figures like Donald Dewar were now able to deliver a fresh constitutional settlement, a task which, whatever their talents, seemed improbable two decades earlier. The Scottish middle and professional classes, previously riven with doubt and uncertainty, were now supportive. Leading institutions such as the universities, vehemently in the opposition camp in 1979, warmly embraced the project. The business community, apart from a few isolated voices, made little protest and indeed committed itself to working with the new Parliament. The silence from all those traditional supporters of inflexible unionism was now almost audible. A sea change had occurred in Scottish opinion which may, at root, have been influenced and exploited by senior pro-devolution politicians but was not created by them. That transformation in mood was generated by deeper forces and these should be briefly described to place Donald Dewar's contribution in a wider historical panorama.

Scotland experienced a traumatic process of de-industrialisation in the early 1980s that brought pain and suffering to many communities. Decline and adjustment were inevitable but the process was hastened by the refusal of the Conservative government under Margaret Thatcher to provide the kind of state support and protection to which Scottish industry had been accustomed since 1945. Between 1976 and 1987, manufacturing capacity in Scotland fell by almost one-third and by an even greater proportion in the west central heartlands of heavy industry.

At the same time, a cleavage opened up between Scottish and English voting patterns. While the Conservative vote north of the border fell into terminal decline, the Tories in the Midlands and south of England continued to pile up huge majorities and establish a veritable monopoly on power at Westminster. Mrs Thatcher's governments rejected the Union as a partnership to be worked out through a consensus and as a discussion combining Scottish and London interests. No account was taken of the consistent opposition to Conservatism in Scotland. From the Tory perspective, the cancer of state control, corporatism and welfare dependency would have to be surgically removed there as elsewhere in the United Kingdom.

Indeed, Mrs Thatcher soon showed her utter contempt for the subtleties of the Union relationship by imposing the poll tax first in Scotland, as an experiment in what soon came to be regarded as a detested form of punitive and regressive taxation. The attack on the corporate state went down almost equally badly, not least because the Scots had gained more than most from the welfare-state reforms after 1945 and regarded the new market philosophy as destructive of the community values they saw as central to their national identity.

All this gave a new impetus to the cause of home rule. The Union, which had been viewed as a benign force from 1945, bestowing welfare improvement and rising living standards, was now also seen to have the potential for repression. Nor was there any machinery in the British constitution through which specifically Scottish interests could be safeguarded in the event of permanent English majorities at Westminster. Under earlier governments, this problem had rarely surfaced. Now, the Scottish people were brought face to face with the awesome reality of the absolute authority of the Crown in Parliament. As Canon Kenyon Wright, chair of the Scottish Constitutional Convention, put it, 'We realised that our real enemy was not a particular government, whatever its colour, but a constitutional system. We came to understand that our central need, if we were to be governed justly and democratically, was not just to change the government but to change the rules.'

But it was only after another Conservative victory, in 1987, that the movement 'to change the rules' began in earnest. The Campaign for a Scottish Assembly (CSA) had kept the torch of devolution alight after the fiasco of 1979 but for much of the 1980s, apart from a few politicians such as Donald Dewar and John Smith, it was virtually a voice crying in the wilderness. In 1988, a group of 'prominent Scots' appointed by the CSA issued 'A Claim of Right for Scotland', arguing the intellectual case for a parliament and recommended the establishment of the Constitutional Convention drawn from all the political parties and Scottish institutions.

It was at this point that Dewar emerged, not simply as a pro-devolutionist, which he had been throughout his political career, but as a significant force influencing key events.

Even if the new political climate in Scotland generated a renewed interest in home rule, there was still no certainty or inevitability that constitutional change would be delivered. British political history is littered with examples of a party's commitment to a particular policy which for one reason or another fails to reach the statute books. Indeed, a devolved parliament or assembly for Scotland had been promoted on and off since Victorian times. In the end, several events and personalities combined to convert the probability of constitutional reform in the 1990s into a certain result. Not the least of these and the essential precondition for devolution, given robust Tory opposition to the policy, was the massive Labour landslide in 1997. Another key factor, however, was the signal contribution of Donald Campbell Dewar.

Carol Craig makes the salient point in her essay that Dewar was exactly the right man in the right place at the right time. When appointed Secretary of State for Scotland in the new Blair government of 1997, it is difficult to think of any other senior Labour politician who had the same commitment, background, stature or aptitude to deliver devolution.

Dewar's pro-devolution credentials were impeccable and went back as far as his student days at Glasgow University, much longer even than his friend and close colleague, the late John Smith. Jimmy Gordon, in his contribution to this book, recalls the Scottish Labour Party conference of 1970 which followed soon after the loss of Hamilton to the SNP in 1967 and further SNP successes in the local elections in 1968. These Labour defeats, in Gordon's words, 'sent shockwaves through the party which made any rational discussion of devolution seem almost traitorous'. Only two Labour MPs spoke out in favour of giving some consideration to constitutional change: Dewar and the late professor of politics and charismatic politician, John P. Mackintosh. Mackintosh's early death left Dewar virtually alone for some years as an enthusiastic standard bearer of home rule. Alf Young reminds us that 'too many in the Labour Party [in the 1970s] either opposed the whole idea of devolution or saw it as a tactical ploy to see off the nationalist advance'.

Furthermore, Dewar was an interesting mix of loyal unionist and cultural nationalist. Dewar's interest in and knowledge of Scottish history and culture was vast. Forging the link between the Scottish past and the Scottish present came easily to him, as he revealed in his eloquent address at the opening of the Scottish Parliament, a speech that was replete with historical reference and allusion. Equally important, however, was his unionism. Under Dewar, Scottish devolution could never be a nationalist project, a stepping stone on the road to independence. Home rule was meant to strengthen the Union rather than weaken it. Donald Dewar's staunch unionism helped to ease the fears of those in Westminster who suspected the whole scheme was designed to appease the Nationalists and might threaten the break-up of the United Kingdom.

Finally, Dewar was one of the few senior Labour politicians who could work the system both in London and Scotland. Linkage between the two was essential to the rapid and effective delivery of devolution legislation after 1997. Dewar was a respected House of Commons man and his time as a Labour Whip had ensured that he was well connected at Westminster. But his knowledge of the Scottish scene and reputation there as a political 'fixer' within the Labour Party were also important assets. Dewar, above all his peers, does seem to have had a long-term commitment to home rule and a focus on its delivery. His political opponent Malcolm Rifkind observes in his essay: 'Donald Dewar often seemed a rather lonely figure not because his colleagues in the Shadow Cabinet disagreed with him [about constitutional reform] but because they could not be bothered to spend much time on the issue. Gordon Brown, Robin Cook and John Reid were far more concerned with trying to demolish Margaret Thatcher or John Major than with the campaign for constitutional reform in Scotland. This was not just because the key to reform lay with winning power at Westminster. It also reflected their own political ambitions. As we saw when the Parliament at Holyrood was created, only Donald made the trek north. Every other of his Cabinet colleagues opted to remain at Westminster.'

It was perhaps inevitable at the time of Donald Dewar's tragic and early death that the media would often give the impression that he virtually alone had fathered the Scottish Parliament. The distance of a few years has allowed for a more balanced perspective on this key issue in Scottish history. As Dewar himself would have been the first to admit, devolution was the product of much longer-term processes and the work of many people. A fundamental difference from 1979 was not simply the crucial advantage of a huge parliamentary majority for the pro-devolution governing party but the political will at the highest levels of that party to achieve constitutional reform. Tony Blair may not have been an instinctive devolutionist but, as Murray Elder points out in his essay: '. . . the "unfinished business" legacy of John Smith, public expectation and the long established commitment of Gordon Brown . . . and others made it impossible to dilute the policy'. Critically also, Blair backed Dewar in the contentious issue of proportional representation for the new Parliament.

The controversial idea of a two-question referendum to endorse the devolution proposals emerged not from Donald Dewar, who was initially unconvinced, but from a committee set up by Blair in 1996 whose recommendations received the full backing of the future Prime Minister. Gordon Brown's role in the process is rarely mentioned but, as John Sewel argues, Dewar's task was made easier by having such a powerful ally at the heart of government who also possessed strong pro-devolution credentials.

In addition, one of the most interesting new aspects to emerge from this book was the role of the Lord Chancellor, Derry Irvine. Irvine chaired the key Cabinet forum, the Devolution to Scotland, Wales and the Regions Committee (DSWR), through which both the White Paper and the subsequent Bill were negotiated. The press predicted personal conflict between them because, 25 years before, Dewar's wife, Alison, had left him for Irvine, taking with her the couple's two children. In his essay, Irvine is at pains to quash the rumour that any disharmony existed. He stresses that the scrutiny and debate in DSWR were indeed intense and demanding but according to him it helped that 'Donald and I were equal true believers in devolution' (though that did not necessarily mean agreement on the course which devolution would take). Plainly the evidence now suggests the two men did work closely together. Irvine also made an important contribution by drafting the chapter in the Devolution White Paper describing the proposed Scottish Executive's relationship with Europe. It was important, too, that Derry Irvine was close to Blair and apparently had, himself, the personal ambition to leave behind him the legacy of a Lord Chancellor who had successfully reformed the constitution.

Nor should the role of the Civil Service be forgotten. A team of the 'brightest and best in Whitehall', the Constitution Secretariat, was put together to piece together the complex legislation and prepare the detailed briefing papers for discussions inside the DSWR. It paralleled a similar high-powered group of civil servants which was drawn from the Scottish Office.

Yet, despite the many hands involved and the favourable political context, the Dewar influence on events remained central, as those who were closest to the action have readily conceded in previous essays. This was the case in at least four respects. First, his decision to encourage Labour participation in the Scottish Constitutional Convention was crucial to the establishment of a wider political consensus for a parliament. Since the debacle of 1979, Dewar was conscious of the need to widen the appeal of a new settlement, to avoid the perception which had helped to wreck the earlier attempt, in Murray Elder's words, the Parliament as 'a central-belt Labour council writ large'. This decision flew in the face of much Scottish Labour opinion at the time, as did Dewar's commitment to support proportional representation for the new parliament. Both initiatives demonstrated that this intrinsically cautious man was capable of decisive action.

Second, Dewar's personal credibility and the widespread respect for him among the general public helped to achieve a clear winning result in the referendum campaign. Even political opponents such as Alex Salmond agreed that the Dewar factor was important in this respect.

Third, Dewar put his own personal stamp on the White Paper which contained the basic formula for devolution and differed not only from the blueprint of the Scottish Constitutional Convention but also from the first drafts proposed by the Civil Service teams. These were rapidly restructured by Dewar and his special advisers, Murray Elder and Wendy Alexander, over a few days of intensive work. The subsequent draft went far beyond the timid proposals of 1979 by suggesting that every area was to be devolved other than those specifically reserved, a complete reversal of the earlier idea which spelt out the devolved areas on a case-by-case basis.

Fourth, all this then had to be argued through the DSWR and the result achieved speedily in order to prevent any rearguard action by the 'Whitehall Warriors' and their departments, who might start to oppose any diminution in their own powers and responsibilities. The essays by Elder, Sewel, Irvine and Alexander all concur on the taxing nature of the discussions in that committee, which contained some pretty sceptical ministerial voices. Equally, however, they also agree that, at the end of the day, Dewar achieved virtually all his objectives.

This essay has tried to provide an interim verdict on Donald Dewar's contribution to an epochal constitutional change in Scotland's history. It recognises that devolution was far from being a one-man band. It also acknowledges, however, that Donald Dewar's place in history is undeniably secure as the pre-eminent architect of that final settlement.

Donald's Legacy . . .

At a front bench meeting when we were in Opposition, I recall Donald's following riposte: 'I don't care if the press is not interested in poverty but I am and we will run a campaign against poverty whether they like it or not!'

Sam Galbraith – colleague and friend

One evening, Donald and I planned to have dinner at Westminster. When I arrived at his office in the House of Commons, some crisis had occurred, the resolution of which took precedence over food. It then being far too late either to eat in the House or to go to a restaurant, Donald decided that as he had promised me dinner, he would cook. And that evening I had the best baked beans on toast I have ever eaten.

Baroness Mary Goudie – friend

Donald was a complex and contradictory man: an intellectual and bibliophile who did not suffer fools gladly; a great but indecisive man; a near ascetic who loved a meal with friends; an agnostic who termed himself a 'cultural Presbyterian' but had mused 'if anything, I think I might be Jewish'; a disastrous dresser who admired 'tidy' women; a paternalist who despised heredity and its flummery while finding the Queen 'a pleasant enough woman'; and part of that dwindling political tribe who loved an argument but hated a row.

Brian Fitzpatrick – Principal Special Adviser 1999–2000

The 'Father of the Nation' label has landed upon Donald. It is certainly not a title he would have picked for himself given his notorious shyness. But he should, and will be, remembered as the architect of Scotland's devolution. I am proud of devolution, Donald was too and, rightly, Donald's name is fittingly synonymous with it. He was also just a really nice person to know.

Lesley Quinn – General Secretary, Scottish Labour Party

Foundations, Frustrations
and Hopes

Wendy Alexander

*Give us a Parliament in Scotland. Set it up next year. We will start
with no traditions. We will start with ideals. We will start with a
purpose, with courage.* – James Maxton, 1924[1]

Donald was proud of Scotland, proud of its people and proud of its
Parliament. Yet for a leading politician he was remarkably free from
personal pride and devoid of hubris. This, along with his essential
decency, endeared him to the Scots. Once, when campaigning with
Donald, someone said to me, 'The thing about Donald is that most Scots
believe that when he sits down at his desk in the morning he wants to do
his best by Scotland. We might disagree with him but we don't doubt his
intentions.' It is high praise from a Scot and it rings entirely true.

Whether as 'Big Donald', 'Our Donald' or just 'Big Man', the
nicknames spoke of the affection in which he was held – a rare
compliment for a politician in modern times. And, ironically, it may have
been because he was not particularly skilled at playing the political game.
Yet in retrospect, failing to play the game seems like strength. Donald
commanded trust. And the genesis of that trust was that he told friend or
foe alike what he believed, rather than what he thought they wanted to
hear.

Donald gave devolution sound foundations. As Tom Devine suggests, history provides the proper perspective for assessing the new parliamentary era begun in 1998. Today, as Scotland approaches the 300th anniversary of the Union of the Parliaments in 1707, I think Donald would have detected many hopeful signs for the future. This concluding essay considers devolution's sound foundations, its inevitable and its unexpected frustrations, and the basis for future optimism and hope.

Foundations

Devolution changed the British political framework irrevocably. The Parliament is now woven into the fabric of the British state; it will endure whatever the complexion of the Westminster government. Like universal suffrage, the NHS or the existence of the Welfare State, it has remarkably quickly become one of the non-negotiable aspects of the political consensus between Britain's major political parties. Of course, future reform is possible but not abolition. Indeed, if Britain is moving inexorably towards a written constitution, then the Scottish Parliament will rightly be seen as one of its principal antecedents.

However, the settlement's durability was not pre-ordained. The Scottish Constitutional Convention had adeptly sidestepped some difficult issues. I wrote in 1996: 'It will fall to the new government to refine the devolution architecture . . . on the form of the Devolution Bill, the future role of the Secretary of State, the details of the financial settlement, the disputes resolution mechanism and the future representation at Westminster.'[2] Arguably, the Scotland Act designed by Donald Dewar successfully navigated all, although both the electoral system and the financial settlement have their critics.

The strength of the Act lies in its departure from the Convention's support for a defined set of powers for the Scottish Parliament. It is often forgotten that one of Scottish Labour's objectives in 1995 during the final revision of the Convention Scheme was that the 'general power of competence' for the Scottish Parliament should be stopped.[3] The Scotland Act, in allowing the Scottish Parliament to range over all areas that were not explicitly reserved to Westminster, adopted a more radical approach and thereby took the most important step in giving resilience to the settlement. The referendum vote then provided a mandate from the Scottish people for the Parliament to be established.

During the preparation of the Devolution White Paper, Donald also actively considered moving beyond the Convention's financial proposals but in the end he honoured the Convention's scheme. He minimised direct references to the Parliament's financial power in the Act, to allow scope for further refinement in the future once the wider settlement had proved its constitutional sturdiness. He saw his first obligation as making devolution work – any further evolution could wait. After all, the successful establishment of a Scottish Parliament had eluded Labour (and everyone else) for a century.

The Parliament's more proportional voting system heralded the arrival of coalition government. By providing for 56 regional list members alongside 73 constituency members, it has also gone some way to breaking down the regional heartlands that exaggerate differences in voting preferences. As predicted, Tory and SNP candidates have been elected for Glasgow, and Labour candidates in the Highlands and rural north-east.[4] The Green Party, Scottish Socialist Party (SSP) and some independents have also gained seats.

The reduction in the over-representation of Scottish MPs at Westminster has taken the heat out of the expected sustained opposition to devolution. The much-anticipated West Lothian question remains a political consequence of devolution rather than a constitutional impediment to it. And the Tories' demand for two classes of MP continues to founder, as 'most English citizens [still] view Westminster as their national parliament'.[5]

As a result of Labour's brave decision to back a policy of gender equality in candidate selection in the first Scottish elections, 40 per cent of MSPs are women, catapulting Scotland into bronze medal position in the international league of women's parliamentary representation in national legislatures.

Donald's choice of a far-reaching, generally ambitious constitutional settlement has undoubtedly been vindicated. The predicted bitter disputes – legal, constitutional and inter-party – have not materialised. His legacy is a parliament faithful to but better founded than the Convention's scheme. It has proved workable in practice and has created many significant advances in Scottish life that could not have been anticipated.

The arrival of the Parliament has changed Scottish politics irrevocably. After 1999, the issue that had often defined Scottish politics in the previous three decades – the nature of Scottish sovereignty – changed for ever. The case for Scottish sovereignty over Scottish domestic affairs had been won. Scotland has a new settlement – built around shared sovereignty – and the Scots' desire for control over their own domestic affairs is now the accepted political orthodoxy. Support for the alternatives to devolution – either no Parliament or independence, at least in the form of support for the Scottish National Party – has receded. After 1999, the 'Scottish question' became how much sovereignty; what kind of sovereignty and how much difference will it make? This shared sovereignty arrived in Scotland just as it was increasingly finding favour elsewhere in Western Europe, with Italy and France also emulating the decentralisation of Germany and Spain. In truth, Britain was rather a 'Johnnie-come-lately' to the shared decision making that is often simply second nature in many other (particularly federal) states. But in Britain it was a veritable constitutional revolution. In short, legitimacy has returned to the strained fabric of the British state.

If he were here today, Donald would have rejoiced in seeing the strengths of a workable partnership with Westminster, effective coalition government, the declining interest in separation from the rest of the United Kingdom, planned voting reform for local government and recognition for hardworking councillors. He would have noted how the Parliament's powerful committee system is bringing a previously unimaginable level of transparency and accountability compared to the days when Scotland was ruled by a Secretary of State who was compelled to spend only Mondays in Edinburgh, then Tuesday to Thursday in London and Fridays in his (it was always his!) constituency. Donald would probably have felt thoroughly vindicated about his willingness to bear the electoral boost that the run-up to the Parliament's creation was bound to give the nationalist cause, believing it a price worth paying for meeting Scottish aspirations for greater self-government.

Donald would have hailed the Parliament's passage of more than 60 pieces of Scottish legislation in its first term: the majority non-contentious in principle, hence often little remarked upon in the media. Yet collectively they represented the most far-reaching and rapid updating of Scots law for three centuries. Instead of going to the back of the Westminster queue, there has been enormously beneficial catching up: modernising of the criminal justice system; abolishing feudalism; civilising the arrangements for mental health and mental incapacity. Measures that do not create extra red tape but which are real, humane, modernising law reform.

He would have revelled in the election of a third-term Labour government, marvelled at recent macroeconomic stability, been delighted by the lowest levels of unemployment since records began and celebrated the fact that 210,000 Scottish children and 170,000 Scottish pensioners have been lifted above the poverty line since 1997. He would likely be astonished at an annual Scottish Executive budget of over £25 billion, up from £16.5 billion in devolution's first year. I believe he would have applauded Jack McConnell's determination to improve Scotland's poor public health – including the ban on smoking in public places – and warmly welcomed recent initiatives to tackle racism, sectarianism and anti-social behaviour, and to attract migrants and fresh talent to Scotland.

And, as only Donald could, he would have openly pondered some of the weaknesses of Scotland's new governing arrangements. He might have dwelt on one, no different from other advanced European countries: the problem of too much regulation, so-called 'regulatory overreach'. One result of the Parliament's principal powers being law making is the inherent risk that legislation becomes the rather lazy answer to every difficult policy issue, so overlooking the downsides of uncalled-for red tape, its perverse incentives and the unintended consequences that follow.

Yet in the years since Donald launched Scotland on its new parliamentary road, the progress has been far reaching. Encouragingly, 'blaming the English' is much less common and certainly less acceptable these days. The old Scottish whinge has been repatriated, at least to only reverberate around our own shores. And whilst its compatriot the Scottish cringe also sometimes lingers on, increasingly the Parliament's wide-ranging powers speak to future possibilities, and its iconic home embraces the future with confidence. So why the sometimes pervasive sense of disappointment?

Frustrations . . .

To understand the cause of the disappointment that has followed the creation of the Parliament, it is necessary to look back before its inception to the initial high expectations coupled with the lack of a common vision for the nation's future.

Scotland was ill prepared for facing up to either of the challenges of changing lives or promoting economic efficiency. From the 1970s onwards, the debate between Scotland's political parties, and amongst the wider public, increasingly came to focus on our constitutional settlement.

In fairness, in the '80s Scotland was not alone in her constitutional preoccupations. But after 1989 and the collapse of the Berlin Wall, others tended to move on while Scotland continued to fixate on her constitutional choices. In the decade following 1989, a new generation of politicians all over Eastern Europe were discovering that 'constitution writing' is easier than 'nation building'. But it would be another decade before Scotland began to discover this for herself.

Of course any analogy between Scotland and Eastern Europe is self-evidently incomplete. The Scottish situation differs decisively in that Scots have always lived in a democracy, albeit one that was severely tested in the '80s and '90s. But the visceral experience for activists campaigning for Scottish devolution has an interesting parallel. When Eastern European dissidents were campaigning for democracy, the political choices ahead seemed straightforward: achieve democracy and justice would follow. Likewise the campaign for devolution was conducted in black and white terms – you were either for it or against it – there were few shades of grey. The Constitutional Convention had served its purpose admirably, allowing a large cross-section of Scottish life to declare 'for Scotland' without having to confront what that Scotland might look like. The coalition around the Constitutional Convention was wide rather than deep and Scottish 'nation building' was left for later.

The challenges of government are fundamentally different. Governing is all about choices between various shades of grey. It is not typically a campaign for schools and hospitals but about the trade-offs between schools and hospitals. Typically it is about the language of priorities and if 'politics is choice; government is decision'.

By 1999, there was already a lot of catching up to do. Scotland's 'nation-building' challenge and the tough choices that went with it had all been pushed to the margins in those years when political accountability and constitutional legitimacy were to the fore. Suddenly, they re-emerged with a vengeance. Home rule had ceased to be a catch-all constitutional answer and had become instead the embarkation point for a national journey. From now on, the call for devolution could no longer be the lazy answer to every awkward question in Scottish life. Standing at last on her own two feet, the nation had to confront challenges common to progressive governments everywhere, such as how to close the opportunity gap or how to improve public services. The Scottish Parliament was also confronted by a series of specifically Scottish challenges such as our poor health and life expectancy record, our relative economic performance and the occasional national predisposition to despondency, if not dependency.

Confronted by this legacy and the absence of a shared policy agenda, Donald and the new Parliament also had to contend with high expectations. In fairness, the empirical evidence suggests that many people's initial expectations, whilst very high in 1997, were becoming more measured by 1999, even before the new Parliament came into being. For example, it is salutary to recall that even in the high excitement of 1997 only a minority of Scots thought unemployment would fall as a result of a Scottish Parliament.[6] And yet unemployment is now at its lowest level since records began and Scotland's employment rate is above that of the United Kingdom.

Expectations for the Parliament, unsurprisingly, typically aligned closely with constitutional preferences – the one in three Scots not in favour of its creation had low or negative expectations, whereas its strong supporters, and supporters of independence, had the highest expectations. Arguably, expectations were greatest amongst the most vocal advocates of devolution and many sections of the media rather than amongst the wider population. Yet, in the years since devolution, Scotland's citizens have consistently been invited to be disappointed and have been repeatedly reminded about the 'disappointments', so eventually they were likely to feel disappointed, even if such self-fulfilling prophesies of failure were often only the outpourings of flawed prophets.

Professor Donald McLeod, writing about the fate of devolution, observed that, 'Contrasted with the tenacity with which we fought for it, the cynicism with which we've welcomed it is extraordinary.'[7] Many observers have pointed to the role of the media. Brian Taylor notes, 'The press had been corralled for too long into the pro-devolution camp. Journalists are seldom comfortable when they can be depicted as a claque marshalled by cheerleaders. Instinctively for some, it felt like time to kick out.'[8]

Yet, with the passage of time, I think it is also possible to discern more fundamental forces at work. Scotland's 'devolution hangover' was about much more than who occupied an editorial chair at the *Daily Record* or *The Scotsman*. Donald fought self-pity in himself and disdained it in others – today he would be asking why, rather than pointing a finger of blame. The explanation lies in Scotland's collective ill-preparedness and the absence of a shared vision for the post-Parliament world as well as misplaced and contradictory expectations.

Scotland's media was not alone in its high expectations. Many of devolution's most diehard supporters were convinced that it could be the platform for much more wide-ranging social and economic reform. And on the back of the Devolution White Paper and referendum successes, highly ambitious hopes did – however briefly – find an echo amongst the wider electorate. As Professor David McCrone has pointed out:

> With hindsight, the late 1990s was a period of unusually high expectations among the UK electorate as a whole, as a discredited Conservative government was swept from office in the UK, with the ruling party managing to return no MPs whatsoever in both Scotland and Wales.

He notes that the subsequent disappointment or downsizing of expectations was not simply a Scottish or even a United Kingdom phenomenon. This disenchantment with political elites also appeared across most of the Western world.

> In other words, the decline in trust and the efficacy of the system is fairly endemic, and it is Scotland's (mis)fortune to find itself caught up in this tide. While most Scots recognise that Westminster is in practice a more powerful parliament than Holyrood, they consistently prefer (by a majority of 4 to 1) Holyrood to be the more powerful – hardly evidence that the whole devolution project has run into the sand. Indeed, the differential between trusting Edinburgh over London remains at a broadly similar ratio of 3 to 1 even though the absolute numbers trusting either tier of government has diminished.[9]

The hopes of Scottish voters for their new Parliament were not about a fairer voting system, a more consensual form of politics, or even more women MSPs, although nor were they unsympathetic to such reforms. When pressed, their hopes for politics, and hence the Parliament, were about a better Scotland. The trouble was that amongst both people and parties there was real confusion about how to deliver such advances. The successful establishment of a Scottish Parliament could not cure all Scotland's economic or social ills or shield people from the quickening pace of global change.

In such an atmosphere, Professor Lindsay Paterson's reasoned assessment of the first year of devolution that, 'Pluralism *is* being renewed, coherent government *is* struggling back to life . . . and distinctive Scottish details of policy *are* once again finding an acceptable place in the Union . . . that is no small achievement and if you are of a cautious *and* patient disposition it is probably much the best of all possible outcomes' would inevitably seem rather tame.[10]

Donald found himself torn: he wanted to uphold the hopes, yet he saw around him little appetite for far-reaching reform. Donald, Professor Paterson noted, 'did not make exaggerated claims', but there was an air of expectation that had its own momentum.[11] He knew that many of devolution's supporters were likely to measure its success in terms of its ability to create a more socially just Scotland and, ironically, his success in 'constitution building' had raised expectations even further. He felt the inevitability of the disappointment acutely but he hesitated about speaking out. Certainly he could not do so before the referendum result confirmed the Scots wanted a parliament. Soon after the referendum victory, and still battling the Scotland Bill through the Westminster Parliament, he quickly became the first Scottish Labour leader facing the first Scottish parliamentary elections. Again, this was hardly the right moment to try to manage expectations, not least when Tory and SNP opponents were attacking the fundamentals of the scheme. And from May 1999, as Scotland's first First Minister, he feared being accused of a lack of faith in either the nation or its fledging institutions. He felt alone, wondering who else was with him now the battle for democracy had been won. Looking back, it is hard not to have sympathy.[12]

By the time of the first parliamentary elections, the media were already coming down from their 1997 constitutional high. Donald wrestled with the inevitability of the coming public reckoning. The media undoubtedly overreacted, so squeezing the space for candour even further: too much straight talking could have invited charges of fatalism and attacks from friend and foe alike. He did not know how to plead for patience, and death robbed him of the chance to try. Sometimes the sheer burden of the business of government simply overtook a man whose attention to detail led him to be described as a 'permanent secretary manqué'. And on the toughest days, when the nation's challenges sometimes seemed overwhelming, perhaps it was easier to simply and dutifully finish the evening's official box.

But mostly his focus was on how Scottish Labour could do better: he knew that the challenge was to demonstrably deliver superior government to that of any previous Secretary of State for Scotland or Westminster government. The air was thick with calls for 'Scottish solutions to Scottish problems'. But as Donald privately acknowledged, a uniquely Scottish solution does not always exist; sometimes just matching, or keeping up with, the rest of the United Kingdom was a sufficient challenge. Donald pondered how Scotland could stay abreast, or even move ahead, of the social and economic reform underway in the rest of the United Kingdom and beyond. He knew and respected colleagues in the United Kingdom Cabinet. He enviously eyed the skills and experience at their disposal. What would it take to make Scotland smarter and quicker? Sometimes he yearned to be twenty – or at least ten – years younger and was daunted by the sheer scale of the reform task but courageously unwilling to disguise its necessity or its costs.

And it was not just a Labour challenge. For all Scotland's parties, rising to the challenge of the new parliamentary era was complicated by the fact that their primary function had been to organise for electoral success rather than develop policy. For over a century, Scotland's political parties had been geared to delivering more seats in Westminster rather than to thinking about how they might legislate in a devolved Scottish Parliament.

It can now only be a matter of interesting speculation to consider how Donald would have reacted had he lived. I suspect his instinct would have been to force his party and the country to confront head-on the lack of a shared vision or common agenda on economic or social reform. Ultimately, he would have led them towards facing up to some tough challenges about how 'righting the social arithmetic' means asking more of ourselves.

Yet, despite all his private misgivings, Donald did not lose his belief in what the nation should aspire to. Until his health deteriorated, I am sure that he believed the new nation would find its feet, face up to the tough dilemmas and emerge better prepared to move decisively forward. That vision for the next stage in the nation's journey is the one he outlined in his speech at the opening of the Parliament in July 1999. He held out the hope of 'Scotland as a good example that remains for generations to come'. As things turned out, he had little more than a year to try to fulfil that hope.

So just as Labour discovered that its famous five election pledges in 1997 could not bear the weight of public expectation of a Labour government, neither could a Scottish Parliament bear the weight of pent-up expectations from many of devolution's diffuse supporters. The arrival of the Parliament was a moment in history that demanded the grand gestures of policy in return. Grand gestures were not Donald's style. But the search for them misses the wide-ranging reform programme he initiated in health, education, housing, land reform, social and criminal justice. What emerges in retrospect is a series of 'good example[s] that remain for generations to come'.

In the first year of the Parliament, when financial resources were still tight, the radicalism took many forms. Donald was Secretary of State for two years and First Minister for eighteen months. All the following measures were begun during his time in office:

- fundamental land reform, including the right to roam, a community right to buy and the abolition of feudalism;
- a change of direction of economic policy bringing together enterprise and lifelong learning to boost Scotland's innovation rate and invest in skills;
- a new social justice strategy, including an annual social justice report;
- free local bus travel for pensioners and free central-heating systems for pensioners and council tenants without them;
- fundamental nationwide housing reform, starting in Glasgow, based on community ownership by tenants, the establishment of the homelessness taskforce and the rough sleepers initiative;
- the promise to build or renovate over 100 schools in the first parliamentary term and the establishment of the McCrone Committee on teachers' pay and conditions;
- a commitment to eighty one-stop clinics for same-day diagnosis and eight new hospital developments;
- abolition of tuition fees and student bursaries introduced;
- the establishment of the Scottish Drug Enforcement Agency;
- the first steps on anti-social behaviour, including the introduction of ASBOs and Drug Treatment and Testing Orders, and piloting the fast tracking of court cases;
- first national action to counter domestic abuse;

- recognition for carers;
- the creation of Scotland's first national parks;
- commencing the modernisation of the support framework for voluntary organisations; and
- a far-reaching Freedom of Information Act.

It already emerges as a remarkable record for such a short tenure. These policies required a Scottish Parliament to give them momentum. Donald along with his Cabinet and parliamentary team initiated this far-reaching policy programme that provides just a few of the answers to the question 'what difference has devolution made?' It is a reforming legacy that endures today and will continue to shape Scotland in the future. One can only speculate about Donald's reaction to more recent policy developments: most would find favour; a few would likely not.

Donald's creed of social justice and economic efficiency altered little throughout his long political career and these were, incidentally, the twin pillars of Labour's electoral recovery in 1997. Less than six months after the opening of the Parliament, Donald went to Drumchapel with the then United Kingdom Work and Pensions Secretary, Alistair Darling, to launch the *Social Justice Report for Scotland: A Scotland Where Everyone Matters*. The document began by acknowledging that poverty knows no devolved–reserved distinctions. It backed the commitment to social justice with concrete targets covering both reserved and devolved areas. Donald was determined to measure the successes and face up to the failures by publishing an annual social justice report. Key policies such as free local bus travel for pensioners and the £350 million five-year anti-fuel-poverty programme to install central heating for all pensioners and all council house and housing association tenants without it were initiated in the spending review of September 2000, shortly before his death. Typically distinctive policies tailored to Scottish circumstances.

But uniquely 'Scottish solutions' were never going to be the whole story for Donald. He believed that proclaiming a policy's 'Scottishness' was an insufficient guide to its desirability, credibility or efficacy. During Donald's tenure as First Minister and since, there have also been a host of measures that mirror advances in the United Kingdom, such as the extension of nursery places to all three and four year olds; the spread of classroom assistants; the reduction of all Primary 1–3 classes to under 30;

health service reform; the huge expansion of modern apprenticeships; and interest in enterprise education. All of these measures have been enacted in the United Kingdom, with Scotland sometimes taking a lead role, sometimes following a policy lead elsewhere – such is the nature of devolution. Donald freely acknowledged that Scotland couldn't be out in front in all circumstances. What he cared about was to be out in front where it counts: in social justice and economic efficiency.

The detail of economic policy was never Donald's forte but he recognised the importance of securing trust on the economy and pursuing economic efficiency in government. He wanted to set a new economic direction in Scotland and stick to it with steely determination.[13] The foundations were laid with the creation of Britain's, and perhaps the world's, first joint Enterprise and Lifelong Learning Ministry. I recall discussing the case for such a ministry with Donald over Sunday lunch in a Glasgow hotel during the first Scottish Parliament election campaign. The new department paved the way for a substantial change in policy direction, begun under Henry McLeish, with the publication of the first Framework for Economic Development for Scotland. In due course, cooperation between business and our universities has improved; a framework for innovation has been established; the financial incentives for industry changed; and Scotland's overseas image has been modernised through Scottish Development International, Global Scot, EventsScotland and the Fresh Talent Initiative. Many of these initiatives were made possible by Donald's decision to bring enterprise and lifelong learning together in one ministry.[14] Professor Phil Cooke notes: 'Scotland has enacted a visionary economic development policy, Northern Ireland a constrained approach, while Wales has adopted a precautionary one.'[15]

As an instinctive pessimist himself, Donald understood our national predisposition to worry. But he also fought debilitating despondency crowding out 'realism', particularly if it was misplaced.[16] Donald, as Malcolm Rifkind notes, was an aficionado of facts. Neither shallow hyperbole nor withering despair was his style. In his dealing with the Scottish business community, he would have listened, always willing to hear frustrations, whilst distilling what was sound common sense from special pleading.[17] He had an enduring affection for and interest in Scotland's universities, doubtless rooted in his love of learning and belief in the liberating potential of education.

Cabinet colleagues point to his belief in cabinet government. He made time for us all and tried by example to discourage the low arts of politics. His personal style of government was inclusive, principled, low key and out of kilter with much contemporary political orthodoxy. His instinctive reaction towards the media was often to seek a low profile, even sometimes when he had important things to say! He always believed in office that he was a privileged representative of the people rather than a political statesman. At a time when Labour's presentation was becoming slicker, Donald was heading in the opposite direction.[18]

Crucially, his style of government has more to commend it than was commonly appreciated at the time. Peter Hyman (Donald's researcher in the early 1990s, who went on to serve for ten years in Downing Street) wrote recently of New Labour's tendency to favour 'momentum, conflict and novelty' at the expense of the 'empowerment, partnership and consistency'. Hyman concedes the former approach was the wrong one for convincing frontline professionals, or indeed for ensuring successful delivery.[19] Donald even at the height of the fashion for the former, instinctively inclined to the latter. And for the most part his policies are creating an enduring legacy.

Donald was also, as Jim Wallace suggests, instinctively anti-tribal, a trait that helped account for the breadth of his appeal. He freely admitted that no political party has a monopoly on wisdom. He constantly wrestled with what he could ask of himself, his party and his country. He was candid about the shortcomings of all three. He worried about how Scotland might face up to dilemmas about future reform that confront every progressive party and nation.

What concerned those closest to him was how onerous he found the burden of decision making. His governmental responsibilities weighed heavily on him when contrasted with the cut and thrust of parliamentary debate, at which he excelled. He disliked conflict, whether with colleagues or officials. Like all of us, he made mistakes. One was to bow to official pressure in 1999 and move Sam Galbraith from the Scottish Office health brief, where he had formed a strong working partnership with Geoff Scaife, the head of the service he had inherited from the previous administration.

In office, Donald even found time to worry about his opposition. He felt the task of Scotland's opposition parties was to hasten, not halt, Scotland's journey of reform; to empathise with the complexities of governing in shades of grey and no longer hanker after the simplicities of an earlier era. Donald believed that Scotland desperately needed a modern, reform-minded opposition. He was right then and he would be right now. If it is ideas that count in politics, then there were few from that quarter.

However, Donald was relieved to see Scottish politics move on from the pre-devolution days where political commitment was too often measured by the depth of one's constitutional ardour. His constitutional achievements meant Scotland's intellectual energies could start to be more focused on 'what we can do' rather than on 'what we cannot'. He hoped the Parliament would give Scotland the opportunity to have a different conversation with herself. As Jack McConnell noted at the opening of the new Parliament building, the new democratic Scotland *is* creating the space for a more self-confident Scotland to emerge. Had he lived, Donald would certainly have welcomed much that has been achieved in the first decade of the Parliament's short life.

Like all politicians' legacies, Donald's is also touched with failure. He was deeply conflicted about how willing or ready either he or Scotland was to embark on a new reforming political journey. He doubted, unfairly, his ability to inspire. So if in his heart he aspired to creating a Scotland that truly made the rest of Britain and others further afield look on enviously, he typically chose not to share it – reasoning perhaps that the time was not right. Whatever his private dreams, his public programme and plans were altogether more practical. Moreover, he recognised the simple fact that the new Scottish Parliament had to learn to walk before it would be ready to run.

Indeed, that very honesty, disdain for shallow hyperbole and lack of grandiosity – both personal and political – endeared him to ordinary Scots. He was uninterested in point scoring, insults, abuse or praise. What mattered was getting started – after so many years of reversals and retreats, to begin moving in the right direction once again. He believed in the common weal, he trusted that the nation was similarly inclined and he was determined to make progress.

As a myriad of contributors to this volume attest, Donald's life deserves to be remembered and his legacy reassessed. The constitutional element of that legacy is secure. He brought to the devolution process a unique combination of vision, commitment and a mastery of arcane legal detail. And despite the contemporary noise, and the doomsayers of the day, his governmental legacy has overwhelmingly proved to be humane, modernising reform. The frustrations expressed by some reflect inflated expectations, unexpected events, real differences of opinion about the nature of the new Scotland and a healthy dose of impatience. But unquestionably, the Dewar years are much more strategic than a reading of the contemporary record would suggest. From land and housing, to educational reform and pensioners' well-being, key themes around social justice and community empowerment emerge.

Hopes . . .

Today, I believe Donald would advocate optimism. Many wrongs have been righted. Scottish politics is exciting again, with the staleness and stagnation of the past just a memory. Young graduates have reasons to stay and the haemorrhage of emigration from Scotland has been stemmed. Granted, too much of contemporary Scottish politics is still about blame and the willingness to attack an adversary instead of the championing of big ideas. But one can detect in many walks of Scottish life a new determination to take responsibility and grasp opportunities. Overcoming the dependencies of the past would always be a journey involving ceasing to see Scotland's problems as someone else's fault and abandoning the vestiges of a blame culture. It will require vigilance against the parish-pump politics, which can afflict any small nation. But Donald would have had contempt for the constant knocking of the nation, seeing it as nasty, nihilistic and fuelling fatalism.

Throughout his political life Donald sought to be 'hard on the issues and gentle on the people', advice that should resonate in Scotland today. Profound economic and social challenges remain: collective challenges that we should not duck. It means acknowledging the enormity of what we are trying to achieve. The transition from *administering* Scotland last century, to *governing* it today, to better *growing* it in the future, takes time. After more than three centuries without a parliament, the pace has markedly quickened. Measured against the ambition of better administering Scotland, the successes are unquestionable, not least in terms of the increased transparency and accountability that the Parliament has brought. The challenge of better governing Scotland is also being realised. Scotland has left behind those endless debates about her identity and moved on to the tougher business of government. Devolution has created a policy laboratory and the Parliament has made great strides, unimaginable in the pre-devolution era, although there is still much further to travel. As Professor Michael Keating has noted, too often policy divergences have arisen because of a failure to follow an English example rather than as a result of pioneering new ideas.[20] When it comes to better growing Scotland, initiatives like the recent Allander Series – which brought some of the world's leading economists to Scotland – point to new opportunities.[21]

As Donald once famously remarked, devolution is 'a process'. Today, Jack McConnell talks of Scotland aspiring to be the 'best small nation on earth'. Achieving this vision will require courage and clarity about principles. Donald's principles, Labour's principles of social justice and economic efficiency, stand the test of time. They endure as we move further into the century in which our Parliament took shape.

After Donald's death in 2000, there began a period of unprecedented growth in Scottish and United Kingdom public spending. Much needed investment and reform followed but too often future ambitions are assessed more in terms of 'cash spent' than 'successful change delivered'. All three of Scotland's First Ministers have spoken about the forces of conservatism that operate in Scottish life. Has the search for 'Scottish solutions' become a way of avoiding sometimes-difficult discussions about areas of Scottish life where reform is needed? Scotland could benefit from a more meaningful dialogue about why we sometimes struggle to embrace radical reform.

The Scottish Parliament, with five of its six political parties drawn from the left or centre-left, has the opportunity to decisively strengthen the common weal but its complacencies can also lead to conservatism. Donald knew how the past could protect us: old ideas, old nationalism, old Labour, even old Tories. But how often is Scotland today instinctively hidebound by what is familiar, resistant to reform? Too often, past patterns of service delivery are elevated to the moral high ground of social justice. Does the evidence justify these past patterns? 'It's aye been' is as insidious in political life as in life itself.

Donald might have recalled that earlier decisive moment in 1988 when he led Labour in Scotland towards the Scottish Constitutional Convention, knowing that only a new consensus could galvanise change. In that step, he signalled his acceptance of future cross-party cooperation in order to move the home rule debate forward but he stood firm against independence or a multi-option referendum. Today, creating a more socially just and economically efficient Scotland means advancing a more far-reaching debate about the riskier changes that will be required.

Scotland must not neglect the need to match her successes in constitutional modernisation with equally far-reaching economic modernisation. The future economic efficiency agenda must go hand in hand with building communities where not only Scottish citizens but also the internationally mobile want to work and live. Attractive professional opportunities and prosperous communities will attract international migrants: they seek out better services, safer streets and good schools.

When it came to social justice, Donald's starting point was often 'what sort of world are we creating for our children? Will it be characterised by more opportunity, more diversity and more security?' The Scandinavian nations have modernised the social democratic model based on such inclusive, citizen-friendly principles. Crucially, their approach to services has been increasingly to empower the users of services: in short, a 'bottom up' rather than a 'top down' approach.

We need to increasingly 'walk the talk' when it comes to empowering communities, patients, parents and pupils. Donald made a significant start with land and housing reform. But can we do more to empower the users of services in the way we deliver health, education, or community regeneration in Scotland today?[22] The appetite for 'handing power back' must grow.

Labour's central commitment for 'righting the social arithmetic' is its promise to halve child poverty within ten years and end it within a generation. Tony Blair first laid out this vision nine months before Donald's death. Donald was a sceptical devotee: committed to the cause, nervous about its deliverability. But he would also have been doggedly determined to do his bit to make this promise a reality. It is a commitment that involves more than raising income, it also means improving life chances.

Donald's interest in and commitment to tackling child poverty were more than theoretical. In the 1970s when out of Parliament, he served as one of the early reporters to the children's panel. Today, he would be troubled by the large increase in recent years in care and protection to children's panels. He would have worried about the day-to-day welfare of the one in twenty children under sixteen in Scotland with a drug-abusing parent, some 41,000 to 59,000 children in all.[23] He would have been harrying officials for solutions about how we collectively help parents whose children risk getting left out or left behind. How could Scotland protect and nurture the future prospects of this generation of under-parented children?

Had he lived, Donald might, or might not, have evolved in office into a powerful institutional as well as policy reformer like his predecessor Tom Johnston. We will never know.

But as in those earlier reforming eras, Scotland needs to continue to build around the principles of social justice and economic efficiency. But it cannot be a soggy consensus that fights shy of defining the choices for voters. We need to be clear about the choices, the inevitable trade-offs, and committed to making the necessary changes. We must abandon consensus as code for preserving the power of vested interests. Embracing reform should never be seen as 'anti-Scottish'. To Donald, an essential element of 'Scottishness' was a commitment to community: a commitment that meant asking more of ourselves as a nation.

So far, post-devolution Scotland has been hungry for politicians' promises. If he were with us today, Donald might be asking whether, as a nation, we are yet ready not for politicians' promises but new collective challenges.

The best political speeches capture a moment and touch the pulse of a nation. Donald's opening speech to the Scottish Parliament did just that when he spoke of:

> a turning point: the day when democracy was renewed in Scotland, when we revitalised our place in this our United Kingdom.
>
> This is about more than our politics and our laws. This is about who we are, how we carry ourselves [and] . . . a very Scottish conviction: that honesty and simple dignity are priceless virtues, not imparted by rank or birth or privilege but part of the soul.

He caught the mood of the country, calling on Scotland to rise to the noblest challenge for any nation: the tackling of poverty and inequality.
I believe the judgement of history will be kind to Donald Dewar. It was Edwin Morgan, in another poetic line penned for the opening of Holyrood, who proclaimed that the new Parliament was 'picking up a thread of pride and self-esteem . . . not ever broken or forgotten'. Donald held that thread with pride and affection.

My last meeting with Donald occurred on the Friday evening before his death, in Labour's Scottish HQ. He had his constituency correspondence on his knee and he was dictating a letter about a constituent's 'leaking windaes'. He died as he had lived, inspiring his colleagues to bring the light of compassion and social justice to politics. Through his leadership and convictions, times have changed for ever and for the better in Scotland. In that powerful speech at the opening of the Parliament, he also spoke of Scotland's 'journey begun so long ago which has no end'. His leadership, straddling the twentieth and twenty-first centuries, saw Scotland take great strides on that journey of change. Unquestionably history will not forget Donald Dewar. But Donald, the quiet conviction politician, would have urged us all not to look back but to look forwards in hope, carrying with us that unbroken thread of pride and self esteem.

You are picking up a thread of pride and self esteem
that has been almost but not quite, oh no not quite,
not ever broken or forgotten

Edwin Morgan, the Scots Makar,
from his poem 'For the Opening
of the Scottish Parliament',
9 October 2004

Appendix One

Donald Dewar: A Chronology

21 August 1937	Born in Glasgow
1961–64	University of Glasgow MA
1964–66	University of Glasgow LLB
1964	Labour Candidate Aberdeen South
1966	Elected MP Aberdeen South
1967–79	Parliamentary Private Secretary to Rt Hon. Tony Crosland, Board of Trade
1970	Defeated in Aberdeen South
1972–74	Reporter to Children's Panel, Lanarkshire
1974–78	Solicitor; Ross, Harper & Murphy, Partner 1976–92
1975–78	Part-time Presenter Radio Clyde
1978	Elected MP for Glasgow Garscadden (later Anniesland)
1979–81	Chairman, Select Committee on Scottish Affairs
1981–83	Labour Deputy spokesman on Scottish Affairs
1983–92	Labour spokesman on Scottish Affairs
1984–97	Member of the Shadow Cabinet
1992–95	Labour front bench spokesman on Social Security
1995–97	Opposition Chief Whip
1996	Privy Councillor

1997–99	Secretary of State for Scotland
6 May 1999	Elected MSP for Glasgow Anniesland
13 May 1999	Elected First Minister
14 May 1999	Signed a 'Partnership for Scotland' with the Liberal Democrats
25 April 2000	Went to hospital for cardiac test
8 May 2000	Heart operation
16 August 2000	Formally returned to work
10 October 2000	Fell and suffered brain haemorrhage
11 October 2000	Death

Appendix Two

Donald Dewar: Speech at the Opening Ceremony of the Scottish Parliament – 1 July 1999

Your Majesty, on behalf of the people of Scotland, I thank you for the gift of this mace.

It is a symbol of the great democratic traditions from which we draw our inspiration and our strength.

At its head are inscribed the opening words of our founding statute:

'There shall be a Scottish Parliament'

Through long years, those words were first a hope, then a belief, then a promise. Now, they are a reality.

This is a moment anchored in our history.

Today, we reach back through the long haul to win this Parliament, through the struggles of those who brought democracy to Scotland, to that other Parliament dissolved in controversy nearly three centuries ago.

Today, we look forward to the time when this moment will be seen as a turning point: the day when democracy was renewed in Scotland, when we revitalised our place in this our United Kingdom.

This is about more than our politics and our laws. This is about who we are, how we carry ourselves. There is a new voice in the land, the voice of a democratic Parliament. A voice to shape Scotland as surely as the echoes from our past:

the shout of the welder in the din of the great Clyde shipyards;

the speak of the Mearns, with its soul in the land;

the discourse of the Enlightenment, when Edinburgh and Glasgow were a light held to the intellectual life of Europe;

the wild cry of the Great Pipes;

and back to the distant cries of the battles of Bruce and Wallace.

Walter Scott wrote that only a man with soul so dead could have no sense, no feel of his native land. For me, for any Scot, today is a proud moment: a new stage on a journey begun long ago and which has no end. This is a proud day for all of us.

A Scottish Parliament. Not an end: a means to greater ends. And those too are part of our mace. Woven into its symbolic thistles are these four words:

'Wisdom. Justice. Compassion. Integrity.'

Burns would have understood that. We have just heard – beautifully sung – one of his most enduring works ['A Man's a Man for a' That']. At that heart of the song is a very Scottish conviction: that honesty and simple dignity are priceless virtues, not imparted by rank or birth or privilege but part of the soul.

Burns believed that sense and worth ultimately prevail. He believed that was the core of politics; that without it, ours would be an impoverished profession.

'Wisdom. Justice. Compassion. Integrity.' Timeless values. Honourable aspirations for this new forum of democracy, born on the cusp of a new century.

We are fallible. We will make mistakes. But we will never lose sight of what brought us here: the striving to do right by the people of Scotland; to respect their priorities; to better their lot; and to contribute to the commonweal.

I look forward to the days ahead when this Chamber will sound with debate, argument and passion. When men and women from all over Scotland will meet to work together for a future built from the first principles of social justice.

But today, we pause and reflect. It is a rare privilege in an old nation to open a new Parliament. Today is a celebration of the principles, the traditions, the democratic imperatives which have brought us to this point and will sustain us into the future.

Your Majesty, we are all proud that you are here to handsel this Parliament and with us as we dedicate ourselves to the work ahead.

Your Majesty, our thanks.

Appendix Three

Notes on Contributors

Wendy Alexander is Member of the Scottish Parliament for Paisley North and served as Special Adviser to Donald Dewar, 1997–98, and in the Scottish Cabinet, 1999–2002. She is a visiting Professor at the University of Strathclyde.

Charlie Allan was a childhood friend of Donald Dewar and is currently farming correspondent of *The Herald*.

Lord Kerr of Kinlochard is a peer, chairman of the Court and Council of Imperial College London, and was a member of the United Kingdom Diplomatic Service from 1966 to 2002.

Lord Gordon of Strathblane is a Labour peer, chairman of Scottish Radio Holdings and founder of Radio Clyde, for whom Donald worked part-time in the 1970s.

Fiona Ross is a freelance broadcaster and former political correspondent of Scottish Television. She was a long-standing friend of Donald's and programme consultant on the first anniversary television documentary on his life.

David Whitton is an experienced journalist and was press spokesperson for Donald Dewar from 1998 until his death.

Alf Young is one of Scotland's leading business commentators. He has been with *The Herald* since 1986, currently as policy editor, and was a colleague and friend of Donald's from the mid 1970s.

George Whyte was Donald's agent in the 1964 and 1966 general elections and a former Aberdeen South Constituency Party Secretary. He is still active in the Aberdeen Labour Party.

Bill Butler is Labour MSP for Glasgow Anniesland and was Chair of Garscadden Constituency Party, 1985–89.

Matt Smith is Scottish Secretary of UNISON and worked with Donald both within the Labour Party and as part of the wider labour and trade union movement.

Rt Hon. Gordon Brown has been an MP since 1983 and was appointed Chancellor of the Exchequer on 2 May 1997.

Lord Elder of Kirkcaldy is a Labour peer and former Chief of Staff to The Rt Hon. John Smith, MP, 1992–94, and Special Adviser to Donald Dewar, 1997–99.

Dr Carol Craig is Chief Executive of the Centre for Confidence and Well-being and was a long-standing friend of Donald Dewar.

Lord Hattersley of Sparkbrook is a Labour peer; both a colleague and friend to Donald, he was Deputy Leader of the Labour Party from 1983 to 1992.

Sir Malcolm Rifkind is Conservative MP for Chelsea and Kensington; currently shadow Secretary of State for Work and Pensions, he was Secretary of State for Scotland, 1986–1990.

Peter Jones was Scottish Political Editor of *The Scotsman* from 1987 to 1995 and Scottish and North of England correspondent of *The Economist* from 1995 to 2005.

Lord Irvine of Lairg is a Labour peer and was Lord Chancellor, 1997–2003. In 1997, he chaired the Cabinet committee responsible for preparing the devolution legislation.

Lord Sewel of Gilcomstoun is a Labour peer. He was a Scottish Office minister, 1997–99, and led for the Scottish Office in the Lords during the passage of the Scotland Act.

Professor Neil MacCormick is Regius Professor of Public Law in Edinburgh University and was SNP MEP from 1999 to 2004. A lifelong member of the SNP, he was also a personal friend of Donald Dewar.

Ruth Wishart is a well-known Scottish journalist and broadcaster and long-time friend of Donald Dewar.

Jim Wallace is MSP for Orkney and was Leader of the Scottish Liberal Democrats, 1992–2005. He served as Scotland's Deputy First Minister, 1999–2005.

Henry McLeish, **Jack McConnell**, **Sarah Boyack**, **Susan Deacon**, **Sam Galbraith** and **Tom McCabe** were all Labour members of Donald Dewar's Cabinet. **Henry McLeish** succeeded Donald as First Minister, 2000–1, and **Jack McConnell** has served as First Minister since 2001.

Professor Duncan Maclennan was a special adviser to Scottish ministers on housing policy from 1999 to 2002 and is currently working as a researcher and writer in Canada and the United Kingdom.

Bernard Ponsonby has been a journalist with Scottish Television since 1990. He reported on the Holyrood inquiry for Scottish Television and produced the first anniversary television documentary on Donald's life.

Professor Tom Devine is Glucksman Professor of Irish and Scottish Studies and Director of the Centre for Irish and Scottish Studies at the University of Aberdeen, Scotland.

Notes and References

Introduction

1 Donald Dewar, quoted in B. Taylor, *The Scottish Parliament* (1999), p. 38.

2 Michael Keating, *Policy Making and Policy Divergence in Scotland after Devolution*, Devolution Briefing no. 21 (March 2005), ESRC Research Programme Devolution and Constitutional Change.

3 Support for housing-stock transfers continues to be Executive policy, but the desire for continuity amongst housing departments and other local interests threatens to swamp community leadership. There is no momentum in the case of large housing transfers for onward second stage transfers, moving homes to more local community levels.

This contrasts with the Executive's position in 2000, which was that 'whole stock transfers to single landlords in urban areas do not realise the vision of full community ownership'. Scottish Executive written response (19 September 2000) to Social Inclusion, Housing and Voluntary Sector Committee Report on Stock Transfers (July 2000).

4 Donald Dewar, reported 11 April 2000 in *Daily Record* and *The Herald*. Donald added 'the key to success is lifting the debt burden and the improvement in homes . . . creating 3,500 jobs, and most importantly, giving better living standards and choice to those in our cities who want to rent.'

5 The Fraser Inquiry was established by Jack McConnell, First Minister, in June 2003 under the Chairmanship of The Rt Hon. The Lord Fraser of Carmyllie QC to report into the Holyrood Building project. His report was published on 15 September 2004.

6 For a discussion of the repeal, see Wendy Alexander, 'Five years on . . . was the Section 28 war worth it?', *Sunday Herald*, 26 June 2005.

Section 28/2a was a controversial amendment introduced by Mrs Thatcher's government into the 1988 Local Government Act, preventing a local authority from 'intentionally promoting homosexuality or publishing material with the intention of promoting homosexuality' or 'promoting the teaching in any maintained school of the acceptability of homosexuality as a pretended family relationship'. It was sometimes referred to as 'Clause 28', because Westminster amendments are called clauses before they become law. It was also sometimes referred to as 'Section 2a' since the effect of the amendment was to insert a new section, 2a, into the Local Government Act 1986.

Donald, the man . . .
Coming of Age

1 The competition known for over 40 years as the Observer Mace after its original sponsors was renamed in 1995 as the John Smith Memorial Mace.

Donald and Labour
His Finest Hour

1 H.M. Drucker, *Doctrine and Ethos in the Labour Party* (1979), p. 1.

2 *Ibid.*, p. 14.

3 *Ibid.*, p. 40.

4 The theory of personality type which has most influenced me comes from Carl Jung's work and is embedded in the Myers-Briggs Type Indicator®. These ideas also underlie David Keirsey's work on temperaments. In his work there are four basic temperaments which are a variation of Jungian type preferences. His four temperaments are Rational (NT), Idealist (NF), Artisan (SP) and Guardian (SJ). I do not think the last two names work well for describing political leadership style and that is why I have changed 'artisan' to 'operator' and 'guardian' to

'governor'. The overall drift of my analysis of political leadership is otherwise within Keirsey's broad temperament theory. Information can be found on his website www.keirsey.com. The site also includes analysis of different presidential styles.

5 Fraser Inquiry Report (2004), p. 6

6 *Ibid.*, p. 55.

7 *Ibid.*, p. 8.

Donald and Devolution
His Obedient Colleagues

1 Based on interviews with civil servants, who preferred to remain anonymous.

Enduring Foundations

1 See J.M. MacCormick, *The Flag in the Wind: The Story of the National Movement in Scotland* (1955), pp. 199–206.

Donald and Scotland
The Modernising Radical

1 See Record View: 'Why won't they listen?', *Daily Record*, 28 April 2000; Record View: 'Donald Dewar', *Daily Record*, 12 October 2000; Comment: 'Holyrood must raise its game', *Daily Mail*, 6 May 2000; and Comment: 'Debt of gratitude to Donald Dewar', *Daily Mail*, 12 October 2000.

2 Scottish Parliament Official Report (SPOR), 16 June 1999, Col. 412.

3 SPOR, 16 June 1999, Col. 405.

4 Interview.

5 Scottish Office News Release 1953/97, '£23 million for tackling social exclusion in Scotland', 8 December 1997.

6 Scottish Office, Consultation Paper, *Social Exclusion in Scotland* (1998).

7 Interview.

8 See, for example, P. Munn, 'Can Schools make Scotland a more Inclusive Society?', in *Scottish Affairs* 33 (Autumn 2000), pp. 116–31.

9 *The Development of Integrated Community Schools in Scotland* (HM Inspectorate of Education, 2004).

10 Interview.

11 'Council Housing: Slum clearance, 2002-style', *The Economist*, 28 March

2002; Scottish Executive Press Release SE 1033/2000, 'Unlocking the future for Glasgow's housing', 11 April 2000.

12 SPOR, 9 September 1999, Cols. 277–8.

13 Scottish Office News Release 0005/99, 'Land reform barriers will be swept away', 5 January 1999.

14 Interviews with colleagues.

15 From Donald Dewar's Brough Centenary Lecture at the University of Paisley on 27 November 1997. Extracts are set out in Scottish Office News Release 1870/97, 27 November 1997.

16 SPOR, 9 September 1999, Col. 280.

17 SPOR, 16 June 1999, Col. 415.

18 From Donald Dewar's speech, 'The Scottish Parliament: the challenges ahead', given at St Andrews on 30 November 1998. Quoted in full in *Donald Dewar: A Book of Tribute* (2000).

19 Press reports, cited in M. Watson, *Year Zero: An Inside View of the Scottish Parliament* (2001), p. 25 and p. 198.

20 P. Jones, 'The First Term of the Scottish Parliament', in G. Hassan and D. Fraser (eds), *The Political Guide to Modern Scotland* (2004), p. 22.

21 Leading article in *The Scotsman*, 13 May 1997.

22 J. Robertson and K. Johnston, 'Error of judgement', *Sunday Times Scotland*, 12 October 1997; H. McLeish, *Scotland First* (2004), pp. 69–70.

23 The Scottish Office press release announcing the cancellation of the prison transfer was written by Alastair Campbell, the Prime Minister's head of communications (information from interviews).

24 Interview.

25 Comment, 'Holyrood must raise its game', *Scottish Daily Mail*, 6 May 2000.

26 SPOR, 24 February 2000, Col. 166.

27 G. Leicester, 'Scotland', in R. Hazell (ed.), *The State and the Nations: The Politics of Devolution* (2000).

28 SPOR, 24 February 2000, Col. 166.

29 Labour Party *Record of Party Conference 2000* (2000), p. 36.

30 Interview.

31 Interviews.

32 Interviews.

33 Interview.

34 Personal recollection.

35 M. Watson, *Year Zero: An Inside View of the Scottish Parliament* (2001), pp. 104–5.

36 'Behave or you will be sacked', *Scottish Daily Mail*, 6 July 2000.

History's Judgement

1 This chapter reflects on the historical significance of the events discussed by other contributors. It was written without sight of the following essays: 'As a Colleague', 'Enduring Foundations' and 'Cabinet Voices'.

Donald's Legacy . . .
Foundations, Frustrations and Hopes

1 James Maxton, *James Maxton and Scotland* (Report of a speech in 1924) (1924), p. 5.

2 W. Alexander and J. McCormick, 'Devolution's firm foundations: home truths for Home Rule', *The Scotsman*, 7 March 1996.

3 Labour Memo, 17 September 1995, quoted in B. Taylor, *The Scottish Parliament* (1999) p. 67.

4 W. Alexander and J. McCormick, 'Arithmetic of an Assembly: home truths for Home Rule', *The Scotsman*, 8 March 1996.

5 W. Alexander and J. McCormick, 'Devolution's firm foundations: home truths for Home Rule', *The Scotsman*, 7 March 1996.

6 L. Paterson et al., *New Scotland, New Politics* (2001), p. 41.

7 D. McLeod, *West Highland Free Press*, 24 September 2004.

8 B. Taylor, *Scotland's Parliament: Triumph and Disaster* (2002), p. 10.

9 D. McCrone, 'A Parliament for a People: Holyrood in an Understated Nation', *Scottish Affairs*, no. 50 (Winter 2005), p. 12.

10 Professor Lindsay Paterson, writing about the early Parliament, noted how 'utopianism is strong in Scotland, despite the strong heritage also of boring Presbyterian pragmatism . . . The campaigning for a Parliament went on for so long that it was bound to attract to itself all hopes of all sorts of social movements who were dissatisfied with any aspect of modern society . . . There were indeed immensely high expectations, and these do indeed seem to have been disappointed to some extent, I have suggested that that was inevitable.' See L. Paterson et al., *New Scotland, New Politics* (2001), pp. 59–60.

11 L. Paterson, 'Scottish Democracy and Scottish Utopias: The First Year of the Scottish Parliament', *Scottish Affairs*, no. 33 (Autumn 2000), p. 61.

12 As far back as 1996, we (W. Alexander and J. McCormick), writing in *The Scotsman* (8 March 1996), recognised that, 'After many years when Scottish politics was largely defined by opposition to Westminster Rule, the central challenge for Scottish political parties will be to offer effective policy solutions able to build an economically efficient and socially just nation.' In the '90s, it was always easier to be clear about the necessary constitutional changes to make the settlement secure than it was to engage in a debate about the readiness of the new nation for the policy challenges that awaited it. The capacity for distinctive policy making and reform had got rather rusty.

13 Discussion before the Parliament's establishment about how it might become an engine for earning wealth as well as spending it was too infrequent and often superficial. Ten years later the question of Scotland's comparative economic performance remains highly contested. Although *Measuring Scotland's Progress towards a Smart Successful Scotland* (Scottish Executive, 2004) provides an important benchmark of Scotland's performance against OECD competitors, there is less agreement about the necessary action in response to economic challenges that are often not unique to Scotland, as the recent Allander Series has explored. See J. McCormick and W. Alexander in S. Tindale (ed.), *The State and the Nations: The Politics of Devolution* (1996). See also D. Coyle, W. Alexander and B. Ashcroft, *New Wealth for Old Nations: Scotland's Economic Prospects* (2005).

14 For example, the Proof of Concept Scheme, the Scottish Co-investment Fund and the new intermediary technology institutes all benefited from the strengthening of the higher education enterprise link.

15 P. Cooke, 'Devolution and Innovation: The Financing of Economic Development in the UK's Devolved Administrations', *Scottish Affairs*, no. 50 (Winter 2005), p. 40.

16 Donald would likely have been saddened by frequent claims of continuous relative decline in the Scottish economy over the last 40 years. This ignores the fact that Scotland is the only part of the United Kingdom to substantially change its relative ranking in the last 40 years, having gone from 85 per cent of the United Kingdom average in terms of GDP per head to over 100 per cent in the 1990s, before slipping back slightly.

17 The consistent underperformance of Scottish Water is unlikely to have found favour, nor would the failure of Scotland's planning system to meet its own targets. I suspect he would also be asking whether the rising support for fishing, farming and forestry is the best way to support Scotland's rural communities. And Donald would not have exempted the Scottish public sector from the need for ambitious reform.

18 P. Hyman, *1 out of 10: From Downing Street Vision to Classroom Reality* (2005), p. 47.

19 *ibid.*, p. 384.

20 Michael Keating, *Policy Making and Policy Divergence in Scotland after Devolution*, Devolution Briefing no. 21 (March 2005), ESRC Research Programme Devolution and Constitutional Change.

21 See D. Coyle, W. Alexander and B. Ashcroft, *New Wealth for Old Nations: Scotland's Economic Prospects* (2005).

22 Typically, schools are monitored through 49 performance measures, each health board through 109 performance measures. Parts of the government machine are under siege from data which is often unwieldy for those at the sharp end to collect, and not necessarily fit for purpose.

23 *Hidden Harm: Responding to the Needs of Children of Problem Drug Users*: The Report of an Inquiry by the Advisory Council on the Misuse of Drugs (Advisory Council on the Misuse of Drugs, June 2003), p. 10.

Selected Bibliography

Alexander, Wendy and McCormick, James, 'Home truths for Home Rule', a series of articles, *The Scotsman*, 7–9 March 1996

Alexander, Wendy, 'Five years on . . . was the Section 28 war worth it?', *Sunday Herald*, 26 June 2005

Cooke, Phil, 'Devolution and Innovation: The Financing of Economic Development in the UK's Devolved Administration', *Scottish Affairs*, no. 50 (Winter 2005), pp. 39–50

Coyle, D., Alexander, W. and Ashcroft, B. (eds), *New Wealth for Old Nations: Scotland's Economic Prospects* (Princeton University Press, 2005)

Denver, D., Mitchell, J., Pattie, C. and Bochel, H., *Scotland Decides: The Devolution Issue and the 1997 Referendum* (Frank Cass, London, and Portland, Oregon, 2000)

Dewar Donald – A Book of Tribute (The Stationery Office, Norwich, 2000)

Drucker, H.M., *Doctrine and Ethos in the Labour Party* (Allen & Unwin, London, 1979)

Harvie, Christopher and Jones, Peter, *The Road to Home Rule: Images of Scotland's Cause* (Polygon, Edinburgh, 2000)

Hassan, Gerry, *Redesigning the State: The New Scotland* (Fabian Society, London, 1998)

Hassan, Gerry, *The Scottish Labour Party: History, Institutions and Ideas* (Edinburgh University Press, 2004)

Hyman, Peter, *1 out of 10: From Downing Street Vision to Classroom Reality* (Vintage, London, 2005)

Jeffery, Charles, *Devolution and Constitutional Change: Delivering Public Policy after Devolution: Diverging from Westminster* (Economic and Social Research Council, Edinburgh, 2005)

Jeffery, Charles, *Devolution and Constitutional Change: The Institutions of Devolution* (Economic and Social Research Council, Edinburgh, 2005)

Jones, P., 'The First Term of the Scottish Parliament', in G. Hassan and D. Fraser (eds), *The Political Guide to Modern Scotland* (Methuen, London, 2004)

Keating, Michael, *The Government of Scotland: Public Policy Making after Devolution* (Edinburgh University Press, 2005)

Keating, Michael, *Policy Making and Policy Divergence in Scotland after Devolution*, Devolution Briefing no. 21 (March 2005), ESRC Research Programme Devolution and Constitutional Change

Leicester, G., 'Scotland', in Stephen Tindale (ed.), *The State and the Nations: the Politics of Devolution* (Institute for Public Policy Research, London, 1996)

Lynch, Peter, *Scottish Government and Politics – An Introduction* (Edinburgh University Press, 2001)

MacCormick, J.M., *The Flag in the Wind: The Story of the National Movement in Scotland* (Victor Gollancz, London, 1955)

McCormick, James and Alexander, Wendy, 'Firm Foundations: securing the Scottish Parliament', in Stephen Tindale (ed.), *The State and the Nations: The Politics of Devolution* (Institute for Public Policy Research, London, 1996), pp. 99–166

McCrone, David, 'A Parliament for a People: Holyrood in an Understated Nation', *Scottish Affairs*, no. 50 (Winter 2005), pp. 1–25

McLeish, H., *Scotland First* (Mainstream Publishing, Edinburgh, 2000)

Marr, Andrew, *The Battle for Scotland* (Penguin, London, 1992)

Marr, Andrew, *Ruling Britannia: The Failure and Future of British Democracy* (Michael Joseph, London, 1995)

Maxton, James, *James Maxton and Scotland* (Report of a speech in 1924) (Scottish National Party, Port Glasgow, 1924)

Paterson, Lindsay, 'Scottish Democracy and Scottish Utopias: The First

Year of the Scottish Parliament', *Scottish Affairs*, no. 30 (Autumn 2000), pp. 45–61

Paterson, L., Brown, A., Curtice, J., Hinds, K., McCrone, D., Park, A., Sproston, K. and Surridge, P. (eds), *New Scotland, New Politics?* (Polygon, Edinburgh, 2001)

Schlesinger, Philip et al., *Open Scotland? – Journalists, Spin Doctors and Lobbyists* (Polygon, Edinburgh, 2002)

Taylor, Brian, *The Scottish Parliament* (Polygon, Edinburgh, 1999)

Taylor, Brian, *Scotland's Parliament: Triumph and Disaster* (Edinburgh University Press, 2002)

Watson, Mike, *Year Zero: An Inside View of the Scottish Parliament* (Polygon, Edinburgh, 2001)

Index